ELWOOD'S BLUES

Elwood's Blues

Interviews With the Blues Legends & Stars

By Dan Aykroyd and Ben Manilla

Backbeat
Books
San Francisco

Published by Backbeat Books
600 Harrison Street, San Francisco, CA 94107
www.backbeatbooks.com
email: books@musicplayer.com

An imprint of CMP Information
Publishers of *Guitar Player, Bass Player, Keyboard,* and *EQ* magazines

CMP
United Business Media

Distributed to the book trade in the US and Canada by
Publishers Group West, 1700 Fourth Street, Berkeley, CA 94710

Distributed to the music trade in the US and Canada by
Hal Leonard Publishing, P.O. Box 13819, Milwaukee, WI 53213

Cover Design by Richard Leeds - BigWigDesign.com
Front cover photo: © Larry Hulst / Retna Ltd.

Library of Congress Cataloging-in-Publication Data

Aykroyd, Dan.
  Elwood's blues : interviews with the blues legends & stars / by Dan Aykroyd
and Ben Manilla.
      p. cm.
  Includes index.
  ISBN 0-87930-809-5 (alk. paper)
  1. Blues musicians--Interviews. I. Manilla, Ben, 1952- II. Title.

  ML394.A94 2004
  782.421643'092'2--dc22

                                2004015467
Printed in the United States of America

04 05 06 07 08   5 4 3 2

Dedicated to Isaac Tigrett
and to all the musicians who have contributed
to the rich tradition known as the Blues.

Contents

Preface

I have listened to the blues for most of my life, and played it and even felt it from time to time. It has been my privilege to witness the performances of many blues legends over the years, as well as legends in the making. And it has been my honor to perform with many of them.

One of our aims with the Blues Brothers was to get our blues idols back in the spotlight, to provide them some gainful employment—not to mention publicity—beyond the vagaries of the road, record label machinations, and the fickle taste of the public.

Now entering its 12th season, *The House of Blues Radio Hour* is also intended to be a haven for blues performers and lovers of this purely American contribution to world culture. Since the program first aired back in 1993, we have showcased hundreds of records, many of them world premieres. We have interviewed hundreds of musicians, label owners, producers, writers, and knowledgeable fans and promoters—people like Dick Waterman, the blues champion who "rediscovered" Delta blues singer Son House and launched Bonnie Raitt on her career. We have done shows highlighting the tenacious blues record labels of today, like Blind Pig, Alligator, and Telarc, without whom the blues would wither on the vine. We have featured a multitude of performers—John Lee Hooker, B.B. King, Robert Randolph, R.L. Burnside, Bill Wyman, Popa Chubby, Keb' Mo', Marcia Ball, and Susan Tedeschi. Some of them our listeners already knew, some of them were heard nationally for the first time on our program.

The House of Blues Radio Hour generally focuses on one performer per episode, to allow as much time as possible for both the artist's music and what he or she has to say about it. But time is our enemy, nowhere more so than on commercial radio; each interview had to be condensed to fit into the hour-long format. What a pleasure then to see, for the first time, the extended interviews here, within these pages, for everyone to experience.

Elwood's Blues is a glimpse of the blues' musical spectra from electrified Chicago blues, straight-ahead rock and acoustic, to gospel, jump, rhythm and blues, Latin offshoots, and soul. The blues' umbrella is large, and many shelter beneath it. Here you will find the juke joint gut-bucket howlers, the unplugged roots players, the elegant songsters, the guitar gods, and the young turks eager to make their mark, all bathed in the hot and cool blue light, sharing their experiences. And you will find rockers like Eric Burdon, Robert Plant, and Aerosmith paying homage to the American roots that made their musical careers possible. Funny, touching, and stirring—these are the stories of the people who live the blues.

—Dan Aykroyd, a.k.a. Elwood Blues

Blues
Legends

LUTHER ALLISON

Soul Fixin' Man

> *"We would just put it together—go in the backyard, hook up the old instruments, bring the cords out the windows."*

A gospel singer in his Arkansas hometown, Luther Allison overcame his fear of the devil's music to become a major force in the second wave of postwar Chicago blues. After his family moved to Chicago, a teenaged Luther received a blues education literally in Muddy Waters's backyard, learning from the likes of Otis Rush and developing a style that took on the rock 'n' soul energy of Little Richard and Chuck Berry. Settling in France in 1980, Allison didn't record for a U.S. label until the 1994 *Soul Fixin' Man*, which ushered in his big American comeback. Luther died in 1997—a year after this conversation with Elwood. Today, Luther's son Bernard carries on his blues legacy.

Elwood Blues: *After your family moved to Chicago, you met Muddy Waters through his son Charles Morganfield. How did that come about?*

Luther Allison: Well, I passed Muddy Waters's house every day on my way to school. I was alone pretty much, and Charles walked out one day and we started talking. He said, "My dad is Muddy Waters and he plays guitar and he got a band." I said, "My brother's name is Ollie and he got a band." And we become friends. Through this, I spent much of my time at Muddy Waters's house, and my parents knew it. My mother would say, "Where's he at?" And my dad said, "Don't worry, he's down at Muddy's

Luther Allison works his Chicago-honed magic onstage in 1997.

house. That's how I got to know Muddy's son, Muddy himself, James Cotton, Otis Spann. Otis Spann was just a perfect gentleman, you know.

My brother at that time had a group called the Rolling Stones. So from Muddy's house to my house where my brother lived in the back apartment, from me in that kitchenette apartment, I had the whole cake, every day. So much that I couldn't even study my schoolwork.

Elwood: *I've heard they'd bring a piano out for Otis, and everybody would jam in the alley next to Muddy's?*

Allison: Oh, that was a thing. You got guys who love music, so what they do, they drink a little bit, they do the whiskey, they do the wine, they do the beer, they do the barbecue, they do the flat-tire fixing, the car wash—all this, and some guy is doing the keyboards or guitar or cardboard boxes or washboard, just making noise, and these guys start to sing. We young ones were going, "Wow, listen to that—this stuff is great."

Elwood: *And then you used to hang out at barbecues with Freddie King and Hubert Sumlin and Magic Sam, right?*

Allison: Those were the younger generation of my guys. Yes, Sam loved to cook and sing with his brothers. And I come from that same kind of cooking family. Freddie was already a big guy, you know. Many times people like

Mighty Joe Young or Bobby Rush, we would just put it together—go in the backyard, hook up the old instruments, bring the cords out the windows in the summertime, and just play music all day long. They would eat, take a nap, go back to it, go out to the next nightclub. People like Freddie, they like to go chase the girls or go shoot a few dice or whatever—"Here's the guitar. I'll be back later." You might not see them for the next weekend. They knew you was not going to do anything but take care of that guitar because you didn't have a guitar.

And we was all one brotherly love trip, trying to learn off each other and trying to say, "Look, this is where we come from, this is where we going, this is what we do." There was no trouble. There was not talk of drugs; there was talk about playing music and maybe drinking some whiskey because if you didn't drink some whiskey, then you ain't no man to hang. So these things happen.

Elwood: *Of all those great guitar players, who was the most influential as your style developed?*

Allison: Elwood, I got to go with Otis Rush. Otis was my main guy. I mean, I love B.B., I love Chuck Berry, Muddy shaking them strings with that slide. My brother, he was good, too, at the time. But Otis Rush, when you heard him you kind of forgot about anything else but listening to the tone of his guitar. He was left-handed, and I could listen to him—as I say today—backwards. He could hold a note and just yank on it a little bit. You saw Albert King doing the same kind of thing. But Otis was a little more mellow. He was not quite as aggressive as Albert King. He could hold it like he was singing a melody. And today he can still do that. Otis is my man. I tell him every day I see him. I say, "Man, you got to get together because you my idol, man."

Elwood: *You were one of the many blues men who made successful careers in Europe. Was it difficult to make that break?*

Allison: It's hard. In the mid-'60s there was people like Jimmy Dawkins, Freddie King, Muddy, a few others was going to Europe. These guys would come back and tell us how much fun they had in France—"The next time we go, we're going to make sure you go." And it just never happened.

But in 1975 or so I got an offer, and in 1976 I went to Europe. I started at the Montreaux Jazz Festival, and I supported Big Voice Odom over in France, John Lee Hooker many times. John Lee Hooker said, "Where's Luther? Get him over here, because I know how to play with him." And it just went on and on and on. I started to go to Europe one, two, and three times a year, all the way from '76 until '83.

Sometimes there was just too much for the American musicians coming from Chicago—couldn't deal with the language, couldn't deal with the fact that, "Okay, I got a little money while I'm there, but I don't know what I'm doing, I don't know how to spend it. I'm totally dependent on someone else." They couldn't hang.

My people said, "Hey, there's a few people here who know who Luther Allison is. Let's make a lot of people know. The thing for you to do is come in and stay." So 1983 I decided to go deal with it. My son, Bernard, was still a teenager, 13 years old or so. I took the chance, and I'm working hard at it. I'm still doing new venues in Europe. I'm being successful in many ways. I just did B.B. King's show with him. Who shows up? Gary Moore. We jammed—my first jam with Gary, although I've seen him a number of times. And B.B. was just in top form as usual.

So that's Europe, where I open the show for B.B. and had the maximum crowd for one of the greatest jazz festivals there, the Antibes. I moved right on to the North Sea Jazz Festival up in Holland with Buddy Guy, Little Richard, and a whole bunch of other folks. So I ain't coming back here to stay until I know that when people are saying, "We want you back," they mean it this time.

Elwood: *Ten years ago the European audiences were digging the blues the way the Americans are today. Why were they so much ahead of the Americans?*

Allison: I think in America we've just been spoiled. We had all of the things we wanted, where we want to place them. With Muddy Waters and Howlin' Wolf and those guys down in Chicago, we got to know what good-feeling music meant. If a ballad blues hit you, you could be sad about it, you could be happy about it. If there was something moving, whether it was funk or rock 'n' roll, then you knew how to deal with it—your attitude was to get up and dance. But today in the States, people say, that's rock 'n' roll—that's for rock 'n' rollers, only. That's the blues, that's devil's music. You don't want to see that. That's jazz—you ain't got money to go there.

Elwood: *Soul Fixin'* Man *was your first release in 20 years in the States, and it had a nice variety of styles—soul, Chicago, and you were one of the first blues guys to start bringing in the rock sound.*

Allison: In the early days when I was coming up that ladder in Chicago, our job was to play a little bit different, be recognized as a little bit different. We all challenged each other—"Buddy Guy and Luther Allison are going to battle it out next Sunday." That's how it happened. I decided that I love Chuck Berry, I love Little Richard, Bo Diddley, Hank Williams. I mean, I'm from Arkansas—we played the blues in any kind of way we could. We learned how to entertain. And when we got a little shot like a flash of a camera, we took that shot. We took chances. My dad said if you don't take chances, you chicken, man, you yellow.

Elwood: *When you did* Bad News Is Coming *you were the only blues artist to have recorded for a Motown label.*

Allison: I think there was a couple more people, but nobody surfaced. I know when I went to Motown, the people in Chicago thought there was big, big future there—"Luther Allison's on Motown Records, we got a chance." They knew I'm not a person to go out there and play the star road. I'm out there trying to make something happen for us. This is what I've been doing through my life, reaching out for somebody else, man. Bringing new turf—"I got an opportunity, I want you to be part of it." And I'm telling everybody today, I don't care who's on top, there's room for somebody else.

Elwood: *Last year you came back and knocked them dead at the 1995 Chicago Festival, and you said to everybody, "Hey, Luther is still here."*

Allison: The talk was, "Luther Allison and Otis Rush is going to jam." It was my big chance to maybe open Otis up. Otis needs somebody who loves him, a friend, somebody that he can say, "Man, thank you for letting me know who I am for an instant." Well, I want some limelight, too, okay. But first, I want Otis to be straight. I want Otis to know I appreciate anything he's doing, and I'm going to go out there and make him play.

So I said, "Okay, what are we going to do, Otis?" "Ah, man, I don't know, what you want to do?" I thought, I'm going to do something I know he can do. So we start a slow blues, something that we can get moving, make him cry, make him use that left-hand vibrato and make me love it. And I'm going to keep leading him, leading him. I'm going to make him burst. And he did.

He sounded so great that day he made me sound good. He gave me a chance to open up. Unfortunately, Eddie C. Campbell kind of got lost in that, because he's playing a Jazzmaster guitar, which sounds between a Gibson Les Paul and the 355 that Otis Rush plays. We're trying to get this feeling going without breaking way down—it just wasn't going to happen. But I kept feeding Eddie C. Campbell, too—take some, take some. Okay, come up. Me and Otis going to do like Muhammad Ali and Joe Frasier. We got to hook it up together. The people loved it, and that was a big push for Luther Allison.

Elwood: *You always put out so much energy onstage.*

Allison: I'm having a great time, believe me. I'm on the edge of my birthday—I'm 57 on the 17th of August, and here we are. People say, "Where do you get the energy?" And I just say, "Look, I want you to get your money's worth. I don't want you to leave here unsatisfied because I went out on stage shucking and jiving. I think a lot of young rock 'n' rollers and blues players and jazz players look at Luther and say, "I'm getting some of this energy." I'm putting it there free to take it. You got to have it. I'm tired at looking at these kids hanging out on the stage, a cigarette hanging out of their mouths and can't move unless they're totally messed up on drugs or whiskey. We don't need that. We need some dancing. Get on out there, Fred Astaire, Michael Jackson, Luther Allison—hey, let's move.

Elwood: *Are there any songs that you never get tired of playing live?*

Allison: "Watching You," "Blue Streak," "Cherry Red Wine," and "Move Away From the 'Hood"—I will never get tired of doing these tunes. I will never get tired of doing "Standing in the Middle of the Road," or "Soul Fixin' Man," or "Back to the Shoeshine Stand." I want everybody to know that if I can't make it in music any farther than I came, I can always go back to the shoeshine stand—but not the cotton field. Forget it.

BOBBY "BLUE" BLAND
Give 'em What They Want

> *"You can't be happy and sing the blues as far as I'm concerned."*

With a vocal style that melds gospel, blues, R&B, and even a bit of crooning, Bobby "Blue" Bland created a body of classic work and gained worldwide fame. Born Robert Calvin Bland, Bobby grew up in rural Tennessee and did his first recordings in 1951 in Memphis. His style didn't begin to blossom, though, until after 1955, when he returned from Army duty and did a series of records for the Duke label. A major hitmaker throughout the '60s, Bland was recording and performing well into the new millennium. Elwood talked with Bland not long after his 1992 Rock & Roll Hall of Fame induction.

Elwood Blues: *You grew up not far from Memphis, in the town of Rosemark, Tennessee. What was your childhood like?*

Bobby "Blue" Bland: It wasn't a bad childhood, it wasn't a good childhood. Rosemark is very, very small—the population I guess would be 200. Basically, I didn't do anything but go to the grocery store and help clean up there, or go to the cotton 'gin, which my dad ran. I used to hang around there and hustle up quarters and dimes doing a little extra work with the people that brought the cotton to be 'ginned. So there wasn't really much to get into and nothing really exciting. You'd have people with jew's harps, harmonicas, and old guitars, and you'd do some of Blind Lemon's stuff, Walter Davis, Big Boy Crudup.

Bobby "Blue" Bland, happy to be singing the blues.

Elwood: *When did you first get to Beale Street?*

Bland: I was fortunate to be there in the year 1947, I think it was, when my mother brought me to Memphis.

Elwood: *Do you remember the first concert you saw there?*

Bland: The first concert would be Rufus Thomas, Rufus and Bones [*Thomas's early performing partner Robert "Bones" Couch*]. They had an amateur show every Wednesday night on Beale Street at the Palace Theater, and people who thought that they could sing, like myself, could go in and try out. They would pay $5 for the top winner, $2 for the second, or whatever it was. I managed to win a couple of nights in a row, and then I had to kind of lay off because you can't win every night—people would think they have it fixed. Rufus was a disc jockey and an entertainer at radio station WDIA. I'd say he would be the first I saw, along with B.B. King.

Elwood: *You worked with B.B. King in a group called the Beale Streeters.*

Bland: The Beale Streeters was Billy Duncan's band along with Earl Forest and the late great Johnny Ace. B.B. was part of the Beale Streeters, but kind of in the upper crust from where we were, which B. has been ever since I've known him. He had his thing going with Sunbeam Mitchell.

Elwood: *Ike Turner was another guy on that scene.*

Bland: Ike Turner did my first recording at Tuff Green's house—he was an important musician in Memphis. Ike was out of St. Louis and was with the Bihari Brothers out of Chicago. The label was called Modern Records; I did my first two recordings, and Ike was doing the engineering, the whole thing.

Elwood: *I understand he was a talent scout for Sun Records. Did you ever record at Sun?*

Bland: Me and Roscoe Gordon did a thing there in the earlier years, "No More Doggin'." "Saddled the Cow and Milked the Horse" was something else that we did. It was just something local; it wasn't nationwide.

Elwood: *I have seen a powerful picture of you back then with Junior Parker and Elvis Presley.*

Bland: WDIA had a thing that they'd do every year called the Goodwill Revue for the homeless. I was traveling with Junior Parker during that time. Elvis would come down and always give us a nice booster, saying that he paid his dues with him. The gentleman in the picture along with Elvis and Junior and myself is Walter Bailey, who is my attorney now.

Elwood: *You toured a lot with Junior. What was that like?*

Bland: I stayed with Junior a little better than eight years. That was the first person that ever took me out on the road. It was quite an experience because I never had been anyplace away from home for any length of time. We went different places, Louisiana, Mississippi, Georgia, Alabama, Texas, St. Louis, Chicago—that's about as far as we got until later on.

Elwood: *What was it like stepping out onstage for the first time?*

Bland: Very, very, very scary, because you didn't know what was going to materialize, you didn't know what was going to happen, how the public was going to accept you. You just have a lump right here in your throat, wondering if the first word that you're going to say would come out correctly and have some kind of meaning or get some kind of response.

Elwood: *I remember the tours you used to do with B.B. King and Albert King. They were always something to look forward to.*

Bland: Oh, yeah, we did something every year before Albert passed. We would have at least a month, month and a half that we would travel and do the larger places, auditoriums and things of that nature. That was real fun, because B. and Albert were my two favorite people and I could learn each and every day from them.

Elwood: *What was the energy on that stage like?*

Bland: Hot, very hot. I think, speaking for B. and Albert and myself, we did a good job because we always tried to make it hot for the other fellow, not arrogant like or anything like that—just make one another work. You do your best, and it was a lot of fun. Being professionals, there was no jealousy of any sort there. It was just a matter of doing what you're supposed to do and give the public what they want.

Elwood: *You've been recording ever since the '50s. How do you keep finding fresh material?*

Bland: Actually, you have a lot of help in that area because people get kind of attached to you as you grow. They know the type of material that you've been good at, that you've been fortunate to sell, and they know the type of story that you like to tell. And I've had some good writers, man—that's been a part of my success.

Elwood: *I read an interesting quote from you about the early blues artists: "They had their particular lyrics during that era, people like Blind Lemon, Big Boy Crudup, Walter Davis. They're the ones who set the pace for all of us." There are a lot of rock 'n' rollers like Rod Stewart who you set the standard for. What are your thoughts on being such a big influence?*

Bland: What makes it good with an entertainer like Rod Stewart, he gets ideas from other singers, but he makes it his own—you can tell it's a Rod Stewart delivery. That's the same thing that I do. If I couldn't do a standard tune any better than the artist before did, there's no point in trying to record it. But it's a very good feeling to have someone take a liking to your music and want to do some of the things that you've already done.

Elwood: *You're known for that growl in your voice. How did you develop that?*

Bland: I used to sing real, real high, like what you call a falsetto. Then I had to have my tonsils removed, and it lowered my voice down to maybe a baritone. I didn't have a gimmick. That falsetto was a little thing that carried over with the ending of a lyric. I was listening to a spiritual record by Rev. C.L. Franklin; he was preaching a sermon called "The Eagle Stirred His Nest," and it caught my ear. I listened to this particular part over and over, and I said, "It looks like I could use this for something." So I started to practice the different squalls that he was doing—I stole the squall thing from him. You have to work it into your delivery, and it has to be on time. I think it was in the late '60s when I started really developing that, got to where I could really use it. That was the start of it, what they call in London "love throat." C.L. Franklin was one of my favorite preachers. I always liked his daughter, too—my favorite singer, Aretha.

Elwood: *You started off in a gospel group, the Miniatures.*

Bland: Yes; we didn't do anything really big. It was just local. We performed every Sunday in the rural area out from Memphis. Actually, my whole background comes from the church. So naturally that's where you get your feeling and your desire and the way I like to sing.

Elwood: *You're one of the important musicians who melded gospel into the blues. How are they different, and what makes them go together so well?*

Bland: It's just a matter of wording. Like, "I love you, baby," or "Oh, Lord," which I use in a lot of my records. It's a matter of phrasing. Spiritual blues and country and western are so close it's pathetic. A lot of good stories come from the country and western side. The greatest writer Hank Williams; Ray Charles did a lot of his material. Ernest Tubb had a blues feeling; "Walking the Floor Over You" had the blues flavor. Some don't like the twang that country carries, but that's just the delivery they had. The lyric is what tells a story.

Elwood: *What makes the perfect blues song?*

Bland: Well, it's about life. Some of the things that I sing about actually happened to me. Maybe you have a girlfriend and you lose her. It's not a good feeling, not if you care for her. Blues is based on feeling, what happens in life. I see things on TV, people that don't have anything to eat, starving. That's the blues. You think of those type of things to change the mood when you're singing. If I have a lyric that has anything pertaining to sadness, I just go back and think of whatever happened or how I felt at certain different times. It helps me to say things better and have more meaning to them. You can't be happy and sing the blues as far as I'm concerned. Maybe some people can, but it's news to me if they do.

Elwood: *Do you think that makes young people today less interested in the blues?*

Bland: Blues is a downer to younger black people, mainly because our history carries a lot of guilt and disappointment. Blues basically was done by being sad, being out in the country and not allowed to do certain things. So young black people, some of them don't want to look back on that era. They want to look ahead the way that Dr. King has brought them up to now. There's no looking back, we got to go forward. But the blues will always be here.

Elwood: *What kind of music are you listening to these days?*

Bland: I listen to a variety—I just don't have one particular thing in my CD player or whatever. I like ballads, I like country and western, like I said, I like blues, I like some Dixieland. I listen to jazz—Stanley Turrentine, Gene Ammons, Grover Washington, Sonny Stitt. I like some bluegrass if they have a story. I listen to people like Nat King Cole or Billy Eckstine or Tony Bennett, Perry Como, people of that nature, when I want to soften up. I had a kind of a learning process with Nat, because he's the only person that I've ever listened to that had perfect diction with a song, that you can hear every word. See, I kind of mumble some things because maybe I get off track, maybe I think that I'm losing time with the music or whatever and jumble up the words—sometimes I say things a little too fast. But Nat was never like that. I got a lot of information from him about how to deliver a lyric. I met him twice before he passed. He was a delightful person to be around, to talk to. He loved the Dodgers and he loved to talk about baseball.

Elwood: *What would you like people to remember about Bobby Blue Bland?*

Bland: I'd like to be remembered just as a good old country boy who did his very, very best to give the people something to listen to and helped them through a lot of sad moments, happy moments, and gave them a lift up if they were feeling bad. In the world today there's not too much happiness, so whatever moment you get of happiness, use it up because it don't come that often.

Elwood on the Air: Christmas

HOUR: 99/52
AIRDATE: 12/25-26/99
WRITER: SHANE SHARKEY

[Cheesy Christmas music]

FEMALE HOST: Hello and welcome to a special Christmas edition of Consumer Probe, I'm Joan Face. Today on our program we have entrepreneur Irwin Mainway. He is the owner of Mainway Novelties, makers of several controversial new toys. Welcome to the program sir.

ELWOOD (as Irwin): Thank You.

HOST: What have you brought for us today?

ELWOOD: Well, first I would like to start with a traditional Christmas icon, a bag of Candy Canes.

[FX: bag of nails being tossed onto table]

HOST: [confused] Well . . . Mr. Mainway this looks like a bag of rusty nails with red stripes painted on them.

ELWOOD: Ya well a . . . they're gonna last a real long time ya know.

HOST: Don't you think that's a little dangerous? Kids might put these rusty nails in their mouths, seeing that they do look quite a bit like candy canes.

ELWOOD: Ya well that's why I put the warning label on the back of the bag here. See, look—"NOT FOR ORAL CONSUMPTION."

HOST: [Skeptically] Okay . . . well, let's move on to your next stocking stuffer.

ELWOOD: Ya. I call this one "Little Johnny Reindeer." It's fun for the kids to dress up around the holidays, know what I mean? This gives 'em a chance to do a little make believe, like they're one of Santa's helpers or reindeer or whatever.

[FX: bag being opened]

HOST: But this is just two pieces of brown felt and a staple gun?!

ELWOOD: Yeah, Pretty cool huh? If ya like that one I know you're gonna love this next one. I call it "The Bathtub Angel."

[FX: Opening package]

See here, it's a set of sponge wings and a halo that actually lights up. Ya just turn the lights out while you're little one is takin' a bath. Plug in the halo and ya got yerself a beautiful glowin' angel.

HOST: [Surprised and disgusted] Mr. Mainway, are you implying that you plug this into an electrical outlet while it is connected to your child in the bathtub?

ELWOOD: Ya . . . well uh, the lights really sparkle off the bubbles and the water, ya know?

HOST: Mr. Mainway, I am shocked at your irresponsible attitude. I think we can all see that your toys are unsafe and should be banned from the market.

ELWOOD: Wait just a minute. You say my toys are unsafe? Anything can be unsafe. Ya take this table for example. I could get a splinter from this thing.

HOST: [Disgusted] Mr. Mainway!

ELWOOD: And this plant ya got here. A little piece of dirt could all of a sudden fly outta the pot and land in my eye here. [Acting like he has dirt in his eye] AHHH! I'm blinded! My eye!

HOST: I'm afraid that's all the time we have today on Consumer Probe.

ELWOOD: I could get a carpet fiber in my toe and get an infection and they'd have to cut my leg off.

HOST: Have a safe and merry Christmas.

[Song: "Merry Christmas Baby"—Charles Brown]

CHARLES BROWN
Second Time Around

> *"Here comes this lady with red hair and sat in the front, and every time I would sing she would say, 'Oh, Charles, ooohh.'"*

For some people Charles Brown showed up in the '80s as an opening act for Bonnie Raitt, delighting audiences with his jazz-tinged piano and vocals. But that tour was actually the triumphant career rebirth Brown's dying grandfather had prophesied. The Texas-born, classically trained pianist first found success in L.A. in the '40s with Johnny Moore's Three Blazers, the trio's hits "Drifting Blues" and "Merry Christmas Baby"—still a holiday staple—propelled Brown on a solo track. He landed in the Top 10 frequently in the late '40s and early '50s, but his career waned with the rise of rock 'n' roll and '60s R&B. Elwood talked to Brown at the height of his resurgence, five years before his death in 1999.

Elwood Blues: *You have a number of W.C. Handy awards, Bammy awards, you've been nominated for Grammys—how does it feel to be getting so many honors at this point in your career?*

Charles Brown: Being 71 years old and not ever thinking I'd have a second time around, it feels good that I'm able to do it and not have any pain. I had really given up—I wasn't going to do anything more in music. I was just given to being older 'cause things hadn't been going right. Just to keep myself going I started working a janitorial thing for a friend of mine. She just wanted me to drive her help, and I would dust these rich people's windows

Once an unsung blues man, Charles Brown sang to thousands late in his career.

in Hollywood and Beverly Hills and Santa Monica. Sometimes we'd do three houses a day, and it was $75 a house for me. That kept me going. I was living in L.A. in a little cheap place, and I relaxed to enjoy the rest of my life and not be on that road.

Elwood: *I understand things started happening after Bonnie Raitt heard you play in Hollywood.*

Brown: I did a showcase at the Vine Street Grill—I hadn't been there in 25 years. This fellow Michael was doing my managing, and he said, "Charles, they should see you now because you haven't lost a thing." We'd been trying to get into the Vine Street Grill, but the man didn't know anything about me. So Michael says to him, "Well, who do you have there now?" And he says, "I have Mose Allison here." "Why don't you ask Mose

Allison who Charles Brown is?" So Mose Allison told him, "You don't know who Charles Brown is? That's where we got all our stuff from." So he says to Michael, "I can give Charles Tuesday and Wednesday night"—which is the worst nights in Hollywood—"I'll give him the door."

I had a band, and we got there early that day. He was supposed to have what you call a mic checkup. We sat there from three o'clock until six, and we were supposed to play at eight o'clock. He comes in late and says, "How you doing Charles," so I said, "Well, I'm not doing so well, because we've been sitting here waiting to get the mic." He said, "I'm too busy myself—I can't do all of this." It made me angry—I said, "I'd like to tell this man to go jump in the lake." So Michael said, "Don't do that, because the *Los Angeles Times* had a great write-up about you and we've just got to do this."

"That night the line was in front of the club from the middle of Holly-wood Boulevard to near the Sunset, waiting to get in. And the club wasn't that big, but he was charging 25 dollars. He took Michael off the door and said, "Nobody's gonna take this money—this is my club, I'm gonna pay Charles." It made Michael mad, and he just said, "Well Charles, we're going right back to the '50s again." I said, "I'll just go right on and try to make it."

We played that night, and here comes this lady with red hair and sat in the front, and every time I would sing she would say, "Oh, Charles, ooohh." So at intermission a guy said, "Do you know who that was? That was Bon-nie Raitt." That was the start of things. I got a notice from the Rhythm & Blues Foundation at the Kennedy Center that I was to receive a Lifetime Achievement Award; it would be $15,000 to spend freely. We never got money like that in our day.

Elwood: *So you go from hassling over money at the Vine Street Grill to being honored at the Kennedy Center.*

Brown: They had a big program; they had Carla Thomas, Rufus Thomas, Lou Rawls, the Memphis Horns. . . . After they give us our awards a TV guy came over to me and said, "Charles Brown, who do you think in the younger generation, be it man or woman, could go and do the blues?" So I said, "I think Robert Cray would be great, and Bonnie Raitt can sing anything." And she was sitting there. I had never met her, and when it was over she said, "Charles, thank you so much." They had a big dinner that evening and Bon-nie was there. She said, "Charles Brown, I heard you at the Vine Street Grill, and you are Mr. R&B—there is nobody like you. I could marry you musi-cally." I said, 'Bonnie Raitt, you don't want to marry me musically. You'd be smelling liniment all night." And she just fell out.

After that I was going along enjoying my $15,000 when somebody told me, "Bonnie Raitt's manager is looking for you; they want you on that tour. They are asking questions about you—do you need a doctor?—whatever you need they will give you and put you on a bus with Bonnie Raitt. You can sit and play and talk and have a good time." And this other guy said, "The way I see Charles Brown going up the racetrack, I don't think he needs a doctor."

Well, we went out on the road in April or May, and we stayed out there till October. Everywhere we went we got a standing ovation, and all the critics gave us A-plus. Then finally Bonnie Raitt tells me, "Charles, with the way these people like you, if you get one-tenth of them to come to see you when you're performing, you don't need nothing else."

Elwood: *Tell me a little about your background, who you listened to and how you got started.*

Brown: I listened to Bessie Smith, Leroy Carr, Blind Lemon Jefferson, all them people way back then, but it didn't strike me that that was my bag. I knew that if I played classical it would give me good technique. So I learned classical piano.

My mother died young and left me with her mother, and she said, "One of these days I want my children to go to California." So when my grandmother died my ambition was to go California. Well, when I got to California, I first came to Berkeley to go to school. I had been a junior chemist, but that wasn't really the thing for me. During the war I got classified 4F because of asthma, so I went on to L.A. and I played for the church, then I won an amateur contest that started the ball rolling. I wanted to go out to Hollywood and play—I didn't want to go on Central Avenue where sometimes you didn't get paid. So I found out what was required, and I signed with Johnny Moore to be pianist and vocalist with his trio. The black entertainers that was anything was with William Morris—Johnny Moore, Pearl Bailey, Count Basie, the Will Maston Trio with Sammy Davis . . . they had the Christmas party and I met Veronica Lake, Dick Haines, all of them, and it as just wonderful.

We got kind of popular in Hollywood, and we were going up to Frisco to play at the Backstage on Powell Street, which was a very fabulous club back in the '40s. We made our first recording, "Drifting Blues," and it swept the country—it was selling for $10 a record because the company couldn't produce enough. "Drifting Blues" made No. 1, and we got the Cash Box award of 1946, so that started the ball rolling.

Up in the corner of the record it said "Vocal and piano Charles Brown," but people figured that I had to be Johnny Moore. So when Johnny Moore did take sick I went on the road for William Morris. We were doing classical because Hazel Scott had set a precedent of mixing classical music and boogie-woogie. We were doing a little blues, but in Hollywood we kept one side of our music for one type of audience and another side for another type— the Hollywood types didn't know anything about blues at that time.

Elwood: *When people talk about the West Coast blues or the West Coast sound, they always mention your name.*

Brown: California had a more of a sophisticated thing; Nat Cole came out of that setting. That's where I learned about saying my words where you can understand them—even today I hear these great singers with great pipes, but you can't understand what the story's about. But we had to dramatize for the young people; if it was a number called, "You Are My First Love," we would sing that in a way that they could understand.

After the war was over people were looking to get away from sentimental songs—they said, "Now we're gonna pop our fingers and have a good time. So then here comes Little Richard, here comes Fats Domino, and later it was Elvis Presley, James Brown.

Elwood: *James Brown told me that one of his biggest influences is Charles Brown.*

Brown: Is that right? You know, when I did "Please Come Home for Christmas" after "Merry Christmas Baby," King Records asked James Brown to do it, but nobody got the sales like my record. It's just like Nat Cole—once he did something, no matter who tried to sing it he couldn't come up to what Nat Cole had done. Today a lot of singers sing so much alike you can't tell who it is, but you know if it's Nat Cole, Ray Charles, Dinah Washington, Billie Holiday, Nancy Wilson. And there's Barbra Streisand, Aretha Franklin—not a lot of girls try to copy after that.

Elwood: *What musicians and singers inspired your style?*

Brown: My grandmother loved Russ Colombo; that sentimental way he was singing, so it kind of put me into that. When we were going to college the Andy Kirk Band was popular, because they were singing beautiful love songs like "Good Bye," and "Until the Real Thing Comes Along," and I wanted to sing that. When I heard Helen O'Connell sing "Green Eyes" and "Take Me" and "Embraceable You," I said, "Well, I can't sing like that," but it gave me inspiration. That's where you get your style—you have somebody in mind even if you can't sing like 'em.

Elwood: *How did you get into doing those bluesy Christmas songs?*

Brown: There was a little heavy-set fella named Lou Baxter who used to follow us around. He was always interested in writing songs. He was having a trouble with his throat—which later on was found to be cancer of the esophagus—and he needed some money. [Exclusive Records owner] Leon Rene had told us that whoever would get a song to us that we would do, they would advance him $500. Lou Baxter gave me this satchel, and I said, "Let me take it home tonight and see what's in here." He had a lot of songs, but I saw "Merry Christmas Blues" and it just struck me, I don't know why. I said, "That should be 'Merry Christmas Baby,'" and I began playing around with words to match that. I figured if I did this, maybe Lou could get a $500 advance.

I thought, what do people like us colored folks want at Christmas time? They'd like diamond rings or Cadillac cars, something they're not able to get. So I said, "Gave me a diamond ring for Christmas, and I'm living in paradise." I brought it back to Leon Rene and told him Lou Baxter wrote a great song. Lou Baxter got the $500, but he didn't live too long after that; he died from cancer. The song went to Chicago and New York, and they just went crazy. The black people related to "Merry Christmas Baby" because "White Christmas" doesn't blend with us. Back then there was a separation of songs that were called "race records." Louis Jordan was the leader of that, but we took him out of first place with "Drifting Blues."

Elwood: *A lot of people don't realize that there were two separate music worlds in the '30s and '40s—white music and black music. A lot of white people didn't hear black music, and black people didn't often hear the white music.*

Brown: Yeah, there were two separate worlds. There were some songs that I liked that were by white people—I loved my grandmother's old Russ Colombo records, and I liked Jimmy Dorsey, Claude Thornhill . . . But it was a separation because you couldn't put a black record into a white store unless it had a white person on the front of it. I remember when they released "Drifting Blues" they had this white girl on the album in the shipment they put into white stores. Some of white people were into the black music, but it was not a majority. But when the rock 'n' roll era came in, everybody begin to mix.

Elwood: *Do you ever get sick of Christmas?*

Brown: They call me Mr. Santa Claus because I come once a year. But that song really kept me in the limelight when I wasn't doing anything—when Christmas time come, it was Charles Brown. So I think I've been lucky with Christmas numbers. "Merry Christmas Baby" sold a bunch, but it was not documented, so we don't how many. We never got the money because I wrote it for Lou Baxter and they put Johnny Moore's name on record. Even though I didn't get any royalties, I am proud of the fact that Johnny's sisters were able to get checks to keep them going when all the brothers were dead.

People ask me, "Why don't you put in for it? You could get that song back? But I'm not interested in getting it back. I let sleeping dogs lie. Other people need money, too—if I had all the money I might just go the racetrack and lose it. I got what I need for myself.

Elwood: *Did you ever imagine that you'd be having a new career, that you'd be singing to a whole new audience?*

Brown: My grandfather, on his dying bed, wanted to see me, and he said, "You've been a good boy, and for you being good to your family and the way you are, down the road you are going to see what's coming back to you. I can't tell you when it's coming, but it's coming." So when people ask me about my resurgence, I say I'm not so surprised, because my grandfather said that down the road I would see good for what I had done. Maybe this is it.

RUTH BROWN
Sympathy for the Devil's Music

> "He ran down the aisle and said, 'Sing it like I taught you.'"

Throughout her career Ruth Brown has triumphed over tough breaks. Stranded in Washington, D.C., in 1947, she took a job that led to her discovery by Atlantic Records. Her debut with the label was delayed by injuries suffered in a car crash, but during her nine-month hospital stay she honed her singing and signed her formal contract with Atlantic. In the 1950s she recorded a string of hits that helped build the label into an R&B power-house, but the next decade found her laboring in menial jobs. Brown fought back once again, building a new career while forwarding the work of the Rhythm & Blues Foundation. When she and Elwood talked in 1997, they touched on some of the stories in *Miss Rhythm: The Autobiography of Ruth Brown, Rhythm & Blues Legend.*

Elwood Blues: *You grew up in a gospel background, singing in the church. How were you exposed to the blues?*

Ruth Brown: Yes, as most of us did. I was exposed to the blues because the blues identifies a way of life, and when you're the oldest of eight children, there are many days that you witness and experience the blues, you see. But of course I didn't get an opportunity to actually sing it until I was about 20 years of age—even though I was singing many, many years before that—because the blues were considered the devil's music, as you know.

Ruth Brown brings down the house with her powerful vocals, and she gets credit for hits that helped build Atlantic Records' house in the 1950s.

And as I used to say, I don't know why the devil's got to have all the good stuff, but he does.

Elwood: *You had to sneak around when you were kid, singing at the USO behind your dad's back.*

Brown: Yes; during the war years. My excuse for being in the USO was I had a day job there working behind the soda counter, making milkshakes. I wasn't doing very well, because between scoops I was sneaking in the back and listening to the band. So I got exposed to the music, but it wasn't really the blues, you know. What we heard were the Tex Benekes, the Glenn Millers, the Andrew Sisters, all the music that was prevalent during the war years. So I ended up doing things like "Chattanooga Choo-Choo." My dad still did not approve of it, because that was still the devil's music as far as he was concerned.

Elwood: *I understand your dad was not averse to giving you a whooping in public.*

Brown: Not at all. He walked into the USO one time when I was up on stage singing, on a Thursday when I was supposed to be at choir practice, at Emmanuel AME Church—I had told a little teensy, eensy lie. I looked down and saw my daddy observing me, and of course he was this individual who didn't have to say a word. All he had to do was give you a look and point a finger that said, "Come on down"—long before that was the slogan of the state of Florida. He took his belt and kind of exposed me a little bit. I guess that's a little different than nowadays. You didn't wait on the punishment. You do the crime, you pay the time, right now.

Elwood: *Years later when your dad came to the Apollo and saw you up there performing, it brought tears to his eyes.*

Brown: And he ran down the aisle and said, "Sing it like I taught you"— yes, he did. That was quite fulfilling for me. I'm sure my dad was probably very frustrated because he had a great baritone voice, and if he'd had the opportunity, he could have become recognized himself. But being the father of eight children, he didn't see that. So I'm sure that some of the time that he was very restrictive was because he saw in me what he might have been. And I always say that I know that this gift that he had was handed directly to me, because out of eight children, I'm the one that got that gift.

Elwood: *As you were a young woman developing your style, who were your influences? Was Bessie Smith one of them?*

Brown: No, I did not know about Bessie Smith. My dad and them knew, but that music was totally kept out of my ear range. I did hear Bing Crosby and Red Foley and Hank Williams. We heard country and western because that's what most of the radio stations were relegated to; I came up in Portsmouth, Virginia, and it was very much country and western. The only outlet we had was a program in the morning called the Mailbag. There was a deejay, God love him, called Jack Holmes, and when my daddy would leave in the morning, no sooner had the front door slammed than we had switched the dial on the radio to Jack Holmes. He was playing things like Sonny Til & the Oreos, the Charioteers, Buddy Johnson and Ella Johnson, Arthur Prysock, Billy Eckstine.

Elwood: *Did you ever in your wildest dreams think some day you'd be out touring with Billy Eckstine and with Count Basie?*

Brown: Never. That's where my self-esteem was. Being the oldest of eight children and in a locale like that, and with the world situation, prejudice and segregation, where it was at that time, I never dreamed for a moment that I would go any further than right there at Chestnut and Race where the USO building was.

Elwood: *When you were still a teenager you went to the Apollo and won an amateur contest. Can you tell us about that?*

Brown: Oh yes. That was 1943, though I remember it like it was yesterday. I rode the bus all the way from Virginia with a ticket that had been paid for by some airmen who had frequented the USO where I was singing. I won first prize singing a Bing Crosby song. The band was Tiny Bradshaw and the emcee was Doc Wheeler, and I remember that when I went onstage I was so nervous I forgot to touch the Tree of Hope—there was something very important about touching that tree. Doc Wheeler said, "Go back, go back and touch the Tree of Hope." It meant something, because in those days you heard the amateur show from the Apollo on the radio all through the South every Wednesday night. When it ran it was as important as when Joe Louis fought. Nothing moved. You could sit on your stoop, and everybody in the block would be tuned to the same thing.

Elwood: *You must have been quite the local heroine when you returned after winning that award.*

Brown: Well, not really, because I was up there without my daddy knowing what I was going for. He thought I was going to visit an uncle, but my uncle arranged to get me on that show. However they did it, they managed to keep him from hearing it the night I was on.

Elwood: *Many years later you were due to come back to the Apollo and sing on the same bill with Billie Holiday, but she didn't like women to be singing with her, did she?*

Brown: That's right. A couple of days before we were supposed to leave, a message came down that there had been a change in plan, and Ms. Holiday or her management, whomever, had decided that it would not be wise for me to be on that bill. So they made it for the following week which, would have put me on with Dizzy Gillespie. En route to the Apollo that Thursday morning—Thursday was the day you had rehearsals—around nine in the morning we had an accident outside of Chester, Pennsylvania. It delayed my arrival for over a year, because my legs were crushed, you know. I spent nine and a half months in Chester hospital.

Elwood: *You put that time to good use, though, working on your singing and your music, didn't you?*

Brown: Yes, and I had not previously signed a contract with Atlantic. They had heard me, and it had been just a verbal agreement. They came to the hospital with the contract, and it was signed in the hospital. Also, for my birthday, for my 20th birthday they brought me a pitch pipe and a book on how to sight-read. I'm still not reading, though.

Elwood: *That was Ahmet Ertegun and Herb Abramson?*

Brown: Yes; they were the originators of Atlantic—this is long before Jerry Wexler came on. At that time Ahmet's father was Turkish ambassador to the United States. They were lovers of the music; when I first went with Atlantic the label was very small, and everybody involved was real family-like. It wasn't difficult to get to talk to one another or go to Harlem together and see shows or visit restaurants.

Elwood: *The label became known as "the house that Ruth built," and it certainly put you into the Top Ten.*

Brown: Ruth is the person that Atlantic built—same thing. And even though in these later years—I'm sure everybody's aware of what happened—with the struggle for royalties, it wasn't vindictive. It was something that I had a right to, as other performers did. In those days we weren't well protected by legal people, didn't know how to read the contracts. The contracts were simple, but not quite so simple, you see? We had no idea about foreign royalties. Everything that we did in the studio, we were charged for. And consequently, every time you looked around, you were in debt, so you thought.

Elwood: *Did your involvement in the Rhythm & Blues Foundation, working to preserve the rights of artists, come out of that experience?*

Brown: Yes, but I must say that the seed money was put up by Ahmet Ertegun and Atlantic Records. The Rhythm & Blues Foundation fights for the rights of the people who were the innovators of this music—artists that came along in the late '40s into the mid-'60s. By the mid-'60s people were better represented than we were, and record royalties had changed. When I went into studios I made $65 and $70 a side. When I read the figures that today's artists are receiving—I never could even write that many zeros.

The music is coming full circle. Films, soundtracks, commercials, you name it, it's there. But are we getting paid for it? Once in a while I get a residual check, and it's a feather in my cap to say, "Gee, they were playing my music on *Northern Exposure*. Even if the check is for $400 or $500 every once in a while, that $400 or $500 will help pay my rent.

Unfortunately the Foundation has come along late, and a lot of the recipients of the benefits are not living to enjoy it. They keep saying, "We'll do this next year and maybe the year after that." Who's got that kind of time? I don't—I'm 70 years old. Who else is going to hire me? The top acts that are big moneymakers are not being as kind as Bonnie Raitt was.

Elwood: *You've recorded and toured with Bonnie. Tell us a little about your relationship with her.*

Brown: She has never ceased to amaze me in her giving back to what she has drawn from—and she'd be the first one to tell you where it came from. She called my name loud every night that she introduced me. It was like giving me a shot in the arm to rejuvenate my career. And she does things that people never read about. A lot of people do things for you, and they got the cameras rolling—"Here's this check in my name; be sure camera number two gets this." Not Bonnie. I call her First Raitt. I'm very glad to call her my friend.

Elwood: *Tell us about another friend of yours, Little Richard.*

Brown: I love Little Richard—Richard Penniman. He says that he heard me do "Mama," and then he did "Lucille." He says, "I love Ruth Brown. I wanted to be Ruth Brown. I wanted to look like Ruth Brown." So we are friends even to this day. We've done many tours together. We don't see each other that often, but when we do it's just like we were never away from each other.

Elwood: *He's the one who took rhythm and blues and turned it into rock 'n' roll.*

Brown: He don't get credit for it, but he did it. He as well as Bo Diddley have been kind of overlooked when it comes to giving out the accolades. Little Richard definitely gets my vote for being what he calls "the Architect." He's right.

Elwood: *You had the opportunity to work with Ray Charles early in your career.*

Brown: Yes; the first time he ever worked with me, in Austin, Texas, he was going to be the house piano man. When I got there we had all this music, and my road manager said, "This is Ray Charles." I noticed right away the black glasses and that he was blind, and I said, "How's he going to play my music?" We still talk about that when we see each other.

I had another incident with Ray Charles and [blind vocalist] Al Hibbler, God bless him. We were all playing a job in New Jersey, and I was sitting in the back of the car just waiting to go on. They were sitting on the front seat. Al Hibbler started up the car and said, "Let's take Ruth for a ride"—the scariest five seconds I've ever lived in my life, with these two idiots.

These are wonderful memories. I'm always rejuvenated when I think how fortunate I was. In those days I had no idea of the depth and the quality and the status of the people with whom I was rubbing shoulders on a day-to-day basis.

Elwood: *You had a rocky start in the business when you got hired by Lucky Millinder.*

Brown: I think Lucky hired me on a dare. He already had two singers in the band, Annisteen Allen and Bull Moose Jackson. I was working at a club in Detroit, and he came in one night with couple of members of the Stan Kenton Orchestra. They were probably celebrating, and he might have had one little wine glass too many. Somebody said, "That's a good singer," and he said, "I think I'll hire her," just like that. I sang about ten songs auditioning for him, and when he offered me the job, the two owners of the club allowed me to go. I traveled with the band three or four weeks and never sang a note. When I finally got to Washington, D.C., on the Fourth of July we played a place called Turner's Arena, and he let me sing two songs. When I got through, Al Grey, bless his heart, asked me to go to the soda counter and bring some sodas back for him, Jimmy Nottingham, Clark Terry, Billy Mitchell—all these guys were in the Lucky Millinder Orchestra. I went to the soda counter and came back with a boxtop full of sodas, and Lucky saw me as I was crossing the stage. He leaned down and said, "I hired a singer, not a waitress; you're fired"—just like that—"and besides, you can't sing anyway."

Well, I was devastated, but it was probably the best thing that he could have done for me, because by leaving me stranded there in Washington—I didn't have the price of a ticket and I only lived about 200 miles away—I got to meet this wonderful woman called Blanche Calloway. She gave me a job at a club called the Crystal Caverns. That's where I was singing to earn money to get home when one night in walked the great Duke Ellington and a wonderful man named Willis Conover, who was the Voice of America at that time on Armed Forces Radio. Sonny Til of the Orioles was with them. After I got through singing, I saw Willis Conover go to the pay phone. He called Ahmet Ertegun, who was in Washington at the time, and told him, "You better come over here and listen to this girl singing at the Crystal Caverns." That's where it all started.

Elwood: *What was Harlem like when you were there in the '40s and '50s?*

Brown: In those days every other corner had music—great music. There was the Top Club, there was the Celebrity Club, the Lido, the Red Rooster, the Shalimar, there was Wells' Chicken and Waffles, the Candlelight Lounge, the Baby Grand, the Palm Café—Oh, my God, there was the Apollo Bar, the Braddock Bar, Club Harlem, the Heat Wave. . . . on 110th Street was the Paradise where you could go any night and hear Lester Young and Charlie Parker and Dizzie just standing up there playing.

Elwood: *The flip side must have been touring through the segregated South.*

Brown: Oh, yes indeed, it was difficult, and that is why I'm such a champion about people not throwing away this music—rhythm and blues was the healer, you know. I worked places where the people in the same room were separated by a rope. And when the music got good, the ropes fell down, with people dancing, touching one another. Nobody said a thing about it, because they were involved in the music. The places we played when there were segregated water fountains, segregated bathrooms—I got locked up a couple times for going into the bathroom; it said "Ladies," and I thought *I* was a lady. I've had my car burned. I've had night court held on me when it said I was doing 35 miles in a 32 zone. But still, what compensated for all of that was riding those buses with the likes of Jackie Wilson and Sam Cooke and the Clovers and the Drifters and Lester Young and John Coltrane and Buddy Johnson, and the Five Keys, LaVern Baker—everybody on one bus, you know? It was very difficult, because we had to get in town in time to go down into the across-the-track black section. Couldn't stay in Howard Johnson's. Couldn't stay in these motels. Couldn't eat in these restaurants. You had to go into the heart of town where somebody would allow you to come into their home and sleep.

Sharecroppers came to those dances, and they didn't pay to come in. They signed the book for the man that was booking the dance, and at the end of the month that money would be taken out. But that one night that we were there was like the calm after the storm after being in the fields all day. That's what made it worthwhile. And the wonderful thing for us was we could get on the bus and leave. Those people had to stay.

Elwood: *You've said you can touch people's hearts without making them mournful. That's the essence of the blues.*

Brown: That's what it is. Blues were once relegated to people of my ethnic background because the music typifies the way we dealt with things, as in the slave trade, when a lot of spirituals were not really spiritual—they were signals, a way of communicating. The high master wasn't aware. He'd just say, "Look at them children singing." But we were singing about something. The blues is the same way, but it is no longer relegated to my ethnicity, because everybody nowadays has got the blues about something, especially men. Society does not allow a man to express with dignity what he feels. He can't cry without someone saying he's a weakling. Why should he not be able to cry? I mean, he's got problems, you know? But when blues singers get up on the stage, they can cry and be real about it.

Elwood: *It's wonderful you were able to tell about your experiences in your book.*

Brown: I thought I'd like to be the one to tell it. I don't want it to come out unauthorized, with somebody saying, "This is what I *think* happened." There may be some things in there that people will gasp and say, "Oh, I didn't know that." I was no angel—there were a lot of things that happened to me that I was ashamed of when I was a young girl. I take the blame for it. But you have to get to a certain place and decide who you are. What I've got is a gift. I didn't pay a dime for this voice. So you take those things that were not good, and you say, "Now I can sing about it." People call it soul.

R. L. BURNSIDE
Juke Joint Genius

> *"The main thing is, everybody has the blues sometime."*

Like his "ass pocket of whiskey," the juke-joint blues of R.L. Burnside is raw, bracing, and powerful. A longtime northern Mississippi denizen, the former farmer learned the blues from his neighbor, Fred McDowell, and got further slide-guitar inspiration in Chicago from Muddy Waters. In the late '60s folk archivists discovered Burnside, and in the '90s his career received a boost from his collaboration with rock maverick Jon Spencer. R.L. went on to release a number of his own records on Fat Possum, several featuring family members Dwayne and Cedric Burnside and Calvin Jackson. Elwood talked to R.L. in 1998, not long after the death of Burnside's friend and juke-blues peer Junior Kimbrough.

Elwood Blues: *When did you get your first guitar?*

R.L. Burnside: Well, when I got married my brother-in-law could play a little guitar, and then he got married and he left his guitar there with me. I played on it, then about a year later I messed around and bought one. One of them high-priced ones, about five dollars.

Elwood: *That was high-priced back then?*

Burnside: Yeah.

Elwood: *About how old were you then?*

Burnside: I started around 17 or 18 beginning to learn. I grew up around Fred McDowell and Rainie Barnette, and I've always liked the blues music. I was 21 before I started playing out in the public.

From stealing cows to stealing the show: R.L. Burnside brings the juke-joint sound to Central Park's Summerstage in June 2000.

Elwood: *Who were some of the guitar players that inspired you?*

Burnside: Well I got a lot from Fred McDowell. And when I went up to Chicago, Muddy Waters was married to a first cousin of mine, and I got a lot of influence from him.

Elwood: *What were some of the things you learned from Fred McDowell?*

Burnside: That was the first place I learned some slide guitar. After I got around Muddy Waters for two or three years, I learned the slide good then. That was in the late '40s.

Elwood: *What brought you up to Chicago?*

Burnside: I just told myself I was going to make a little more money. I came up there and worked for two or three years, and I got off and went back down to Mississippi to visit for a couple of weeks and got married. And I've been back ever since. People have always given Mississippi a bad name, but I think it's a good country. You never heard tell of nobody starving to death down there because there is rabbits you could hunt or go fishing or some cows you could steal or something. You could eat.

Elwood: *Stealing cows?*

Burnside: Yeah. Steal chickens and stuff like that, you know.

Elwood: *When did you first start recording?*

Burnside: My first recording was in 1967. A guy by the name of George Mitchell, he came through the country. I was working on the farm then, driving the cotton pickers and combines and things. He came and got Rainie

Barnette, Fred McDowell—he was just looking for some blues players. He came on up there, and every night when I came out of the field we would sit up there and record until one or two o'clock in the morning. Then in '68 he wrote and asked could he make an album out of it. He left his phone number and I called him. I told him yes, okay. And when the album came out, that was my first tour, about the last of '68 to Montreal, Canada. I was playing solo then, and I got up there to play, me and Robert Pete Williams, a guy from New Orleans. We was going together with Robert Junior Lockwood; he was already out there, and we got lost on the subway and passed the place, and we were late getting back there and they was hollering for me on the stage—"R.L. Burnside, from Coldwater, Mississippi!" I didn't even have a chance to go to the restroom, just got on the stage, started playing, people standing all around there, sitting down, and Robert Junior Lockwood and his wife sitting over there in the tent; he waved and hollered over my way.

For the first couple of songs, man, I was nervous; I couldn't hardly play. But then I was drinking pretty good, you know, so I was getting high so I wouldn't be too nervous. After about a couple of songs people got to hollering and carrying on and twisting, and I got the feeling then, you know. I went on and played, and the people was glad at that.

That was the first time I got to meet Lightnin' Hopkins and John Lee Hooker. When I came off the stage I went over and talked to Robert Junior Lockwood and his wife, and he said, "You really done a good thing, man, I'll tell you what. I'm glad to see you again, but I can tell you got a whippin'." I said, "What do you mean?" "Lightnin' Hopkins and John Lee Hooker are there in the dressing room." I said, "Oh, man, I'm playing some stuff behind them guys?" Man, I could have been sold for a penny then. I got in there, and they said, "Yeah, Burnside, I don't mind anybody playing my music as long as they don't mess it up. Man, I didn't know nobody could do that but us. But you done it just like us." I said I sure appreciate it, but I could have been sold for a penny.

Elwood: *How did you feel when you saw your album for the first time?*

Burnside: I was really proud of it, but the people looked like they were gladder than I was. "Yeah, man, you were really great. I want to get one of your albums." That made me feel better. But right then I never thought I would be touring like I am now. I just figured, because I was still working on a plantation, I was just touring maybe once or twice, maybe three times a year. But after I got to touring often, I had to move off the plantation and rent me a house. But still, for a year or two I would go play and do some day work for those guys when I wasn't touring. But I got to where about 14 years ago I gave up farming, I don't do nothing but play music now.

Elwood: *When you were working out in the fields, did you ever think about playing music full time?*

Burnside: Yeah, I wanted to. Always have wanted to do it, but back then I never thought I could do it, you know.

Elwood: *When did you meet up with Junior Kimbrough?*

Burnside: I had heard of him for about 20 or 25 years, but I meet up with him about 18 years ago. I was just going by a place one night, and he was playing there. I was carrying another guy to a store, and he said, "Let's stop by here. Junior Kimbrough is playing up here." Okay. I went on up there, and there he was playing. He got where he let me play after he got tired—they wanted to rest him up a little bit. He'd heard of me and I'd heard of him, you know. And I played a few numbers, and the people they liked the both of us. He was living up near Ashland then, and I was living down just about to Coldwater. But he would always get in touch with me if he was playing somewhere; he wanted me to go help him out and play. I would do the same thing about him. That's where we started getting together.

Elwood: *Did you like his music when you first heard it?*

Burnside: Yeah, oh, yeah.

Elwood: *You guys used to travel together for Fat Possum Records.*

Burnside: Yeah, we was out on a tour together a good many times. Then when we wasn't touring, every weekend he would have his juke joint open, and we would go play there. So we had a nice party going. He was a good guy. He liked women and he liked to drink, but he was a good fellow.

Elwood: *A lot of people might not know what a juke joint is like. Can you tell us a little about that?*

Burnside: Back in those days there wasn't no special place to have a party, so people in these old houses would give a party there on Saturday night. They would start say, nine, ten o'clock and go just as long as the people stayed there. Drinking whiskey and gambling, playing music all night long. Have a good time. People would be breaking the floor trying to dance and carry on.

Elwood: *Do you remember when people started to recognize your music more often?*

Burnside: Well, me and my boys put out a couple of albums, and I put out one in Harlem and another out in California, but then blues just went away after a while, and then you had to have a band to play; people wanted to dance and carry on. So me and my boys started up again and came out with this other album, and that got me known and starting to move around a little bit. What really I think got the young people turned on to me was me being out there opening for Jon Spencer.

Elwood: *How did you meet Jon Spencer?*

Burnside: He heard that album we had out, and he called Fat Possum and asked could we open for him. I'd heard of him, but I'd never heard him play. I said, "Yeah, we'll do it." Anything to make a little money, you know.

We got out there and the first place we played at the guy asked me, "You ever heard these guys play before?" I said, "No, I haven't." He bought me a package of earplugs and said, "You're going to need these."

When they played they would always want us to come back and jam with them at the end. And we would be in the dressing room after I come offstage, sitting there talking and drinking and carrying on, and I'd be telling a lot of old funny stories. "R.L., man, you ought to do an album about that." I said, "Oh, man, you know ain't nobody going to buy that." "R.L., you just don't know, yes they will." I said, "Well, I'll let you know."

I'd been back home a couple of weeks, and me and some friends of mine were sitting out there in my yard drinking some beer and some corn whiskey. My daughter ran out there, "Daddy, telephone." I said, "Bring it here"—I had one of them cordless phones. "Hello, R.L. This is Jon. You ever decide to do that album?" I said, "Hell, if it don't help me it can't hurt me none. Come on down and we'll do it." About two days, they came down to Hollow Springs, rented one of them big hunting clubs up there, and we did the album in about four hours. But they had the hunting club rented for a couple of days, you know—all the equipment and every thing in there but we did the album in about four hours.

Elwood: *What was it like out on the road with Jon Spencer?*

Burnside: It was great. We had some T-shirts and some albums with us and the fifth night they had sold about three T-shirts and two albums. We got to Harlem, and they said, "Man, we're going to have to do that 'Ass Pocket of Whiskey' tonight." I said, "No, man, we ain't going to do that in public. I had never been doing this, you know, out in the public, but I'd like to sit up in the dressing room and talk that old stuff. But we were sitting back in there drinking, and I got out there and went to singing and I was dancing and hollering and cussin', and Jon hollering back at me, and the people went wild over that. That night we sold out of T-shirts, CDs, and everything. You take right now, about everywhere we play there's some-body hollering at me: "R.L., 'Ass Pocket of Whiskey.'" I think it caused me having more younger people at the places where I was playing.

Elwood: *Do you like being on the road?*

Burnside: Yeah, as long as I got my health and strength and feeling good, I love being out there. I just don't like to be out there too long. I love to go back home and be with my family. The first time I was out on tour I stayed out two and a half months—we was overseas for two months. I just told them I will never do that no more. Right now, Fat Possum could get me shows all the time if I could agree to go stay a month. But I won't do that.

Elwood: *What inspires you to write a song?*

Burnside: I just heard other people play some. I play some songs behind other people and some I just make up myself. At home I sit and think and I play some of it, and I got me a little recorder so I record that part. Then the next time something come to me, I write that, and I just put it together.

Elwood: *A lot of times when you do someone else's song you don't stick to the traditional lyrics; you add your own.*

Burnside: Yeah, that's the main thing—that's the Mississippi blues. It ain't 12-bar blues. You add your own lyrics to it.

Elwood: *Tell me more about Mississippi blues.*

Burnside: I think they have the blues because they tell how people have been treated in Mississippi a long time ago, but I think the main thing is, everybody has the blues sometime. You get broke and you want something and you can't get it with no money, you got the blues. You get out pretty late at night and you drive up to your house and you meet your cat when you open the car door—"She ain't here, she ain't here." You got the blues then, bad, man.

Elwood on the Air: Tiny Piano

HOUR: 03/40
AIRDATE: 10/4–5/03
WRITER: MERLE KESSLER

ELWOOD: Welcome to The House of Blues Radio Hour. I'm Elwood Blues. And . . . (interrupted)

[FX: Ding Dong.]

And that is—the door.

[FX: Door opening.]

What is it? I am trying to do a radio program here.

SALESMAN: The House of Blues Radio Hour. I know. That's why I'm here. I have something that will cause musicians everywhere to breathe a sigh of relief.

ELWOOD: A royalty check?

SALESMAN: Ha ha! No. Elwood, have you ever asked yourself why you don't play piano?

ELWOOD: Because I don't know how?

SALESMAN: Because you don't want to throw out your back lugging a concert grand to and from a gig.

ELWOOD: Usually there's a piano already there—

SALESMAN: But I can eliminate those trips to the chiropractor. With this—

ELWOOD: It looks like a tiny piano.

SALESMAN: I call it . . . Tiny Piano. I know what you're thinking.

ELWOOD: You are insane?

SALESMAN: How does a big lug like me get his fingers to play such a bitty thing? Well, with this.

ELWOOD: A Barbie hand glued to a thimble?

SALESMAN: It's Ken, actually, but let me put it on my index finger, and give it a listen.

[FX: Tiny piano noises.]

ELWOOD: I think I will stick to the harmonica.

SALESMAN: Wait! How about this?

ELWOOD: One piano key?

SALESMAN: Middle C.

[FX: Middle C on a piano.]

Easy to carry, slips in a pocket.

ELWOOD: But it's only one note!

SALESMAN: You'll be right some of the time.

ELWOOD: No thank you.

SALESMAN: There are 87 more! Collect 'em all!

ELWOOD: Thank you!

[FX: Door slam.]

But no thank you. I believe we have the piano situation pretty much covered.

[Song: "I Got a Woman"—Ray Charles]

RAY CHARLES

That's What He Said

> *"I don't care how many tracks you have, if you don't get no feeling into it, it doesn't matter about the tracks."*

In the '50s and '60s Ray Charles blended gospel, blues, jazz, and country sounds with his own emotion-drenched vocals to create a style of music that would shape the course of rhythm and blues. Blind from age six, Charles brought his prodigious talents as a singer, piano player, bandleader, and arranger to such classic tracks as "I Got a Woman," "What'd I Say," "Unchain My Heart," and "Hit the Road, Jack." In his 50-plus years as a performer, Charles found success in jazz and country music and on the pop charts, but he'll always be known as the Father of Soul. Elwood had this conversation with Charles in 1994. Brother Ray died on June 10, 2004, at age 73.

Elwood Blues: *On* The House of Blues Radio Hour *I've interviewed a lot of people, and so many of them—from James Brown to Robert Plant—say they got their inspiration from you.*

Ray Charles: I really do appreciate that a lot. You know, I've been around quite a long time, and it's good to know that somebody's paying me some attention. [*Laughs.*]

Elwood: *The question is, what were your influences?*

Charles: It was a variety of things. That's why I like to think of myself as a utility musician—I'm not a specialist in anything. I'm not a blues singer,

Genius at work: Ray Charles gets the feeling in a 1983 show.

I'm not a jazz singer, I'm not a country-and-western singer, but I'm a singer that can sing the blues, I'm a singer that can sing jazz, that can sing love songs, you see.

As a kid, of course, I was around the blues in my neighborhood—that's where you heard Muddy Waters and Tampa Red and Blind Boy Fuller and Big Boy Crudup and people like that. That's one influence. And then, of course, we went to the Baptist church, and I went to all the revival meetings and the BYPU [Baptist Young Peoples Union], so I had that type of influence.

And then, being in the South just about the only radio stations you could get were country stations, so I became very much in love with country music—on Saturday night my mom would let me stay up so I could hear the Grand Ole Opry. Then, the gentleman who lived next door to me, Wiley Pitman, was an excellent boogie-woogie pianist so I got to hear a lot of that; he started me off when I was just a little tot, two or three years old. So my music came to me from different sources.

Elwood: *What does it take to be a good blues singer?*

Charles: That's a great question, because you can't just say it's any one thing. First of all, it's important to have a little talent—that would help, let's face it. But to be any kind of singer you have to have feeling, and feeling cannot be taught. You can teach a person notes, you can teach them to play an instrument, or they can go to voice school and you can teach him how to sing. But the one thing you can't teach is feeling. That is the key to any kind of singing—can the person make what they're saying so real that you believe whatever they're singing about. It's same as an actress who plays a part on the screen that's so real you forget that it's just a play. That's what feeling is all about, to make whatever you're singing about believable.

Elwood: *Where does the blues come from?*

Charles: I think that the blues came from people having trouble. I think the blues came from people having hard times. I think the blues came from people being mistreated. I think the blues came from people having bad relations with their loved ones, or being mistreated or depressed or oppressed. The blues is a way of expressing how you feel inside; you can sing about it, and you're getting it out of your system. It's kind of like crying. It don't resolve a thing, but it makes you feel a little better.

Elwood: *Yet it can be happy music, too.*

Charles: But then that's life for you. You can take anything and turn it around. But I don't think the blues came from happiness. I may be wrong, but my gut feeling tells me the blues came from trouble.

Elwood: *A lot of people point to Louis Jordan as one of your influences. What made him special?*

Charles: The main thing about Louis Jordan is that when you heard two bars, you knew it was Louis Jordan. He had a style of his own; he did not sound like anybody else. It's just like Nat Cole would sing two words and you knew, or Frank Sinatra or Barbra Streisand or Aretha Franklin. That is the key. Louis Jordan also had this little band, the Tympani Five, that was very different; nobody around at the time was doing what Louis Jordan was doing. He did a lot of music that was very comical—"Ain't Nobody Here But Us Chickens," "Run Joe," a lot of fun music.

Elwood: *Your first hit, "It Should've Been Me," had that same kind of humor, and it had that syncopated Chicago blues feel.*

Charles: Well, it was blues. That's the thing, you know; there's so much you can do with music. That's what makes it such a beautiful art. You can go in any kind of direction you want. You can be very dramatic, you can be humorous, or you can be sentimental about whatever you want. When we did "It Should've Been Me" it was like going into the studio and saying, "Hey man, let's have some fun." You know, that song is kind of like rap. That's why I tell people I don't want to hear nothing about no rap—I was doing rap years ago. "It Should've Been Me" and "Green Back Dollar Bill" ain't nothing but talking.

Elwood: *You got criticism early on for secularizing gospel music. How did you feel about that?*

Charles: I could understand what people were saying. When I started out, as I said earlier, one of my great influences was the church, so naturally when I started to sing in my own way in my style, that influence came out, just like the blues in me came out. I came up around spiritual music, and so when I sang, some people felt, "Oh, he's bastardizing religion." But it just shows you about how times change. The next thing I know everybody was doing it, and they started calling it soul music. I say *uh-huh!*

Elwood: *How did "What'd I Say" come to be.*

Charles: In the latter part of the '50s—boy, that sounds like I'm ancient—we were playing dances in those days, you know; we didn't play too many concerts like you do now. The dances would start at about ten o'clock and go until two, or nine to one—always four hours. Usually we would play the first two and a half hours, then you would have a half-hour intermission, then you came back and you played that last hour. So one night we got back after intermission, and I went up on the stage and I sang and sang. When I'd sung everything I could think of we still had 15 minutes to go, so I said, "Tell you what guys, whatever I play y'all just follow me; girls, whatever I say you just say it; and we just started doing "do papa do, dodoom, do wah do . . ." And the people started dancing and going crazy. We did this a couple of nights, and somebody said to me, "Hey, man, you guys have a record on that? 'Cause that's great, man." I said, "No, there's no record, it's just something we do on the stage."

So I call Ahmet [Ertegun, Atlantic Records cofounder] the next day and said, "Man, I'd like to come in and record a song. We're playing this thing out here on the road, and the people love it." He said, "Well, hey, come on in and do it." One thing about when I was with Atlantic, I had all the freedom I wanted, anything I wanted to do musically. They never hassled me, they just said, "Anything you want to do, Ray, you do it." They never got in my way. It was very, very nice. But that song was truly an accident, because I was just trying to kill time. If you listen to the lyrics of "What'd I Say," I'm sure you know that there is no continuity at all—they're just lines thrown together, just verses; there is no story line. I'm just rhyming lines. The reason that it worked is not because it's a great song, but, I think, because it had such a great beat.

Elwood: *Since we're on the radio, I have to remind folks that you recorded some of your early songs at a radio station.*

Charles: Yes we did, as a matter of fact, I think we recorded at two radio stations, one in Atlanta and, if I'm not mistaken, at a radio station in Miami. It was very strange, man. We were trying to record, and we had to stop and break and let the man give the news. It was a very fun thing.

Elwood: *You've seen music go through all these changes, from recording at a radio station, up to recording at a 48-track digital studio. Does all that technology help or hinder your creativity?*

Charles: It doesn't affect me one way or the other. You know, the first little recording I made—it wasn't licensed or anything—was done on a wire recorder. I bet you haven't heard of a wire recorder, have you?

Elwood: *Well, actually I have.*

Charles: You have? Well, that's a surprise. [Claps.] Well, don't tell nobody, okay? From wire recording, we went to these big, round discs that they were recording on when I started recording professionally. "Transcriptions" is that what they called them. Then tape came in, and you had mono, then stereo. At first, stereo was the safety, and the mono was the one they used to put out the record, which was very strange. I remember from the mono to the 2-track to the 4-track, 8-track to the 16-track, and then they had 24-track, and now you have the digital with the 48-track.

But I'll tell you something, I don't care how many tracks you have, if you don't get the music down and you don't get no feeling into it, it doesn't matter about the tracks. People who are into the technical end of it, we get hung up about it—we want EQ, we want the echo chamber. . . . But in the end it's all about what the public hears—that's what it comes down to. You can record in your bathroom, and if the music is right, the people won't know nothing about all this other stuff. So it was recorded on a digital 48, so what?—what did it sound like, man? Could I snap my fingers to it, could it make me cry, did I get an emotion from it—that's what it's all about.

I'm not knocking technology. You can go in and you do your tracking, and then the string section can come in and the trumpet section come in later and all this stuff—you can do all of that and get a cleaner sound. But you know what, one of the greatest things today is to go into the studio and do everything live. That's really something. There ain't nothing like that feeling of having live people in the studio and everybody moves together. Whatever happens, it happens spontaneously—although it gets the engineers crazy, because they can't control everything like they want to.

Elwood: *You were such a big part of the* Blues Brothers *movie. I don't think* *people realize that you gave me and Jake such a hand in helping us with our vocal styles, helping us learn how to sing.*

Charles: Oh, come on now—the truth of the matter is that I was the one that got all the help, believe me. Talk about being out of my league—I know nothing about movies; I was really out of place. You guys guided me and made me feel really at home. I had a marvelous time.

Elwood: *Jake told me, "Ray Charles is such a gentlemen; he took us aside and walked us through this stuff."*

Charles: Well, turnabout was fair play. It just goes to show you, we help each other, baby. That's what makes it nice.

JOHNNY CLYDE COPELAND

Man Facing Southwest

> *"Texas blues is pulled between Kansas City and New Orleans—it's got a New Orleans funk in the Kansas City swing."*

By the time his '80s recordings brought him renown, Texas native Johnny Copeland—nicknamed "Clyde" during his stint as a boxer—had been battling it out in blues clubs for more than three decades. A mainstay at Houston's legendary Shady's Playhouse, Copeland took his scorching guitar style and brawny vocals on tour with Albert Collins and other greats during the '50s and '60s. After a rough transition to New York in the mid '70s, he capped a resurgence with the award-winning *Showdown!* with Robert Cray and Albert Collins in '86. Despite poor health, he continued touring until his death in 1997. His daughter Shemekia [page 188] now carries on his tradition with her own passionate blues vocals. Elwood talked with Johnny Copeland in September 1995 as he was awaiting a heart transplant.

Elwood Blues: *Do you remember the first blues player you heard when you were growing up in Texas?*

Johnny Clyde Copeland: Yes—the first one I went to see was T-Bone Walker. I was 14 or 15. They would have T-Bone Walker, Gatemouth Brown, just a whole big show, and I'd go see T-Bone. I was crazy about the man.

Bringing it home: Texas-born Johnny Clyde Copeland goes for the big notes.

After we got our band together we was playing down in Galveston for a man named James Manfield. T-Bone was playing in Houston that night, so Mr. Manfield says, "If you guys play good tonight, I'll take you over to Houston after the show and introduce you to T-Bone." We got through that night, and sure enough, he put us in the car and drove back to Houston, and we went to the matinee.

When we got in the matinee, T-Bone was sitting at the bar and eating. We all jumped out of the car real fast, and we beat Mr. Manfield inside because he had to park the car. We saw T-Bone sitting at the bar, and we're just standing there looking at him. A little bit later Mr. Manfield walked in and said, "T, I want you to meet these young musicians. They want to meet you." We just stood there looking at him, and he said, "Man, I'm sure glad somebody said something. I thought they come in to jump on me." Imagine four husky kids—we were like football players—and we just run up on him. But he was a great gentleman.

Elwood: *What was it about T-Bone's music that you dug?*

Copeland: You name it, I dug it. Out of all the blues people I ever met in my life, T-Bone was the most favorite. He is the one who made me want to sing the blues.

Elwood: *Who were some other people who influenced your playing?*

Copeland: Most of my influences come from the Texas side—T-Bone, Blind Lemon Jefferson, Gatemouth Brown, Lightnin' Hopkins.

Elwood: *What did you like about Lightnin' Hopkins?*

Copeland: The humor, I think. All his stuff was real humorous. It was more of a happy blues.

Elwood: *You have Gatemouth Brown sitting in with you on your new album, along with another guy from the border country, Lonnie Brooks.*

Copeland: Gatemouth and Lonnie, they right off the Louisiana line, in the swamp country. Johnny Winter is from down there, too.

Elwood: *What's the difference between the swamp sound and the Texas blues sound?*

Copeland: Texas blues is pulled between Kansas City and New Orleans—it's got a New Orleans funk in the Kansas City swing. And the swamp music is a little more New Orleans, you know. It's closer to New Orleans but there's actually a great difference in the sound.

Elwood: *When a lot of younger people think about Texas blues, they might be thinking just about Stevie Ray Vaughan. But there's a big history of Texas blues long before Stevie.*

Copeland: Well, I tell you, Stevie was the first one that made it real known and got Texas blues around the country. He had movie stars coming here. So what can you say? He was well known. He got there at a good time. But he wasn't no overnight success like people think he was. He played blues around for nothing for years in Austin from the time he was about 16. So he wasn't really an overnight success like people think he was.

Elwood: *You have a strong connection to another great Texas blues man, Albert Collins.*

Copeland: When I was just getting started I got a chance to go with his band, which was more experienced than the band I was with. I learned a lot from that band. He had two horns, saxophones, piano, and we had been working with just two guitars and a drum. I stayed with him about six months. That was my first real gig.

Elwood: *There's a good story about an offer you had to tour West Texas, and they promised you some clothes.*

Copeland: I was playing with Albert's band at the time. A guy named Big Frank stopped me on the street and he told me, "I want for you to go out to West Texas with me, and I'll give you 25 bucks a night." It was after the weekend, and I put my clothes in the cleaners, and I would get them out Friday. But he was leaving Thursday. So I said, "Well, I can't go because all my clothes are in the cleaners." He said, "I'll buy you all the clothes you need, so don't worry about it, and I'll give you $25 a night." $25 a night was a lot of money, so I said okay. Well, we get out there and didn't none of the gigs pay off, and I didn't get no clothes—I had to wear the same thing every night.

But when we got back, his brother-in-law made me the bandleader in his club, Shady's Playhouse, and that's where I got started on my own. I was bandleader over some real experienced musicians. I learned a lot from them.

Elwood: *When you came to New York in the '70s, was there a good blues scene going on?*

Copeland: Nah. In '75 when I come here, if I had told somebody, "Say man, I'll come play in your club and you don't have to give me nothing," he would say, "Let me think about it." It was that bad. Blues, gospel, and jazz was like five percent of the whole market, and the best you could get to do an album was $5,000 from any company. But it'd take $5,000 to cut a record.

Elwood: *Right now the blues are definitely hot in New York and other big cities. Why do you think it's come around?*

Copeland: Well, at the time I was telling you about, music went as far as it could go, all the way to disco. That's what it was all about when I got here. And there wasn't no more singing or artists with different styles like you had in the '50s and '60s, like a Sam Cooke or Jackie Wilson or Brook Benton or Aretha Franklin. So people had to go back to the roots—it had to come back around, you know,

Elwood: *When you first came to New York you were playing a jazzier style, weren't you?*

Copeland: Well, I always related to jazz because I kept a lot of jazz musicians around me from the Shady Playhouse thing. Most of my band was jazz musicians, and they played the blues. In them days, there wasn't a lot of guitar instrumentals floating around, so our instrumentals consisted of things like "Body and Soul," "What Is This Thing Called Love," them kind of instrumentals.

Elwood: *In the late '70s and early '80s, a lot of great blues men came through New York. You must have had a chance to hook up with a lot of them.*

Copeland: Oh, yes. We used to go down to the Lone Star a lot—Brooklyn Slim used to play there every Tuesday night. That was about the only blues going on in town. And then after a while, the Lone Star started bringing in a lot of Chicago blues people, and they brought in Albert Collins and Lightnin' Hopkins and a lot of others.

Elwood: *In 1985 you and Albert Collins and Robert Cray had a big hit with the album* Showdown—*it got a Handy Award and a Grammy. What was it like cutting those tracks with those guys?*

Copeland: You know, I've been knowing Albert all my life, and I met Robert later through Albert. It was great to get the chance to do a record with Albert. A lot of things I wanted to say to him I did on the record, because at this time, he was living on the West Coast and I come to the East Coast, though he left Houston in '65 and I didn't leave until '75. I always followed Albert pretty well through my career, you know. Me and Albert got some pretty good records in our time in Texas. He got a song called "The Freeze," and three or four years later I got a tune called "Down on Bended Knee."

Elwood: *What was Albert like?*

Copeland: He was a country boy. He loved to drive trucks and work on trucks. He was that kind of person. He used to play at night and work in the day at a place where they changed tires in Houston, and it looked like he'd have more fun doing that job than he would playing music. He loved that kind of stuff.

Elwood: *Debbie Davies, who played in his band, said that touring with him was great because a lot of time when he'd leave a town, there'd be somebody who was really into the music and they'd travel with him for a while.*

Copeland: Well, he knew a lot of people. Everybody that was into him was really into him. They liked him. If he said, "Come on, make yourself at home," he meant it. So you could go with him.

JAMES COTTON
Schooled in the Blues

> *"He drank half and I drank the other half, and he give me the band."*

James Cotton's musical journey destined him to blues greatness. His mother provided early inspiration, and he traveled straight from the family's farm to an apprenticeship with Sonny Boy Williamson. His connection to Sonny Boy landed him a gig with Howlin' Wolf, and after leaving Wolf he recorded for Sun Records' Sam Phillips. In 1956 Muddy Waters brought Cotton to Chicago, where they played together for a decade. Cotton's 30-year solo career has produced nearly 30 albums that have embraced both soul and rock 'n' roll. When Elwood talked to the tireless blues man in 1996, he had just recorded *Deep in the Blues* with young blues lion Joe Louis Walker and jazz bassist Charlie Haden.

Elwood Blues: *You left home at age nine to live with Sonny Boy Williamson and learn from him. How did that come about?*
James Cotton: Rice Miller, who is better known as Sonny Boy Williamson number two, had this radio show in Helena, Arkansas—"Welcome to the Biscuit because it's King Biscuit Time." I listened to that show and started to play the things that I heard Sonny Boy play. And then about two years later I was sitting on the company porch—my stepfather, Marco, had taught me how to drive tractors and things like that when I was seven, eight years

Urban legend: James Cotton brings his blend of city and country blues to Central Park's 2003 Summerstage.

old—and Marco said, "Well, the farm ain't no place for you." And he take me to Helena, Arkansas to meet Sonny Boy.

Marco told me to tell him that I was an orphan, and Sonny Boy was going for it. Marco said, "I just want to get him a job with you. He's got a talent, and I don't want to see him go to waste." So Sonny Boy took me on. I stayed with his group until I was 15, 16 years old.

Elwood: *That must have been something, being a nine-year-old kid and all of a sudden learning from the best. What was Sonny Boy like?*

Cotton: Well, he had his ways. He liked his moonshine, and he had a fast temper and a quick pocketknife.

Elwood: *Now, you played with him for six years and then you connected with Howlin' Wolf. How did that come about?*

Cotton: I stayed with Sonny Boy six years, then he and his wife had a falling out for some reason. She moved up to Milwaukee, and I guess things were going bad for Sonny Boy. We come in from a gig and he saw his house falling in, falling down. So he just kind of gave up Arkansas. We were playing that Saturday night, and he walks up to me with a bottle of seven-grain whiskey and says, "Stand up and let's drink this." He drank half and I drank the other half, and he give me the band. It didn't stay together long because I was too young to do the right thing with it—stayed together a couple or three months. All the men resigned; I was a crazy, hard-headed kid, you know.

Elwood: *So that's when you hooked up with the Wolf?*

Cotton: Yes, I stayed with Howlin' Wolf. He moved from Mississippi to West Memphis, Arkansas, and he had heard about me from meeting with Sonny Boy.

Elwood: *You must have been 14 or 15 years old. Could you play in the clubs at that age.*

Cotton: No, the first club that I really played was the Hippodrome in Memphis, Tennessee. They had roadhouses, you know, somebody's house where they'd take the bed out and set that in the back yard, and we'd go have a party. That's the type of places that we played.

Elwood: *When you hooked up with Wolf, was that when you started doing sessions for Sun Records and Sam Phillips?*

Cotton: That was after I left the Wolf. I stayed with Wolf a couple of years, and I played on Wolf's first records, "Moaning at Midnight" and "How Many More Years." And after that, I started a band in West Memphis, Arkansas, and then played on a radio station, KWEM. A fellow knew me from playing with Howlin' Wolf, and one day he come and ask me would I like to do a record. I told him I'd love to. I did "Cotton Crop Blues," "Straighten Up Baby."

Elwood: *And that fellow was Sam Phillips. Were you blowing harp on "Cotton Crop Blues"?*

Cotton: I played the drums. There were only two of us, me and the guitar player. I had a '51 beer-case box one summer, hardly been around.

Elwood: *But if Sam miked it the right way, I bet it sounded good.*

Cotton: Yes, well, it sounded good.

Elwood: *What was it like playing with Wolf?*

Cotton: Wolf was a very nice guy. He was strict about his music, like he wanted his music played note for note every night. Same notes, nothing different. When you went to see him play, you heard just what you heard on record. If a guy messed it up, he wouldn't be there the next night.

Elwood: *I've heard Muddy Waters was like that, too.*

Cotton: Yes. They were very serious about it.

Elwood: *Later when you hooked up with Muddy, who were you replacing?*

Cotton: Junior Wells—they had been on tour down through Georgia, Alabama, wherever, and West Memphis. And some kind of way, Junior left the band around there and came back to Chicago. Muddy had heard about me being in West Memphis—he had heard records of me with Howlin' Wolf. Howlin' Wolf moved to Chicago, stayed with Muddy for a while, and Howlin' Wolf told Muddy about me and he came looking for me.

Elwood: *Now, you didn't believe it was Muddy at first. How did he convince you?*

Cotton: Well, he really didn't. He said, "I'm playing in Memphis tomorrow night," which I knew, because I heard it on the radio. And I'm thinking about what he's saying—I didn't believe him. Then he said, "I'm looking for a harmonica player. If you come on tomorrow night, if you make it, you can go back to Chicago with me if you're free." I said yes. So he gave me the address where they were staying, which I knew anyway. He went back to Memphis, and I got in my car and went to the place, and I saw this sign, Muddy Waters and the Hootchie Cootchie Boys. I said, "Maybe he is," you know. And I went to Muddy's room. Jimmy Rogers was there, Edgie Edmonton, Bob Hatley, and Otis Spann. I read these names before; I said, "Maybe this is the guy."

The next night I showed up at the Hippodrome with my amplifier, and they came in, set up. Jimmy Rogers put a little amp up and everything. We played a couple of songs, and then they called Muddy up there. And this was the last of the show. When I heard his voice I said, "Yes, that's him. I ain't got no problems now."

Elwood: *Were you nervous when you were playing with Muddy that night for the first time?*

Cotton: Yes, because I could play but it was a whole different style of harmonica playing. Little Walter played more up-to-date city blues. Sonny Boy played the country blues, and Sonny Boy was my idol and I played just like him. And I didn't have the tone and all that stuff, but I could play. So Muddy recognized it right away. He gave me the job, and I followed him to Chicago. I was in Chicago three years before I recorded with him. But I used to go watch him do it all the time, and I was steadily scuffling, trying to be a guitar player. He wanted the harmonica to be just like Walter, so that kind of made me learn to play twice. I was kind of handicapped there. I couldn't do what I wanted to do or what I felt, and that was kind of funny for me.

Elwood: *I guess the two different styles blended into one James Cotton style.*

Cotton: Yes, they kind of mixed together. After a while, I finally told him, "Hey, I'll never be no Walter, man, you got to trust me." I must say, Walter was one of the better harmonica players that I ever heard. He was soulful. He was sort of like the Beatles. He not only changed the style, he changed the times. He'd take this harmonica and did magic work with it.

Elwood: *Was Little Walter one of the first people to play through his own amplifier instead of using the PA system or just playing it cold?*

Cotton: No, Sonny Boy played with the amplifier when I first met him.

Elwood: *Does playing through an amp change your style a lot?*

Cotton: No, the amp don't play the harmonica, you do. The amplifier makes it louder. You can put treble or bass on it or what have you, but it won't play the harmonica. You have to play that yourself.

Elwood: *What was it like playing with Otis Spann?*

Cotton: Well, that was beautiful. I become a musician in Muddy's band around people like Otis, when you finally feel that you are one of the musicians and you got something to give to the band, and the band gives you something back. Otis was one of the best blues piano players in the world. These people didn't deal with you too much if you wasn't up to their standards. But I could feel that coming around because we were getting to be like brothers, and it was a good feeling. Just even to see them guys, you know, I said, "Wow, I made it with them."

Elwood: *Were you touring or just playing around Chicago?*

Cotton: Well, Muddy went on tour about twice a year, but he'd be out for like three months at a time. And the rest of the time we'd just play around Chicago, which was good for me because we were playing five or six nights a week. It made us tighten up.

Elwood: *After Muddy's band you started playing with a lot of different musicians. You played with Paul Butterfield, you played with Johnny Winter, a lot of people.*

Cotton: I made records with them. Butterfield I taught how to play—well I didn't teach him how to play. He could play, but he didn't know what to play. He didn't know the songs. I said, "You got to know some songs." I told him every song has its own style. That's how you tell them apart. I showed him that and then showed him how I was doing it.

It's a funny thing; I was with Muddy Waters, playing a little club there called Smitty's Corner, all-black club. Michael Bloomfield, Paul, Elvin Bishop walked through the door. Now, Muddy Waters owed the government a little tax, so he thought it was the tax man. Muddy said, "Oh, they going to get us." We hadn't been seeing white faces around there, you know, so we just know for sure that that was it.

Elwood: *Who stepped in on the harmonica when you left Muddy's band?*

Cotton: I went and got George Smith. I loved Muddy, you know, and I couldn't leave him without a good harp player. And I think George Smith was the best. I got him on the L.A.-to-Chicago train to play with Muddy.

Elwood: *What was Muddy like as a person?*

Cotton: He was a beautiful cat, good person. A number-one blues man. And he was crazy that his music be dead right. To keep you in line, when you miss a note, he would fine you ten dollars or something.

Elwood: *How did that record with Johnny Winter come about?*

Cotton: Well, we did a record with Muddy again. John wanted to play on Muddy's record, and I played the harp on it and we were on tour for about five or six weeks around that. The record sold a million copies or something. Later on Johnny come to Chicago to record on the Alligator label, and they said they wanted the best harmonica player in the city, and they called me.

Elwood: *Now, it was after that you put together a little collaboration with Magic Slim and Pinetop Perkins.*

Cotton: Oh, yes. I always had a high-energy boogie band, so I wanted to slow down and have younger guys in the band. They could have played rock 'n' roll—we did do a little rock 'n' roll. I wanted to do the blues, and I know Pinetop, Magic Slim, and them people was going to play blues. So I got together with them, and we did an album for Alligator.

Elwood: *The blues means something different to each person. What does the blues mean to you?*

Cotton: To me the blues is the life I live. Some of it's been good, some of it has been sad, some of it has been happy. It's the combination of things, I think. Coming out of Mississippi, my family stayed on the farm—very poor people. We sometimes didn't know where we would get our next meal from. That is the sad blues. And then sometimes it was going good. That was a good feeling. Then when I left home and found out what life was all about doing it for myself. I've had ladies I've been in love with and they broke my heart, and I couldn't get it across in words. So that was sad blues. I've had them break my heart and come back. That's happy blues.

BO DIDDLEY
Beat Generator

| "I just want what's mine.
I don't want nobody else's." |

With a name that's synonymous with the beat he made famous, Bo Diddley is a pillar of rock 'n' roll. On his self-titled 1955 hit, Diddley laid down an African-rooted rhythm that has since been exploited by artists from Buddy Holly to Bow Wow Wow. Born in Mississippi as Ellas Bates (later using his adoptive surname McDaniel), Diddley studied classical violin before taking up blues after hearing John Lee Hooker. In the '50s and early '60s Diddley logged a number of R&B hits for the Chess label—only one, "Say Man," topped the pop charts—all featuring his raucous, rhythmic guitar and irresistible vocals. Still touring in 2004, Bo talked to Elwood in 1995 shortly after recording his major-label comeback, *A Man Amongst Men*.

Elwood Blues: *What was happening when you were playing "I'm a Man" and other early songs? What was going on in your career?*
Bo Diddley: Muddy Waters, John Lee Hooker, Jimmy Reed, all of these people had Chicago sewed up, and I couldn't play like they were playing. I tried, it just didn't work. So I developed my own thing, which was called rhythm and blues, and then Caucasian brothers started picking up guitars and kicking Steinways down the basement stairs, and it became rock 'n' roll. This was what I called our stupid years, that black and white mess. They had to separate the music in order to get it played, because a lot of deejays were so messed up back then—they wouldn't play black records because the stations was owned by white people. They said, "No, you ain't playing no

A man amongst men, Bo Diddley stands alone in his contribution to blues and rock 'n' roll.

black records in here." Like the machine was going to turn black. I never figured this out, man. America's got a lot to overcome, a lot to learn because there was so much hypocritical mess going on back then, and some of it's still lurking right now.

When the music started to be played by my Caucasian brothers, everybody freaked out. White parents were telling their kids, "You ain't playing that in here," the same as black parents was telling their kids, "You ain't playing that mess." My mother told me, "Don't bring that guitar in this house."

Elwood: *Why is that?*

Diddley: Well, that was religion, our raising, what we were taught as children. Big bands was okay. Church music was okay. But guys like Muddy Waters and all of them was playing blues—they were devil people.

White kids wasn't even interested then. And then all of a sudden I came up, Bo Diddley. And white kids started saying, "I want to play a guitar like that dude."

The only rhythm music that was going on then was church music and Gene Autry—[*sings*] "I got spurs that jingle jangle jingle." I listened to it and I says, "The guitar has got to be able to do more than what I hear these dudes doing." So my sister bought me one, and I started beating and banging on it and taught myself how to play. I had a lot of people worried because I came up with something that sounded like six or seven people, and I had to tame myself to play and carry the bass and the middle and the lead and all that at the same time. When I started to put a trio together and got a bass player, it was hard for me to stay away from the bass line. And I just kept on and kept on, and I'm still learning. I'm 65 and I'm still learning.

Elwood: *That Bo Diddley beat has been used by so many different people. Tell us how that came about.*

Diddley: That's something that I stumbled upon. People keep trying to tell me it sounds like hambone [*the shave-and-a-haircut rhythm*]. That's a lie. If you write hambone down, it's not the same notes as Bo Diddley.

I feel that I was defrauded on this because somebody started talking about public domain. That's the biggest lie I ever heard in my life, and I couldn't do anything about it because I didn't have no funds to get a lawyer. And there's so much bootlegging. I ran into one night before last—another bootleg 45. I'm owed millions. I used to say—because I didn't have no concept—that it was $400,000, $500,000, something like that. I should have been kicked in my butt about that figure, because it's a lot more than that that people haven't paid me. If the government can find me, those people can.

Some people don't understand. They look at me and say, "Bo Diddley has got all this money." You know why? Because they bought my records, man, and they bought the same record maybe three or four times, because one they wear out and they go get another one. And I can't blame them for thinking this, but I want to say to the United States, to the world, that things haven't been good with me. And I'm saying to the young musicians out here, watch who you dealing with, baby. You think about it real good before you trust mama, you understand? Because mama ain't going to trust you with her pocketbook, you dig what I'm saying? It's a business. It's glorified at first, then it turns into a business where they'll turn your lights off in your apartment just as quick if you don't pay that bill. One of the biggest things that hurts musicians is to try and to force somebody to open up their books and tell you the truth and pay you the money that they are supposed to give you. I just want what's mine. I don't want nobody else's.

But I'm glad that I wrote what I wrote. I had no idea what I was starting. You know, I walk up and down Hollywood Boulevard, and I ain't got no star out there. I'm the sucker that started all of the rest of them and built the highway that they're running up now. I haven't seen one for Muddy Waters. I haven't seen one for John Lee Hooker, Jimmy Reed. Why don't we have one? There's some people out there got names I think ain't got no business out there. [*Note: John Lee Hooker received a Walk of Fame star in 1997. Muddy Waters and Jimmy Reed had yet to honored as of 2004, when Britney Spears was scheduled to receive a star.*]

Elwood: *Elvis Presley is an early rock 'n' roll musician who has a star. What do you think of his contribution?*

Elvis was a great man—I really mean that. But they shoved Elvis down everybody's throat with money, doing something like the Elvis Presley Hour. People I was dealing with didn't have the money to put on a Bo Diddley Hour. That's how I learned that a radio is a device to program your mind. If you start playing "When the Saints Go Marching In" every morning when the dude gets out of the bed, pretty soon he'll start humming it. When a deejay says, "I'm going to break a record for you," he knows just about how many times he's got to shove that dude in your ears before you turn around and go back.

Elwood: *Do you feel that people are starting to look back to the roots of the music?*

Diddley: No, no. The past is gone. I'm looking for new things to deal. I refuse to be in a rut, sitting in a mudhole spinning my wheels and going nowhere. I'm more intelligent than that, smarter than that, cleverer than that. This new thing that I got going will freak you out.

People put you in the slot. Chuck Berry, me, Fats Domino, we all in slots. Freddy Cannon—he in a slot. I was talking to Freddy the other night, and I wanted him to cover this country tune. And he's telling me, "I can't sing country." I said, "Uh-huh, when I finish with you, you going to be country." Because I feel that he can do something other than what he's been doing. I've always been a country music lover, and I always tried to figure out how to do it because it's different from rock 'n' roll. It's like playing church music. It's a different lick, and I finally got the lick.

The time is gone for just knowing your language and nobody else's. The Japanese come here and can speak English because it's mandatory in Japan, I think. Even if they don't learn nothing but how do you do, hello, goodbye, and thank you, they say it with dignity and expertise. A Japanese dude walks up to me in New York and says, "Hey, what's happening, man. I saw you in Tokyo." That told me something, brother. We better get off of our buns and quit running up and down the streets. Our youngsters, quit running up and down the streets shooting and killing one another and terrorizing neighborhoods. These kids need to learn something constructive and quit being destructive.

Elwood: *On you new CD you talk to the kids.*

Diddley: The new CD has a song called "Kids, Don't Do It." I'm trying to give our kids something to think about—get away from the gangs. Get out of them, you don't need to be in it because you might lose your life, you dig? I try to tell these kids we need to keep this country within a circle that's together, that's good, not full of crack cocaine, reefer and all that garbage. So I say to kids, don't do it, clean up your act. A lot of kids, they talking about role models. I never used none of that crap. I might drink a little rum and orange juice. If they want to test me for drugs, they ain't going to find nothing but some orange juice and milk and water. Some Diet Coke. And hey, I feel good. I'm not downing kids, I'm trying to talk to them because I love children, I got children. I'm a grandfather, and I just think that it's time somebody said something.

Elwood: *You've been doing benefit concerts for the Chicago Coalition for the Homeless. Can you tell us more about that?*

Diddley: Since I was raised in Chicago, I'm committed to trying to help some of these people that have nowhere to go. So I say to the homeless people in Chicago and the homeless people in Los Angeles and anywhere in the United States or in the world, if I can help, I'm the man. I go and try to help raise a little money and if I can raise enough just to buy each person a loaf of bread, I feel that I've done something, because I was fortunate enough to have that talent to go out and do this to try to help people. But I am not for people sitting on their buns every day and drawing unemployment checks. Look at the streets, how dirty they are. Go out and work. Help your city. You get the check every week. Put in four or five hours sweeping the streets and help clean the city up. I don't see anything wrong with that.

I could fall into that same bag if I didn't get off my buns and try to make something out of myself. There's no guarantee I was going to be Bo Diddley, but I had to try. So I tried and I stumbled onto what I'm doing now, and it works. It's been working for me for 39 years, and I am happy as something else, man.

BUDDY GUY
Sweet Home Chicago

> *"After I met Muddy and Junior Wells and Howlin' Wolf, I didn't get cold no more."*

Buddy Guy is the reigning monarch of a blues lineage that stretches from the prewar South to current-day Chicago. A sharecropper's son, Guy left Louisiana in 1957 to head for Chicago, where he fell in with residing greats such as Muddy Waters, Otis Rush, and Magic Sam. In the '60s at Chess Records, Guy made a number of now-classic singles as well as backing Waters, Howlin' Wolf, and others, and in the '70s he teamed with Junior Wells. Though he was a fixture in the Chicago scene and a hero of guitarists like Eric Clapton and Jimi Hendrix, far-reaching recognition didn't take hold until the '90s, when his Grammy-winning album *Damn Right, I've Got the Blues* launched him onto the international circuit, where he remains today. That momentum was still strong at the time of this 2003 interview.

Elwood Blues: *Tell us about your life before you came to Chicago. What was it like growing up on a plantation in Louisiana?*

Buddy Guy: We didn't have running water. We didn't have electric lights or nothing like that. We used to have to drink water out of the creek; our drinking water was rainwater and we never got sick with anything. So if I'd have to live life over again, I would do the same thing again. As a little boy, I didn't know what a guitar was or anything like that. I would use rubber band stretched across the wall until I figured out I could use screen wire. I

Buddy Guy, playing blues to live and living to play the blues.

used to pull the screen wire out of screen window, and I would try to make guitar strings out of it. The mosquitoes would get in and my mother would say, "Well, I know I put a piece of screen at that window, and these mosquitoes still in here"—it would be all stripped away because I was breaking the wire trying to stretch it as tight as I could. I would take a lighter-fluid can and put a stick in the head of it and four tacks on each end, and I had me a full string guitar. Couldn't bend the strings, though.

Elwood: *What was a typical day in the life of a sharecropper?*

Guy: Well, you worked from sunup to sundown when you got big enough, and I started that at about six and half years old. We had the cotton and corn, the chicken, the pigs. The plantation I was on, the guy had a lot of cattle, maybe four or five thousand. Soon as I got big enough to ride a horse, I had to see about that, too. I mean, you do everything—you didn't have just one job. When I got to about 11 or 12, I had to start driving the tractor, riding the ranch and doing everything else. The only day we had off was Sunday. When I got big enough it didn't matter if it rained, because I still had to ride the cattle and feed 'em and so on. But when you were working in the fields, if it was raining you had your day off. That's when I just banged away.

At one point we had a little sandlot baseball team on Sunday afternoon. It was nine men on each side, so if one didn't play, you couldn't play. Finally we got an old battery radio—I must have been about 14 or 15 then—and every Sunday evening they play the blues records, Lightnin' Hopkins or Muddy Waters or someone like that.

Elwood: *Did you try to play along with the radio?*

Guy: No, I would just bury my ears as close I could to the radio 'cause my Mother was Baptist, and they always figured blues was the devil's music. But that didn't stop me from listening to it.

Elwood: *When you look back on that time, what was the best thing and what was the worse thing about that life?*

Guy: Well, the best thing about it was my mother and father never did have to lock their doors. You could leave your house open and wouldn't nobody go in there. The worse thing about it is there wasn't any future there. My parents always told me, "We gonna try to send you to school," which was impossible. And then my Mother taken a stroke and I was the oldest boy, so I definitely had to go to work then. I didn't even finish my first year in high school. They always wanted to see us grow up and start thinking of leaving because you eat to live and live to eat—that's all the sharecropper ever had.

Elwood: *That's a different song than "I live the life I love, and I love the life I live."*

Guy: Right—Willie Dixon wrote that song after he came to Chicago. I had a lot of conversations with him concerning what we're talking about now. It was a little rougher on the older people than it was me, because some of those guys had to steal away. I didn't have to steal away.

My dad died at 56, and I think my mother was 62, and I wonder how they made it that far. People ask me, "What do you take? How do you have so much energy when you play?" But all I have to do is think about playing two or two and a half hours, and think that back then they had to go from sunup to sundown. When you flash that across your mind, you say, "My job is easy now."

Elwood: *Did you ever get to see anybody play guitar in those days?*

Guy: We had a guy who used to show up every Christmas with a guitar, and he would hit a few licks. My first electric guitar was the late Lightnin' Slim. He came through one Sunday evening and plugged up, and I stood there and said, "Well, guitars don't sound like that." I traced the wires down and looked at it, and I said, "I don't believe this guitar is sounding this loud." I got to know Lightnin' before he passed away. He had his little band there in Baton Rouge, Louisiana, and once or twice a month they started bringing people like B.B. King, Big Joe Turner, and Guitar Slim to a place called the Temple Roof. That's when I really got aware that these guitars were being heard. It wasn't in the background with the horns drowning it out. It's got the volume now.

Guitar Slim was so wild, man. The first time I saw him, they brought him to Baton Rouge where they'd rent these little halls where there wasn't no seats. I was the first one there so I could get close to the stage. The band would play an hour or so before they bring him on, because when he come on everybody would stop buying drinks. When they say, "Ladies and gentlemen, Guitar Slim," I hear a guitar but I didn't see nobody. Then all of a sudden, somebody brought him in like you take your little baby and put him on your shoulders and go walking. I said, "Man, I gotta learn how to play guitar, 'cause that's what I wanna be."

Elwood: *Did you ever get to see any of the older Mississippi guys, like Son House or Fred McDowell?*

Guy: [Blues promoter] Dick Waterman—who was Bonnie Raitt's boyfriend—brought Junior Wells and me out on the road in '66 and '67, and he had Fred McDowell and Son House and them coming out of Mississippi doing the colleges. Muddy told me, "Oh, yeah, I learned a lot from Son House myself." So I said, "Well, I have to meet this guy." I got to sit down and drink with him, and we'd be up until like five o'clock in the morning. He said, "Here your breakfast, Buddy"—a shot of whiskey. "If you want me to sit down and play the guitar, you've got to have a drink with me." I said okay, if that what it takes.

Elwood: *What was your first big break playing music?*

Guy: I left Baton Rouge—we played little clubs for 50 cents or 25 cents—and I came to Chicago. I didn't ever think I was good enough to be a professional musician; I came to Chicago looking for day work and got stranded. One night I went up on the stage with Otis Rush and played a song, and someone called Muddy Waters came by and slapped me and convinced me not to go back to Louisiana. I was trying to get my train fare back. The next thing I know people were calling me and asking me did I want to play.

Elwood: *I guess when Muddy Waters slaps you and tells you something, you listen.*

Guy: Before he died he still would do that, man. He used to look at me and Junior Wells and all the young kids and call us his children. He used to tell us, just call me the Old Man now and you better listen, and I always did. Him, Sonny Boy, Wolf, Walter, all of them would do that.

Elwood: *When you moved to Chicago there were clubs like Peppers, Sylvio's, Theresa's Lounge, Zanzibar—all these legendary names. What was that scene like?*

Guy: When I was in Baton Rouge everything closed down at 12:30, 1:00—everybody works and gets up early. In Chicago we had the steel mill going 24 hours a day, the stockyard 24 hours, and hundreds of thousands of people was working. In the clubs they had what you call a "Blue Monday Jam," and at seven in the morning these bars was full of people who got off work at that time. I'm saying, "This is too crazy, I can't stay here." I came here September 25, 1957, and within a month and a half, it was so cold I was saying, "Even geese and birds go South when they get cold. What am I doing here?" But after I met Muddy and Junior Wells and Howlin' Wolf, I didn't get cold no more, man.

So every bar you went in was full of people. Some of the musicians didn't stick with it, but they played well enough to keep you in there to listen. Earl Hooker was the best slide guitar player I ever seen, and I would find him there. Lightnin' Hopkins wasn't here—he was from Texas—but just about every great blues player that I learned something from, I met them here in Chicago.

Elwood: *What was your favorite spot to go see Wolf or Muddy?*

Guy: You mentioned a lot of favorite nightclubs. The most famous blues club was the 708 Club—that's the address, 708 East 47th Street. When I made it in there, I looked out in the audience, and there was Little Walter, B.B. King, and Muddy Waters watching me, and I was playing with just a drummer and a keyboard player. This was 1958, and I didn't have no records out. I was playing their music, and I was so shaky I wanted to start crying. I looked out there and said, "What am I gonna play now? They're sittin' here, and I know I can't play it as well as they did." But I was so hungry I had to play because the guy had hired me. So I just started singing "Sweet Little Angel." I was trying to avoid B.B. King when I came off the stage, but he walked around and caught me and say, "Son, come here, don't run away from me, I know you're shy. I can look at you and tell that." I say, "Yeah, man, if a few people hadn't taught me how to drink wine, I probably would have left here." But he told me I would be the only one who could take his place.

Elwood: *What else did you play that night?*

Guy: I played "Further On Up the Road," by Bobby Bland, then I went into some Jimmy Reed stuff—I didn't meet Jimmy Reed right away, because he was a heavy drinker and he was out a lot. I even had to play a Fats Domino number. They had jukeboxes in places then, and if you didn't play the numbers that was being played on the jukebox, you wasn't gonna get that little gig, which was paying $2 a night.

Finally, I got this great drummer, Fred Below—who made all those hit records with Little Walter—and a keyboard player. Most blues players were sitting in chairs when I came here, but I had seen Guitar Slim and T-Bone Walker in New Orleans . . . I get so excited, I never could sit down and play. I have to move.

After that, they start having battles of guitars here—Otis Rush, Magic Sam, Freddy King, Luther Allison . . . oh, man. I knew I couldn't play as well as Earl Hooker and Sam and Otis and them, but I'd watched Slim with that 100-foot guitar cord. So there was about two feet of snow one day, and a guy came up to me and said, "Boy, they in there waitin' on you now." I say, "Let's bring that long wire outside, and when they call me, I'm comin' in the door playing." and I came in the door, and they say, "The winner is Buddy Guy with a pint of whiskey"—that's all you'd win, and I didn't even get a drop of that."

Elwood: *What did it feel like when you started hearing British bands like the Stones and Cream playing the material that you guys had been playing for years?*

Guy: At that time I was working at Chess, and every time I got ready to do a session behind Muddy Waters or whoever, I would go in before the session started and I would turn that guitar up, and they would come out and tell me, "Don't play that shit in here, man—that's noise." So I would calm down and play just like they wanted.

About a year and a half or two years before Leonard Chess passed, he sent Willie Dixon to my house to get me. Willie Dixon told me, "Put your suit on." I thought, "Well, I know he's not calling me to let me make a record for myself; this means I'm probably being invited not to come down anymore. They were paying about $30 a session, and that was big money for me then. But Willie slaps on a Cream record, bends over, and tells me, "I want you to kick me because you been trying to play this stuff for us ever since you come here, and we was too f-ing dumb to listen to you. Listen to what they're selling millions of records with." So I sit there and I look at him, and I should of kicked him, but I did not.

But thank God those guys came along. Back in the '60s they had a television show called *Shindig*, and they was trying to get the Stones to do the show. They said, "We'll do it if you let us bring on Muddy Waters and Howlin' Wolf. And they was like, "Who is that?" I think Mick Jagger was the one who said, "You don't know who Muddy Waters is?" We named ourselves after one of his famous records."

Elwood: *In the '70s and '80s, between the time you and Junior Wells were still touring and before* Damn Right, I Got the Blues, *styles like disco and funk got popular, and it must have been hard to make a living playing the blues. What kept you going?*

Guy: I opened a small blues club on the South Side. Clubs were disappearing after the riots in the '60s, and I saw no place for a Buddy Guy or a Muddy Waters or a Eric Clapton. I said, "I'm not going to quit playing my guitar, but if I have to I'll go back to work in the daytime and play at night. You know, Muddy Waters and even B.B. King wasn't making a lot of money. But we just loved the music so well we wasn't gonna quit playing.

This is what happened when we were playing the smaller blues clubs: My club, the Checkerboard, couldn't hold but 90 people or less. So you couldn't bring anybody in there and pay them enough to play for two and half hours for the same group of people, because the cover charge was only a buck or a buck and a half, and you got to pay somebody eight or nine hundred dollars. There's no way you could do that. That's when the word got out that Junior Wells and Buddy Guy weren't playing anymore. We'd have to play 40–45 minutes and then turn the crowd over in order to make $15 or $20 apiece, so people were saying, "They're washed up because they won't play long." I said to my manager, "I gotta go out on my own." He said, "There's nobody gonna come see you unless Junior's there." I said, "I gotta take my chances." The first gig I had was up north here at a club that holds about 250 people, and it was full. He looked out and said, "I guess you're right."

Now when I go play the big outdoor concerts and they say I can't play but 40 minutes, I feel like saying, "I'd rather not play at all because they fans are gonna blame it on me. I was playing in Ireland once, and they had a big digital clock up there. They said, "You watch that clock—if it passes a certain minute we charge you"—it was like $300 a minute. Well, I said, "I'll stop 20 minutes early, and you can pay me $300 a minute."

Elwood: *These days you're out there touring and you have your Chicago club going. Do you think it's a better era for the blues?*

Guy: You know, blues is being ignored a lot. At one point I thought it was the lyrics, until the rap and the hip-hop came out and I heard some of those lyrics. A lot of people ask me why blues is sad. But all blues is not sad. When you hear B.B. King singing, "I've got a sweet little angel, I love the way she spread her wings"—I don't think that's sad. I guess I could call myself and all the other great blues players dummies, because we was just playing it for the love of music, not the love of money.

JOHN LEE HOOKER
Boogie Father

> *"I had both of them, the sweet and bitter."*

Not every postwar blues great traveled the road to Chicago. John Lee Hooker's path led from the heart of the Delta—Clarksdale, Mississippi—through Memphis and Cincinnati and then to Detroit during the city's wartime boom. Hooker didn't linger in day jobs, though. Armed with a guitar, a gruff voice, and his potent boogie rhythms, he found his way to the Hastings Street club scene and a local record label, and then to the top of the R&B charts with "Boogie Chillen." More hits followed on the Modern label, as well as recordings for other companies under such pseudonyms as Texas Slim, Delta John, and John Lee Booker. In the '60s Hooker became a hero to the Brit-blues bands as well as to L.A.'s Canned Heat, but his career languished somewhat in the '70s and early '80s. In 1989, however, *The Healer* began a series of collaborations that would help bring "the Hook" widespread recognition for his contributions to the blues. John Lee Hooker died in 2001 at age 93; he and Elwood had this conversation in 1993.

Elwood Blues: *What keeps you going, keeps you playing the blues?*

John Lee Hooker: I love people, and it shows when I play into my music. I'm a pretty humble person when it comes to that. I don't look at how much money I got or how much success I got. I look at the people of the world who made it possible for me to be where I'm at today, and the success that they give me.

John Lee Hooker onstage in 1988. He couldn't copyright the boogie, but he definitely owned it.

I'm just always low key. I like small honky-tonk places, the small bars, to go in there and get up on the stand and sing a song or two and get myself a beer. I don't want to hide out from people. I want to sit there with them, you know. A lot of them be shocked and surprised to see me in these places. "Oh, what John Lee Hooker doing here." I say, "Well, just like you I like to have some fun with some down-home blues." It's real honest music. I go to see so many blues singers in so many places. They ain't making much money, but they're having fun. And I want to have fun with them. Anyway I can reach out and get them by the hand, I'll do it.

Elwood: *Who are some of the people who helped you along the way?*

Hooker: Well the first person that really helped me was a guy in Detroit called Elmer Barber. He the one that discovered me. He had a little old record shop down Lafayette Street. I used to go to his shop at night. He heard me and said, "Oh kid, you got a voice." And he would take me there and record me, and we would eat and drink wine till two or three o'clock in the morning. I would sleep during the day whenever I wasn't working.

Then he brought me to Bernie Besman on Woodward Avenue. They had a big, big record store, and he had a little label called Sensation. I walked in there, and he turned me over to Bernie. All these songs that I wrote, he would tell people that he wrote the song—you look on the records, you may see his name on a lot of them. But he made the way for me after Barber got me going. He got me on Modern Records, the big label. His label couldn't handle "Boogie Chillen"—that was a big one. I recorded it on Sensation label, and he released me out to Modern Records.

That's how I started out working for little bars and going to what I love so much, which I do now. When I first come to Detroit I wasn't married—I come at a very young age. I got married, and all my children was born in Detroit, grew up there. I've seen the hard times and the good times—I know what the hard way is. I know what it's like to come from the nightclubs, to scuffle, and then into the big time and be a big star. I know how to cope with it. That's always in the back of my mind, what you have to come through. I won't forget my roots.

I look at the people in the streets, sleeping in the streets—hard time. I wonder why these people have to do that. If we get out and reach out to those people, it might would be a better world. I can't save the world, but I cannot forget about the poor people working in the plants and the fields and buying John Lee Hooker's records. Wasn't for them I wouldn't be here. And that's the reason I love people.

Elwood: *What were some of the clubs you played in when you were first starting out?*

Hooker: Well, there was the club in Detroit called Apex Bar. Wasn't too much, about three times bigger than this room. And there's a place in Detroit called the Black and Tan—had a lot of fun there, small club. Stuff like that. I got a lot of memories back in Detroit. When I was coming up there it was good, it was beautiful city. People could just go out and there wouldn't be no fear. But now it's a different world.

Elwood: *It was a boom town back then.*

Hooker: Ooooh, it was a boom town. Everybody could get a job. I was there with all that. I was kind of a kid growing up there.

Elwood: *You were talking about record labels—I started keeping track of all the record labels that you recorded on.*

Hooker: Oh, that's hard.

Elwood: *This is just a short list—I got Modern, VeeJay, Chess, Blues Way, Liberty, Gone, Tomato, ABC, Impulse, EMI, Specialty, United Artists, Green Jewel, Stax, King, Fantasy, Chameleon, Charisma, Charley . . .*

Hooker: I never recorded at Charley. But lot of them labels, some of those labels get it from other companies. Like Stax. I never recorded for Stax, but they bought some of my stuff, you know.

It's a natural-born jungle out there, but you can't stop doing your music on account of that. You just got to try to fight your way through and stay in there. That's what I did. I knew I ain't going to find all honey. You find lots of bitterness out and then lots of sweets. I had both of them, the sweet and bitter.

Elwood: *Some of your songs have crossed over into rock 'n' roll. How is rock related to blues?*

Hooker: Rock come from the blues. Rock 'n' roll come up with Chuck Berry. He was taking from the blues, saying everything we were saying about a man and a woman, a woman and a man, but saying it in a different way, polish it up, you know. But it's the same thing. It's running in the same stream, it's in the same boat—you're rocking in the same boat.

Elwood: *One of your most famous songs is "One Bourbon, One Scotch, One Beer." When was the last time you had bourbon and scotch and beer together?*

Hooker: Well when I was drinking I used to have it all—one bourbon, scotch, beer, anything come on, I would do it. Now I drink a light beer once in a while. That's a good song; I'd like to do that over. There's a different generation now—it would be something they never heard of. They would love it.

Elwood: *It could be like "Boom Boom." The new version is killer.*

Hooker: That's what I'm going to do. I'm going to bring back a lot of that old stuff and update it for the generations that haven't heard of that because they weren't old enough.

Elwood: *Another song that's been through lots of different versions is "Dimples."*

Hooker: Yes, a lot of people did that. That was a big one. Everybody's doing the boogie now; I originated that with "Boogie Chillen." Everybody jumped on the bandwagon; ZZ Top and everybody else, you hear them doing the boogie, which is good for me. They know who it come from. That keeps me up there, alive, you know.

Elwood: *It's too bad that you can't copyright the boogie, or that Chuck Berry couldn't copyright his famous lick.*

Hooker: There ain't nothing you can do about it. Like people do a lot of James Brown, his dance, his beat. But he can't copyright that. You can copyright the label, but you can't copyright a beat. If we could, I could get paid for a lot of money. But hey, nothing I can do about it.

Elwood: *You just did an album with B.B. King,* Blues Summit. *What was it like getting together with him?*

Hooker: For years and years I've been wanting to do this, and I can't begin to tell you a what thrill it give me. Me and him sitting there together, side by side, two masters—I would say over 100 years of blues sitting there together. He got Lucille crying like a baby, and I'm sitting there just singing like I never sung before. I was so happy inside—now here I'm singing beside Mr. B.B. King. I guess he feel the same way, you know.

Elwood: *Tell me about the big tribute they did for you at Madison Square Garden a few years ago.*

Hooker: That's the biggest thrill of my life, to look out there and see hundreds of thousands of people, and they all were there just for me. How could this happen? I was so full. I was crying, tears in my eyes—I stood up on that stage and had on my dark glasses to keep people from seeing the teardrops. I think I've never have a greater day. That was the highlight of my life.

Elwood on the Air: Memorial Day

HOUR: 00/22
AIRDATE: 5/27–28/00
WRITER: ANDY VALVUR

[FX: horns honking, city street atmosphere]

ELWOOD: OK folks—this is a once-in-a-lifetime event. Hey buddy . . . you gonna buy something or just fondle the merchandise? Remember, all sales are final. Cash only. No refunds.

TRIXIE: Hi, Elwood. What are you doing?

ELWOOD: Oh. Hello, Trixie. I am just having a little garage sale. You know, Memorial Day is here and as red-blooded Americans, we have a duty.

TRIXIE: We do?

ELWOOD: Absolutely. To mark the beginning of summer, we have to pile into a huge piece of Detroit steel, load her up with fossil fuels and take off on a tarmac adventure. And with the price of gas these days, well . . . I have to sell some of the Blues family heirlooms.

MAN: Hey, how much for this tie?

ELWOOD: Two hundred dollars.

MAN: Are you crazy? It's a ratty old tie.

ELWOOD: My man, that is no ordinary necktie. Muddy Waters personally gave it to me after a show one night at the House of Blues in Chicago.

TRIXIE: [stage whisper] Elwood—Muddy never played at the House of Blues in Chi . . . [Elwood covers her mouth] mmmmmgggggghh

MAN: I don't know . . . it seems like a lot of money.

ELWOOD: I understand, we all have to save our pennies. How about this pair of socks . . . from Sonny Boy Williamson.

MAN: They're still damp!

ELWOOD: That is genuine Sonny Boy Williamson sweat. And a bargain at seventy-five dollars.

MAN: That's gross. How much you want for the pile of junk?

ELWOOD: My man, that is a 1973 Dodge, Polara. I got it at a Mt. Prospect Police auction. It has a cop motor, a 440-cubic-inch plant, cop tires, cop suspension, cop shocks, and no catalytic converter so it uses regular gas. In other words, the Bluesmobile. And it is not for sale.

MAN: If you ask me it's still a piece of junk.

ELWOOD: Well, nobody asked you.

MAN: How much for the guitar strap?

ELWOOD: Ah, I can see that you are a discerning collector. That belonged to blues man B.B. King. And it can be yours for a mere hundred bucks. I will even throw in a letter of authenticity and the new House of Blues Road Trip Blues CD.

MAN: Is it any good?

ELWOOD: Any good??? Check this out.

[Song: "Pontiac Blues"—Sonny Boy Williamson]

B.B. KING
Beale Street and Beyond

> *"Whatever song I play,
> I'm playing it tonight like
> it's the first time."*

The King of the Blues as well as its worldwide ambassador, B.B. King has been a touchstone of musical intensity and integrity throughout his six-decade career. Born in the Mississippi Delta and raised on gospel and country music, King found early guitar inspiration in the music of Lonnie Johnson and T-Bone Walker as well as Charlie Christian and Django Reinhardt. In 1946 he left the sharecropping life to head to Memphis with his cousin and blues mentor, Bukka White. King immersed himself in the Memphis scene and worked for a time as a deejay, finally cutting his first tracks and landing a recording contract in 1949. He has seemingly been on the road or in the studio since. In 1969 he brought blues into the mainstream with his signature tune "The Thrill Is Gone"—performed as always on his beloved guitar Lucille—and well into his eighth decade he continued to thrill audiences with his incisive guitar style, emotion-drenched singing, and amiable stage presence. Elwood talked to King in 1995 as he was working on the CD-ROM *On the Road with B.B. King* and preparing for his 70th birthday.

Elwood Blues: *Through the years I've talked to a lot of people who got turned on to the blues not only from your music but from your stint as a disc jockey. Just about everybody who talks about that period mentions Peptikon.*

B.B. King: Yes, that was a tonic. When I first went to Memphis I went to the radio station and I saw this person in the studio, from the outside

Staying young one song at a time: The great B.B. King keeps it fresh with help from Lucille.

through the picture window. I didn't bother him until I saw the red light go off, because I knew about recording, but when the red light went off I knocked on the window and he came to the door and let me in. He asked me, "Son, what can I do for you?" And I said, "Well, I'd like to make a record and I'd like to go on the radio." So he called the general manager of the station, Mr. Ferguson—the person I was talking to was Nathaniel Williams, but everybody called him Nat D. So he told Mr. Ferguson what I had said. Mr. Ferguson looked me over, very wise man, and said, "We don't make records but we might be able to use you; come on in."

Now, a friend of mine, Sonny Boy Williamson, was over in West Memphis, and I had been on his radio show—he let me do a tune on it. He was

Riffing on the King: Ruth Brown

"B.B. King is the sweetest, the kindest, the most dedicated blues singer in the world. When he sits down, he is still singing the truth. I'm very proud to say that we still enjoy a friendship where there's many good memories, good stories to tell—I love that man. He's the biggest star I know, but he's always approachable."

advertising for a tonic called Hadicol. Well, *my* introduction to radio would be advertising Peptikon, which was a product they were just putting out. That very evening they put me on advertising Peptikon for ten minutes—ten minutes! They thought up a name for me that very evening—"the Beale Street Blues Boy." Well, my name is Riley B. King, so it wasn't hard for me to just put in that "B" and leave the Riley off. I liked the idea. A little bit later they wanted me to write a jingle. Here I am a guy that don't know anything about writing anything, hardly my name. But I came up with it. [*Sings*] "Peptikon sure is good, you can get it anywhere in your neighborhood." That was the beginning of B.B. King. And at that time it was Bee Bee.

Elwood: *Does anybody call you Riley now?*

King: I don't hear it too often but yes, a few people call me that—all of my friends that have known me for a long time, or some people that just want to remind me that they know my name.

Elwood: *You started out singing in the church. Can you talk about your transition from gospel to blues?*

King: Yes—I wanted to be a gospel singer. It's never left me, I still like spirituals, still enjoy them today. When I was about 14, 15, I used to stand on the corners of Indianola, Mississippi, my hometown, and play. I would not panhandle like some people I see, but I was still hoping in my heart that somebody would come by and put something in the pot. I would mostly be singing gospel songs because that's what I had planned to be.

T-Bone Walker, Charles Brown, Louis Jordan, and those types of people were very popular on the charts at that time—when I say charts, each little café would have one of these Wurlitzer jukeboxes with the records that was popular at the time—so I would hear them. And some people are devilish, you know? They'd come by and say, "Do you know 'Caldonia'?" Most times I didn't know all the lyrics, but I'd go and sing the part that I did remember. And usually when people asked me to sing a gospel song, they would always praise me and pat me on the head and say, "Son, that is great. You keep it up, you're going to be great one day." But they didn't tip. The people that would ask me to sing songs like "Caldonia" or whatever, they would always tip me: "Hey, can't you see that boy playing his heart out, give him something."

And at that time, I was one of the number-one tractor drivers on the plantation, and the top salary was $22 and a half a week. But on an evening, say like Saturday evening, I might make $50 or $60, sometimes even $100 singing. And this in itself motivated my wanting to be a blues singer. I was in it because I liked to do it, but I was also in it because I wanted to do better than what I was doing. And I still enjoy that today.

Elwood: *Thinking about the old days, you often point to Charlie Christian as an influence. How did you first hear him?*

King: I learned about him from the Benny Goodman group. They used to have these things—today, they call them soundies; we used to call them "peanut vendors." It's a machine that you put money in and about three minutes of film would come up. You never knew who was coming up—they didn't have it marked up like Benny Goodman is going to come up this time, or Jimmy Rushing and Count Basie. You had to hope for whatever. Watching those vendors, I had a chance to see Charlie Christian. And I was starting to hear about jazz, like Dixieland jazz from New Orleans and so on. And watching Benny Goodman and seeing this guy work was just so amazing, hearing the sound that came from the guitar. I wasn't used to hearing electric guitar. Where I lived, even if you gave me an electric guitar I couldn't have played it, because we had no electricity.

I can remember how people used to make me go to bed when I was 10 or 12. They had lamps, and they'd put you in there, and man, they'd blow that lamp out, and then they'd be sitting in there talking about ghosts—scare me half to death. So I said then, if I grow up to be a man, I'm going to have electricity, and in every room there's going to be some light as long as I'm around. And believe me, today at 69 at my apartment, some light is on all night when I'm there.

So the only time I heard electric guitar is when I would go to town and listen to the records and stuff. Because the records that was made then—especially the blues—most of them was with acoustic guitar. But I heard electric guitar, and Charlie Christian had that certain something that nobody else had.

Riffing on the King: Carlos Santana

"I discovered more and more that it is grace to be able to play like B.B. King. He doesn't have any habits, like drugs, though he does have a habit of playing on the road—the guy can't get out of the road. He's a shining example of consistency and dignity and carrying that 'King' crown very high for all of us."

Riffing on the King: Buddy Guy

"The one thing all of us guitar players picked up from B.B.–the rock players, the acid rock, and everything–is how to squeeze the string without using the slide. He's the one that brought that out. Every guitar player I see, I tell them, 'Y'all should put two B's on your guitar.' He smiles every time I tell him that."

When I was 18 I went in the Army, but I didn't stay very long. At that time the plantation owners had a system with the local Selective Service. A lot of them was growing produce for the Armed Forces, and being a tractor driver I only took partial basic training. I had a friend that went in the Service the same time, and they shipped him to Europe. When he came home, he had been to a place called the Hot Club of France and he met Django Reinhardt. He brought me some records of Django Reinhardt, and I fell in love with him. That was another jazz guitarist.

Elwood: *One other person you cite as an influence is Lonnie Johnson.*

King: Oh, man. I found some live footage on Lonnie Johnson when we was doing this CD-ROM. He's one of my idols. He recorded with Duke Ellington, he recorded with Mahalia Jackson, with Louis Armstrong—he recorded with many people of various styles of music and he fit in. He was like the link in the chain of whatever musical style he might be in. And a grand old man. I wanted to be like him. I still do.

Elwood: *Over the years you've done work with prisoners and done a lot of recordings at prisons. How did that came about?*

King: I never lived in Chicago like a lot of my friends did when we left Mississippi. Some went to Chicago, Detroit, and even New York and other places. When I left Mississippi I went to Memphis. But after I had started to travel and had made quite a few records, I went to Chicago. My agents booked me into a place called Mr. Kelly's. Well, Mr. Kelly's was known for jazz, never for my kind of music at all. But for some reason my agent and they agreed that I could be the one that would kind of integrate it.

So I went to Mr. Kelly's—a very fabulous club—and I was scared half to death. At that time there was a newly appointed director of the Cook County Correctional Institution, a black guy named Mr. Winston Moore, I believe. Mr. Moore called me—I don't know how he happened to know me; maybe he was a fan or something. He said, "B, it's a first for you at Mr. Kelly's, and it's a first for me at Cook County, so why don't we both do a first and play for the inmates"—well, he called them the residents—"play for the residents here."

And I thought about it, you know. It really hit me. I didn't know what to do, so I called up my manager, Sid Seidenberg in New York. I said, "Sid, Mr. Moore has asked me to play over at the Cook County Correctional Institution and I think I'd like to do it. What do you think I should do?" He said, "Well, what I would do is invite the press, invite some other artists, and then I would get the record company to record it"—thinking like a manager, you know.

To me it made a lot of sense. And so I told Mr. Moore we would, and we did. The Chicago papers interviewed a lot of the inmates. We found there was a lot of young people there, black and white, that had been arrested but they hadn't come to trial or anything—two-thirds of them didn't have money to bail themselves out. The Chicago papers played that up real big the next day. They mentioned the fact that these young people, some of them had been there for months, and when they came to trial, if found guilty or innocent they wasn't compensated for all the time that they spent there.

A few months later one of the TV networks did an in-depth story on that kind of thing, and they changed the system somewhat. That made me so happy that I started to do more and more of that kind of thing—that's how I got into it.

At that time, I had never had a family member in prison that I knew about, not even close friends. My cousin Bukka had been in trouble once, but that was when I was a kid, so I didn't know that much about it. I'm saying that because not too awful long ago, I've had a family member in one of the prisons where I played. But before that it wasn't because of a family member. And thank God at this time, at age 69, I've only been in jail for speeding, and that was only for overnight.

Elwood: *How did that happen?*

King: I was in Mississippi on my way back to Memphis at the time, and I was coming through a little town that's popular today because of the gaming there. But at that time, there was no gambling or anything like that. I was coming through, really speeding, and the state trooper caught me. He said, "Well, I got to take you in because you from out of state. So he took me into the little town where the jail was, and then they found out that the justice of peace was not in town. I remember calling my father in Memphis. I said, "Daddy, I'm down here in jail." He said, "Are you all right?" And I said yes. He said, "You didn't hurt nobody or nothing?" No. "Then you all right?"

Riffing on the King: Junior Wells

"B.B. is never too busy that if a young person comes around and says, 'Could I speak to B.B.,' he'll say, 'Let him in.' He's so courteous, and it means so much to me and everybody else."

Yes. "Then I'll see you tomorrow." *Bam*, he hung up the phone. So I had to stay there all night in this little jail, and the next morning when Dad come down, it cost $35 to get me out and he never let me forget it. I stayed out of trouble from there on.

Elwood: *Traveling as much as you do and playing so many shows, how do you keep your music fresh?*

King: You're going to make me give up my secrets now, but I'll gladly do it for you. One of the things I do—which may not be proper for some—is I play each night like I feel that night. In other words, I don't try to play "The Thrill Is Gone" like I did in 1969 or 1970, when I first made it. I play it tonight like I feel it tonight, the best I can play. That's what keeps it fresh. Whatever song I play, I'm playing it tonight like it's the first time.

Elwood: *You've won so many awards and honors in your career—Grammys, the Rock & Roll Hall of Fame, the Blues Hall of Fame. Of all of them, what has meant the most to you?*

King: You know, that's hard to say; yes, the Grammy Awards and honorary doctorate degrees, all of this is great. But meeting the president—in the office of the most powerful man in the world and he takes time to sit and talk with me, a little boy from Indianola, Mississippi, black at that—is very impressive to this guy. I met President Bush while he was in office, and now I've met President Clinton. Man, that is a couple of the greatest things to ever happen to me.

TAJ MAHAL
Eclectic Purist

> *"Music was the ingredient in the bowl that made you say, 'Okay, I can deal with this soup.'"*

With his respect for and mastery of the blues tradition, Taj Mahal could have easily forged a monolithic career as a roots revivalist. His intelligence and artistic curiosity, however, have led him to explore a multiplicity of traditions, from West African, Caribbean, and Latin styles to zydeco, gospel, and R&B, as well as Hawaiian music. Born Henry St. Clair Fredricks, Taj Mahal began his eclectic musical education by listening to his father's short-wave radio at home in Springfield, Massachusetts. After graduating from college, Taj gigged in Los Angeles on his own and in a band with Ry Cooder, and he emerged as a solo artist in '68 with a self-titled album whose spare, honest sound helped set the rules of the blues revival. Thirty-plus years and numerous recordings later, he remains a champion of traditional blues while continually expanding his global musical vision. When Elwood talked to Taj in 1995 he had recently released the R&B-influenced *Dancing the Blues*.

Elwood Blues: *A lot of big-name rock artists—people like the Allman Brothers and Aerosmith—all point to Taj Mahal as their introduction to the blues. How does it feel to be in that position?*

Taj Mahal: It's flattering—I don't hear an awful lot of that. It's interesting geographically, too. Aerosmith developed their thing in Massachusetts,

Global vision: Taj Mahal performs at London's Barbican Centre in 2004.

where I grew up, and the Allman Brothers are from Georgia. They clicked with this tune called "Statesboro Blues" on the first album we did [*Taj Mahal*]. There aren't too many songs about deep down in Georgia; they're usually beyond the ears of the young listeners. Believe me, your music will sound a whole lot better and you'll be a lot happier if you have some idea where the roots of it are coming from, and how it affects your own roots. The only reason I got into those things is that I liked the music in the same way that a lot of young people like it today, but it just wasn't deep enough for me. So I started trying to find out what else was happening, what made this stuff sound real good.

Elwood: *Tell us about growing up in Massachusetts and your own musical journey.*

Mahal: Well, the music is in the culture, you see. The biggest thing people don't understand about me is that I'm African-American and I'm African-Caribbean, and I'm also part Native American—Cherokee. My father's people are from the Caribbean, and my mother's people are from South Carolina—she grew up with Dizzie Gillespie's family. My father's people emigrated to the United States because they wanted to have their kids out of the islands. So already we're working on some different levels, with a mother who's interested in education, going to college in New England. My parents were very open, but there was a tug from the intellectual bourgeois community that said you take the best of what the society has to offer and then you basically shove everything else out the door. But to me that sounded like a lot of people were throwing the baby out with the bath water.

I heard music coming from lots of different directions, from classical to big-band stuff. I would go cut the grass at Aunt Bessie's house—she wasn't my real aunt—and she would have Jimmy Reed and Muddy Waters and James Brown, Dinah Washington and Big Maybelle, and it was like, Whoa!

Elwood: *What big bands were you hearing?*

Mahal: Count Basie, Jimmy Lunceford, Jay McShann, you know, the jump bands, Louis Jordan, Wynonie Harris. But there always was something that was definitely deeper than that. One of the things that got to me was that country and western music seemed to have a vibe that was very similar to the older traditional music. And I kept trying to figure out why the country guys had great guitar sounds. It was also interesting to see the people who were supposed to be in the know, who were talking about the music, and then the people who actually liked it. It was about being wild, you know—these cats were wearing their leather jackets and got their hair slicked back. They were going for it big time, dancing, and a lot of times the music would hit and these cats would start fighting.

I lived in this little New England town that was kind of quiet. There were 14- or 15-hundred black people in the beginning when my parents came there, and it started getting bigger. The pool of people came from the South and the West Indies and Africa and from Latin America, and music was at the center of the whole thing. Eventually, the various things that went on with urbanization in the '60s and '70s led to the downfall of the inner city, and everybody moved out. So they had their little riot, and the two places that didn't get burned down was the liquor store and the record shop. It cracked me up.

Elwood: *So tell me about the record store. What was the first record you ever bought?*

Mahal: It would have to be something like *The Paragons Meet the Jesters* or some kind of really inner-city blues, doo-wop group. My favorite tune was "Speedoo" by the Cadillacs. Now, years later, I know why I like "Speedoo"—it ain't nothing but Mississippi melody No. 2, only it's a little smoother because they're singing it quartet-gospel style, so you soften it and you woof the notes a little bit more. It ain't as raw as hearing Muddy Waters or somebody like that singing.

Back then, people would come up and just be singing stuff. You hear somebody sing something, you go, "Where did you learn something like that?" I mean, who could teach you that, you know? It wasn't only blues like that. There was Latin music and African music and music from Central or South America with an Afro base. That had the same kind of effect on me, and it became a thing I wanted to play. Music was the ingredient in the bowl that made you say, "Okay, I can deal with this soup."

Back in those days, to be in touch with where songs are coming from, we didn't have books, cross-references, computers. These days you can take a line, say, "I left my baby and she never said a mumbling word," and if that's the only thing you remember out of the song, you can go to the Blues Institute, and they'll tell you the various songs that have that line.

Somebody said that if you want to hear the real spirit of the blues you got to go to Mississippi, hear somebody sing it from Mississippi. It's true. That place put something in the blues. If you hear them sung by somebody else you know that that's where they come from. They can't sing it unless they go down there.

Elwood: *What took you to Mississippi the first time?*

Mahal: I went to Mississippi through a lot of different aunts and cousins and whatnot, some blood relatives and some just extended family. People that lived up the street from me were from Gulfport, Mississippi. Then when we moved across town people that lived up the corner were from Clarksdale, the Nichols family. We used to go and hang out there. Them cats was serious. They were like Original Joe—he's this mythical character who, because he ain't got nothing, he always figures out how to do something, you know? These guys would take radios and turn them into amplifiers. They'd get up there and play their one or two or three tunes, and that stuff would just be cooking. The Ryan boys lived downstairs; they were all doo-wop singers. There was a guy came up from North Carolina when I was 11 or 12, Linwood Perry—this cat was cutting it up. He's still living around town. Garland Edwards was cutting it up, too. He was more like rock; he blended the rock and rhythm and blues thing.

You, know, Chuck Berry was the synthesis of the aspirations of a lot of young black players at that time, to be able to be popular and still cut it the way you wanted to.

Elwood: *They used to call Chuck's music hillbilly music.*

Mahal: Well yes, the early stuff. Whether people want to acknowledge it or not, country music got black roots. And whether people want to acknowledge it or not, blues in the United States has to some extent white roots. If it was sung in some African languages, it would be different. But it takes the African sensibility and brings the experience through English, and that makes it available to everybody. That's why it's a world-class music—that's what I try to tell people all the time. They think it can't be all that important. But they don't get a chance to travel outside of the United States and see how big this is. Whole societies are trying to get more information about it because of what it does and how it feels.

Elwood: *Did you ever get a chance to play with Howlin' Wolf?*

Mahal: No, but I went to see him play live a lot of times. We saw him at a club that probably held about 300, 400, 500 people. It was unbelievable, like there was no room for nothing but what he's got to say. He was just one of the most intense cats in the world. I listen to him a lot; *The Rocking Chair Album* was my favorite album—some great playing on that, and it's wild.

We had a blues festival at the old Milwaukee Braves Stadium. I came down to do soundcheck, and I walked down one the passageways and I backed right into Wolf. I turned around, "Oh, yo, what's happening, Wolf, how you doing?" "Oh, man, I'm all right, what you doing?"

Elwood: *What about Muddy Waters?*

Mahal: That's another one I got into really early, because although Wolf played guitar some, Muddy had another kind of style. It was interesting how—in view of all the sophisticated players around, like Tal Farlow and Kenny Burrell and Grant Green—these guys came along as country players full on with their instrument. They could stand up at a party or sit down at a party and make everybody enjoy what they were doing.

Elwood: *Muddy is known for his slide-guitar style, of course. What's special about slide?*

Mahal: Oh, it depends on who plays it. Sound-wise, the emotion would probably be the thing, because you're sliding instead of pulling, bending, or fretting the strings—you get a talking, conversational kind of thing. B.B. King can do that with a single string—he takes the single string and plays like a slide guitar. So he accomplishes the same thing.

For me, the whole thing connects back to the string players in West Africa, and you can chase the development all kinds of ways. There's different kinds of rhythmic development. The United States has a specific range of meters and times that everybody else wanted to get. No matter how slow they played them back there, they don't play them like that here. Only the older guys do. I just came back from Europe, and all these young Africans that I met love John Lee Hooker, because with him the rhythm hasn't changed.

The tendency for the blues players and the rock players is to get caught up in a lot of clichéd music. But to get the magic to come through those notes, you got to play them slower; they have to have a little more value. That's where you need the background, listening to lots of other people. Then you have a real solid foundation.

Elwood: *On your new album you've included "Sitting on Top of the World," a song that has a long history. When was the first time you heard that?*

Mahal: I actually heard a country recording of that first. I used to listen to radio late at night, you know—couldn't sleep, my mind jamming all out there, wanting to hear something else. Some music would transfix you so you would not move a muscle—you would be like protoplasm and a big ear, just taking in the whole experience. Other times the music would get you up and you would want to dance, or you would think, "I'm going to make sure we have that record when the dance comes around on Friday."

Anyway, one night I was laying up listening to this English skiffle kind of trip, and I heard a woman named Nancy Whiskey doing this song called "Freight Train." After the song was over, I said, "That is not an English song. That song came from the United States." I don't know why or how, I just knew that—there's no way those guys could think of those notes like that. Sure enough, the song came from the United States. It's the same way with "Sitting on Top of the World." It's one of those songs that just by the lyrics and the way it was put together, I knew it had come out of the black experience. There's a lot of songs that travel around from one tradition to another.

Elwood: *For you, what's the connection between rock and blues?*

Mahal: Well, rock is just faster. Some rock 'n' roll is an attempt to play rock 'n' roll that was attempting to play blues. And then some rock 'n' roll is an attempt to play rock 'n' roll that was trying to play rock 'n' roll that was trying to play blues. And it goes on down the line and mutates into some other form. Sometimes it's like a guy can't sing a certain kind of way, he hiccups his way through the song and the next thing you know, it's a style. Or over a period of years a bunch of guys keep missing the fourth or fifth change in the blues and it becomes a kind of a surf style—It's a little thinner, a little bit washed away.

They talk about Robert Johnson—I love Robert's music and what he represents. But Robert got great promotion; that's really what happened to him. There's some guy that Robert was supposed to have gone off and hung out with. Now we finally get a record of this guy, and all of a sudden everybody's going, "Well, Robert learned a lot of stuff from him." Robert just speeded it up to the tempo that we know now.

I think that "I'm a Man" by Bo Diddley or by Muddy Waters—both of those songs have had a tremendous affect on rock 'n' roll. Plus the whole Wynonie Harris, Louis Jordan kind of thing.

Elwood: *What's important about "I'm a Man"?*

Mahal: My personal vision is that it combines the male topic that everybody worries about—"Well, am I or am I not"? It says okay, here's how to chant it. It's also a very strong mating call, because it's got that burlesque beat—there's no mistake about what you want, what you think, what you want to do. And don't think women don't pick up on stuff like that. I mean, even the worst version of I've ever heard, it either hits them in the head, or it hits them in the red chakra, you know what I mean? It's the transference of that energy.

When that song came out the young people wanted to be a part of something, feel something else, do something else, really feel the grip of life moving through them, feel the sap moving through their bones. But the music they had coming from their parents or what was being allowed during that time—these are Eisenhower years, you know—it was pretty cold. I remember going, "This is what it's about?" And then that new music came along, and that was more important than anything else.

Elwood: *What about the jump stuff, like Wynonie Harris?*

Mahal: That's the bunch that really set the whole rock 'n' roll lineup. They came from about '45 to '52, '53. There were all kinds of people in there—one of the singers who precedes a whole line of women is Wanda Jackson. She sounds like a white country singer who grew up around the blues, kind of a counterpart to Hank Williams but not as maybe traditionally country-sounding. Wanda Jackson was somebody that Brenda Lee clearly listened to.

I'll take Wanda Jackson over Elvis Presley any day. For me, Elvis got about three songs, the biggest one being "Mystery Train." That's an example of when these rock 'n' roll guys would listen to what's being played—it's blues and it's moving at a certain tempo—and then they think of some intelligent, creative ideas to add to this already perfect gem. That's a very hard thing to do. I ain't heard a rock 'n' roll band play that good for a long time.

Elwood: *Where does that song come from?*

Mahal: Oh, it's a Mississippi tune. It's like there were ten melodies to come out of Mississippi, and every one of them is attached to a branch that makes a bunch of songs that are out there now. It's a very exciting thing. We're not talking about professor stuff, where you got to sit around and rub the hair off your head on some college wall. No, it ain't about that. It's a history and a situation that's like a living thing. You get inside of it, and it goes on forever and ever.

BROWNIE McGHEE
Strong Medicine

> *"That's what we did, just get out there and go playin' and people comin' around, and he'd sell his medicine a dollar a bottle."*

Though folk-blues fans worldwide automatically link Brownie McGhee's name with that of his longtime partner Sonny Terry, McGhee was an artist in his own right, carrying on the Piedmont blues tradition and finding postwar success in the earliest R&B. Born Walter McGhee in the east Tennessee foothill town of Kingsport, McGhee got acquainted with guitar after a crippling attack of polio. In his early 20s a March of Dimes operation got him back on his feet, and he immediately took his talents on the road throughout the Southeast. He met with blind harp player Terry during a series of Okeh sessions in 1940–41, and the two teamed up afterward in New York. After the war McGhee recorded with Terry and on his own with various R&B labels, and in the late '50s the folk revival helped the duo known as Sonny Terry & Brownie McGhee gain a permanent place in the blues pantheon. The pair finally split up in the mid-'70s, and Sonny Terry died in 1986. Elwood talked with McGhee a year before his passing in 1996.

Elwood Blues: *You and Sonny Terry were one of the longest-running teams in music. Is it true you didn't get along too well sometimes?*

Brownie McGhee: People thought we were arguin', but we were never arguing about the money, because we were always goin' for the biggest

Brownie McGhee took the folk-blues sound worldwide; here he performs at the Royal Festival Hall in the 1960s.

stake. Our deal worked this way: We never went a place and went back for the same money. We had an agent that was excellent.

From the time we got together and started workin' I found that I could not tell him what to do. I had to play with him what he played, and he played behind me what I played. And he supported me the best of his ability, which was excellent. It was his way, and you couldn't beat that. I won't never find another harmonica player like Sonny, because there is no more like him. Sonny was the one and only.

Elwood: *What happened when you and Sonny split up?*

McGhee: Sonny Terry and I was together until I quit the agency. When I quit the agency, that broke up Sonny Terry and me. They booked me and Sonny together, but we had separate contracts—you didn't know that we wasn't a team. And it worked. We'd have had no fights onstage because we didn't have to, because his side of the show was just as good as my side of the show. And my side of the show was as good as his side of the show. What you gonna load the wagon on one end for? Oh, we had a good time.

Elwood: *What set Sonny apart?*

McGhee: Sonny was a natural. He had a "whoop," which was a natural voice, and a harmonica, which made him exotic. Sonny got sounds—trains, dogs, whistles, hollers, whoops, screeches, and yells that we used to have years ago in the country. We had a thing where we'd go and yell, and you would know my yell from another guy's yell because it would come from my house, and it would echo a different echo.

Elwood: *When you first started you were doing the old-time medicine shows. What was that like?*

McGhee: That was far back out into the woods, where they made medicine and pills with vines, and that medicine would cure anything. [*Laughs.*] This old doctor would sell it as long as he had somebody draw a crowd—making money from a medicine show was just as easy as taking cake from a baby. And that's what we did, just get out there and go playin' and people comin' around, and he'd sell his medicine a dollar a bottle. I did a lot of that. There was a lot of con work in it too, you know. They were taking people's money.

Elwood: *Was there a lot of traveling?*

McGhee: Wasn't much travelin' 'cause it was bad travelin'. You had to travel on an old truck. Back in those days they started with solid rubber tires—when they wore out, you were runnin' on hard rubber. It was tough road—dirt, back in the woods.

Elwood: *When you were young did you figure you would make your living playing music?*

McGhee: I graduated from high school on June the 4th, 1936. I had my diploma in my pocket, and I was looking for a school to go to. I was very fond of education because I had polio when I was five, and I figured if I could go to school I could get a job where I could sit down. Study something, be a lawyer or a doctor or something. I could be something. But I didn't realize it took money. Tuitions got in my way, and it drove me to a talent scout. He heard me playing my guitar down in the ghetto in North Carolina—"So, would you like to make records?" "Yeah I want to make records." That was the beginning of Brownie McGhee.

Elwood: *When did you start making your living from music?*

McGhee: Oh, from the time I got into New York and got situated after '41–42, '43. After '47, I begin to go big time. I created bands and trios, and my brother [Granville "Sticks" McGhee] come out with a big song, "Drinkin' Wine Spo-Dee-O-Dee." I was on that—helped to create Atlantic Records, which they don't give me credit for. But I got my brother to do "Drinkin'

Wine" for Atlantic, and I wrote songs for them. I used to write under other names for different companies because I was qualified—Spidey Sam, Big Tom Collins, Tennessee Gabriel. [*Laughs.*] Anything you can think of. And if a song sold, I'd come right along behind and cut it.

In England they'd be debating it—"That's Brownie McGhee. I know that's him. Ain't nobody plays that certain chord." "But see, could be someone caught up with him." [*Laughs.*] So eventually I went to England and confessed that those guys were me. And I started cuttin' records in England. They still sell 'em.

Elwood: *When did you first start playing with Sonny?*

McGhee: I hung around in Harlem and started to play in the streets. That's where Sonny and I started playing together. He started singing with me in '43. I was making pockets full of money, and I said, "You get half of this money, baby. If I do five songs, you'll do five, we'll split 50–50." That become teamwork, no agreement. And so it went that way on contracts.

Elwood: *What was it like up in Harlem at that time?*

McGhee: Harlem wasn't what I thought it was, because blacks didn't care for blues. They started to like the blues after Jackie Robinson hit the Dodgers, made it on the team—1947. I wrote a song called "Baseball Boogie" dedicated to Jackie Robinson. They said, "Who is that guy?" "That's the guy who plays on the street." The *Amsterdam News* give me a big write-up—had my picture on the front page. Then I began to get recognition in clubs in Harlem and also downtown.

That was a change in respectability—Jackie made a great change by getting on the Dodgers. That gave my song a lot of strength and lot of respect. I made my professional debut in Carnegie Hall with "Baseball Boogie." All I had to do was walk up and down the street and sing that baby.

Elwood: *So you hit a home run with that song.*

McGhee: I did!

Elwood: *Was that your first hit?*

McGhee: I wasn't thinking of no hit song. I sold it to a record company, Alert Records, and they made records, and the first batch they sold, they sold to another company. I recorded for any company that opened in New York City. Any company that didn't have a name, I give it a name. [*Laughs.*]

Elwood: *Were you surprised when white audiences started embracing folk-blues in the '50s?*

McGhee: The folk idiom was pretty strong down in the Village—peoples' songs and peoples' unity. Togetherness was what they were working for at that time, people getting together and thinking about [Senator] Joe McCarthy and all that. We could go downtown and sing in old theaters, have big shows until after midnight. And get jobs! I started recording for Mo Ashe, who now has got my whole collection in the Smithsonian Institute. It's paying good money now. At that time I was getting $10 when I needed it. But it was worthwhile. I loved it. Whatever companies I recorded for, I still got a bit in existence.

Elwood: *What about some of the other people you worked with, like Lightnin' Hopkins. What was he like?*

McGhee: Lightnin' Hopkins was a great guitarist. We only played together in clubs. We did make a trip to Japan together: me, him, and Sonny. Otherwise when we worked we didn't work together, because every man had his act. And they couldn't pay because some of these acts was very expensive. Lightnin' was very expensive, you know. And you bet your life that Sonny and Brownie wasn't cheap.

I went with Harry Belafonte three years, and I went on Broadway with Tennessee Williams's play [*Cat on a Hot Tin Roof*]. Those things put you in a category. Harry Belafonte he covered a lot of territory, and I covered it too. When I left him I went around the world with Sonny, going back to the same spots he went. Filled the same joints.

Elwood: *What about Leadbelly?*

McGhee: Lead was great. I played with Lead a little, and I lived with him not quite a year, on East Ninth Street. He was great—he was a guiding light. The songs that Lead did survive nowadays with every type of artist. But if it hadn't have been for the Lomaxes [folk music archivists Alan and John Lomax], Leadbelly would have been out of the picture. The Lomaxes got in there and got his material out and got him his percentage. They did more for him than anybody I know of.

Elwood: *What did you think when the white musicians embraced your music and everything started turning into rock 'n' roll?*

McGhee: In 1960 my wife and I was sitting up in the Catskill mountains out in the woods, I said, "I think I got a big one. I wrote a song—'The Blues Had a Baby and the World Called It Rock and Roll.' And she says, "Honey, I think that's pretty; I think that's nice." It had no women in it, you know. She didn't want me to scandalize women—she wanted me to speak things about women that was important. She said, "Honey, why don't record that?" I said, "Got to give it at least 15 years. The right person gets it, and it'll live forever." I recorded it the year after my wife died, '75. Muddy Waters did version number two. Nobody else seemed to have got the idea of what it says.

The blues was never regulated—W.C. Handy did that when he wrote down "St. Louis Blues." It lost its taste of being free. My daddy used to say, "He left out the flavor out of the 'St. Louis Blues,'" because there was a whole lot of words in there—my daddy knew them all. Bessie Smith sold the blues because she performed an act with a glass in her hand, although she's a great singer. Lady Day [Billie Holiday] come along and she was a great singer; you couldn't take that away from her. That was blues.

Elwood: *It seems like there's a big resurgence in the blues now.*

McGhee: It's a universal thing. Nobody wanted to play the blues until it become a title that they could get involved with without saying "blues"— you playin' blues." "No, I'm playing rock 'n' roll." Guy is sitting up here playing, "I'm going down South, I may not be back till four." And he says, "Now I'm playing rock 'n' roll." That's what I'm talking about.

Elwood: *There's a re-release you appear on that's called* Rediscovered Blues, *but it was originally called* Down South Summit Meeting. *How did that recording come together?*

McGhee: I was the guy that got that together. I went to Ed Pearl and another club owner and a record company, and I said, "Do you know what's happening today? Lightnin' Hopkins from Texas, Big Joe Williams from Mississippi, Sonny Terry from Georgia, Brownie McGhee from Tennessee is all in the same town. And you guys are going to let it get away? Somebody ought to put somethin' together and get a record—a record of us live. Cut us in the studio. We can do it."

They said, "We can't muster up but a hundred dollars." I said, "Well, don't worry about. We're not going to let a good thing get away." We walked in the studio to rehearse and out of the rehearsal become the *Down South Summit Meeting*.

Under my chair you saw a bottle of scotch. Under Lightnin's chair you saw a bottle of whiskey. Under Big Joe's chair you saw a bottle. Under Sonny's you saw a bottle. [*Laughs.*] We all had a jar of whiskey under our chairs, but you'd have to look for it to discover that. We created our songs from what we were talking about—what we thought—the meeting. That's the way the album happened. It wasn't nobody suggestion what we sing about. That become the *Down South Summit Meeting*.

Elwood: *Had you four played these songs together before?*

McGhee: No sir. We had never been on a stage together—nobody but me and Sonny. Sonny and I could get on the stage with anybody, providing they could play behind us. [*Laughs.*] We didn't try to play behind people 'cause we had our own sound. We were geniuses at our work. And I didn't fool around with it. I let people know that, but I didn't let 'em know the secret about following us: Two wrongs make a right, provided you make the wrongs at the same time. If you can't make a wrong with us, you can't play with us.

If I'm playin' a seven-bar blues and you playin' an eight-bar blues, you play a seven-bar blues with Brownie, and then you right. If you play the twelve-bar blues and I do a ten, you do a ten. Makes it right. Can't be wrong, baby! Twelve-bar blues is twelve-bar blues. Ten-bar blues is ten-bar blues. Don't argue with me, and don't make me believe that ten and ten ain't 20. I worked 40 years with Sonny, and Sonny never knew what it was about. I never tried to change him from his style of playing. I never tried to change him and tell him that he was off meter, 'cause he wasn't wrong. If anybody off meter, it was me if he's leadin'. I supported him to the best of my ability, and that was all.

LITTLE MILTON
His Blues Is All Right

> *"I'll keep doing it as long as I enjoy it, and I'm enjoying it to the utmost right now."*

Born in Mississippi and seasoned in postwar Memphis, James Milton Campbell—a.k.a. Little Milton—brings deep blues roots to his soul- and R&B-influenced style. The son of farmer and blues man Big Milton, Little Milton started playing guitar at age 12 and was gigging by the time he was 15. His career led him to associations with many of great blues performers and record labels—including Sun, Chess, and Stax—and he shepherded his own stable of future stars at Bobbin Records. When Elwood interviewed Little Milton in 1994, he was still hard at work bringing his rousing shows to fans worldwide.

Elwood Blues: *I understand you learned the blues from Sonny Boy Williamson back in the postwar era. What were those days like?*

Little Milton: Those were great days. People like Sonny Boy Williamson—the Rice Miller Sonny Boy, now, not the first one—I learned a lot from him and people like Willie Love, Joe Willie Wilkins, Elmore James. Being associated with such blues royalty—that's what I call them—I was able to learn what this thing is all about. That has helped me even up to today. [*Blues harmonica pioneer John Lee "Sonny Boy" Williamson died in 1948. Harmonica great Rice Miller, a.k.a. Sonny Boy Williamson, died in 1965.*]

Back a long time ago, Memphis was sort of a drop-off point. If you could make it to Memphis, you might meet just about anybody. There used to be

Keeping it real: Little Milton puts his energy into his music, not his ego.

a place there, Sunbeam's Domino Lounge, and when you were off work you could go sit in and have jam sessions. You'd run into a whole bunch of people. I met some of the greatest guys in the business: Roy Brown, Big Joe Turner, the late Johnny Ace—in fact, all the ones I just mentioned are no longer with us. You feel like you're in the company of royalty when you're around that kind of people, and you hope some of the good things about them will rub off on you.

Elwood: *Why is that so many blues greats such as yourself came from the Mississippi Delta?*

Little Milton: I really can't answer that—that's a little too heavy for me. But I guess maybe when you speak of Mississippi, you speak of a Southern state—a lot of people call that the Cotton Curtain. There was a lot of common labor back in those days, and they say people that did a lot of hard work got the blues a lot. Being a Southerner myself, I identify with that gut sound, you know, that root type of thing that they say usually comes from the South. But you've got a lot of people that sing the blues that didn't come from the South. But maybe in those days it basically did.

Elwood: *Who were some of your influences?*

Little Milton: Oh, that's easy. The late T-Bone Walker as far as the guitar and guitar style—the way he teased one string at a time and made it sing. He one of the greatest guitarists in the world. Of course, I listened to some of the Lonnie Johnson stuff, and I listened to some of the country and western stuff, the steel guitars, you know, the singing type guitars.

Elwood: *In the early '70's you had success with a country tune, "Behind Closed Doors." How did that happen?*

Little Milton: Well, Charlie Rich did that song—it was a great song, in my opinion—and it was strictly country and western. I thought, wouldn't it be wonderful if I could introduce it as an R&B song. It's just a very soulful song. The people at Stax Records agreed with me, and of course I did my homework and did it my way, and it turned out real nice.

Elwood: *In the '50s you worked with the Willie Love Band and then with Ike Turner. . . .*

Little Milton: Now, that we have to straighten out. A lot of the reporters have a tendency to get that mixed up. Ike Turner and I never did work together in the same unit, like in his unit or mine. We've been friends for years but never worked together—we worked on gigs together.

Elwood: *So one band played before the next?*

Little Milton: Yes; somebody always got to open and somebody got to close. Sometimes he would open and sometimes I would open. Ike Turner was the one who took me into the recording studio for the very first time, which was Sam Phillips's legendary Sun Record Company in Memphis, Tennessee.

Elwood: *Do you recall ever seeing Elvis Presley at Sun Records?*

Little Milton: Well, what I do remember about that time, there used to be three or four young white boys coming to the studio. I found out later that one of them was Elvis. They'd be in the control booth with Sam Phillips. He was his own engineer. Then there was Jerry Lee Lewis and Carl Perkins I found that these three guys would come around and sort of hang out and observe what we were doing, you know? But on a personal basis, no, I never met him.

Elwood: *So you must have influenced their music because they're coming in and listening to you.*

Little Milton: I'm pretty sure we did. You know, it's so strange that when

Sam Phillips does his interviews and he mentions those old days of Sun Records, he has a tendency to leave out the black artists that really was the foundation of Sun. Like the Junior Parkers and so many more around the Memphis area and from Chicago and from Mississippi, of course. Ike Turner was very instrumental in the foundation of Sun Records. He took a lot of artists in there to get them recorded.

Elwood: *Tell us a little more about some of those people you mentioned.*

Little Milton: Well, it's not that they meant so much to me. It's just that they were doing great jobs of performing and recording, and they had some decent hit records. Little Junior Parker, he was the one that did "Mystery Train," which was covered later by Elvis Presley—you know, "train I ride 16 coaches long." It's the artists themselves would give the other artists more credit than, say, what Sam Phillips would do, and that sort of bothered me. I think without a good foundation, the building just don't stand, and they were the foundation.

Elwood: *Didn't you create a label way back, Bobbin Records? Can you tell us a little about that?*

Little Milton: Yes, I had moved from Greenville, Mississippi, to East St. Louis, Illinois. A radio station that is still going here, KATZ, the general manager at that time was Mr. Bob Lyons. We became good associates, and he said he was going to be instrumental in getting me recorded on Mercury Records—I think at that time the president of Mercury Records was a friend of his. So we recorded "I'm a Lonely Man," a tune that I wrote, in the radio studio—we just set the mikes up, and everything was done right there. We sent it off as sort of a test tape, an audition tape, to Mercury Records. He sent it back to us with a letter that it was junk, and do not send him such things any more, ever. [*Laughs.*]

That sort of peeved us off. Bob Lyons said, "Milton, if you're really interested in helping me, go and set up the distribution points where we can distribute these records, and we'll start our own label. I said, "Why not?" So I took off with it and got some press, of course, and in about two weeks we had a hit. Then the man from Mercury called us back and said, "Hey, what about that record?" We said, "We don't need you now—it's junk so it's ours. [*Laughs.*] We also had Albert King, Fontella Bass, Oliver Sain, Walter J. Westbrook, and people like that.

Elwood: *Tell us a little about Albert King.*

Little Milton: He was different—he was his own man, but nothing is wrong with that. He was a great talent. He'll be missed.

Elwood: *You've had over 40 years of live shows, and you always get kudos for your performances. Tell us about what everyone considers your anthem, "Hey, Hey, the Blues Is Alright."*

Little Milton: [*Laughs.*] Elwood, let me tell you this: I was in Europe touring with Magic Slim and the Teardrops and the late B.B. Odom. We did six weeks over there, and I felt we needed something real strong to close the show. The European audiences respond so well, but some of the places we played at they didn't quite speak English. But if you just keep repeating something over and over . . . I got to thinking, and one day I sat down and started to write "Hey, Hey, the Blues Is Alright." I tried it a couple of times and it caught on, but all I could do was just keep repeating "Hey, Hey, the Blues Is Alright." It was going over so well that I decided I'd write some lyrics to it. Fortunately, it has been dubbed as the international blues anthem of the world, and that really makes me feel good. You get that little groove thing with the band really kicking it, it really goes good.

Elwood: *It sure does. When we mention your name, people remember that particular song.*

Little Milton: Well, that's great. You know, I discovered that when we do festivals and what have you, it's a perfect tune to close the show with. If I'm not on the festival, sometimes I've gone to see other artists—some of them wouldn't know that I was there and some of them did know—and I always thought it was a great tribute when they closed their show with it. The audience just loves it.

Elwood: *You've had a very large influence on a lot of the rock, blues, and soul artists of today. For instance, we talked with Jimmie Vaughan on the show, and he thinks you are God's gift to this earth.*

Little Milton: [*Laughs.*] Well, that makes me feel good to know that I played some part in influencing somebody into performing the type music that has been so good to me, that I love so deeply. I suppose I'll keep doing it as long as I enjoy it, and believe me, I'm enjoying it to the utmost right now.

Elwood: *What are you doing right now?*

Little Milton: We're doing what we always do: we're working. We do basically nine months out of a year, and we usually do three to four nights a week.

Elwood: *What do you think of the musicians these days? Is there anyone that you think is really good or who shows the deep blues roots?*

Little Milton: My thing is about feeling, it's about "for-realism." I think as long as you got somebody that's doing what they really enjoy doing, playing what they really feel instead of just going through the motions—any musician doing that has a tendency to be great. We're talking about the Bonnie Raitts, the Robert Crays, and naturally the older guys: B.B., myself, Bobby Bland, and so many more. This is the tradition that the younger musicians are going to have to hang in there with, and a lot of them are doing that.

Elwood: *What other words would you like to leave with the younger people to help them with the blues?*

Little Milton: First of all, I would say to them stay away from the drug scene. Try to be as for real as you possibly can. Enjoy what you perform. Be the best that you can be as a performer, as a person. Try to not get the big head—it takes way more energy to be nasty with an attitude than it does to be pleasant. Remember money don't make you. If you're blessed by the grace of God and you work hard, you might make a little money. And hey, keep doing what you enjoy doing. I hope that's the blues, simply because the blues is all right.

CHARLIE MUSSELWHITE
Past, Present, Future

> *"Sonny Boy'd play one with his nose and one with his mouth. If you were sitting in, you didn't want to use his harmonicas."*

In the mid-1960s Charlie Musselwhite helped foster a new blues audience with an electrified style that was grounded in the sounds of traditional Southern blues. Growing up in Mississippi and then Memphis, Musselwhite joined the Chicago migration at age 18, honing his skills on harp and guitar amid the city's early '60s blues scene. Musselwhite moved to the San Francisco Bay Area in '67, gigged and recorded throughout the '70s, and finally broke through to worldwide recognition in the late '80s. He continues to be a major contemporary blues voice as well as a link to the music's past. Elwood talked with Musselwhite in 1993 after the release of the back-to-the-roots CD *In My Time*.

Elwood Blues: *It's great that someone of your chops and your credibility can take on rural blues. There's a realness to it that most people can't achieve.*

Charlie Musselwhite: It's fun for me to be able to play that old style. You can't fake it, either. It's got to be coming from the heart. I listen to everything from Charley Patton to Charlie Parker; if it's got feeling and it's coming from the heart, it's for me. The feeling that you get from it is the kind of thing that takes you through the world, through your life, and it gives you inspiration to keep going. No matter what comes up you keep getting up.

Traveling the world on his rural-style blues, Charlie Musselwhite performs in London in June 2004.

Elwood: *Do you remember the first time you heard the blues?*

Musselwhite: I remember different times, early things. Where I grew up in Memphis was on a dead-end street, and at the end of that street there was woods and then you'd come to a little creek. And on the other side of the creek there was some fields where people would work. When it was real hot the only way you could get cooled off was to go down by the creek and lay on the shady side.

I'd do that—I was like seven, eight years old—and I would hear these people singing while they worked. They would be singing work songs and blues, and it sounded so good. The way it sounded was just how I felt, because I was kind of a lonely kid. I was an only child, and my parents had broken up and my mother worked. She left in the morning and didn't get back at night until it was dark. I didn't like the other kids rather too much. Playing in the woods and being alone and hearing the singing—it really caressed your heart to hear it.

Elwood: *Where did you learn harp?*

Musselwhite: Well, first I had harmonicas just as toys, because back then they were cheap. I would play along with records—I had gotten into finding old blues 78s in junk stores in Memphis; you could get them for a nickel or a dime. And I would hear harmonica players on the radio. Rufus Thomas had a show every night on WDIA, and his theme song was "Hootin' the Blues" with Sonny Terry. I liked the sound of it, and I started teaching myself.

In later years I got to meet Will Shade, a harmonica player who had the Memphis Jug Band and recorded a lot in the '20s and '30s. He was one of the first harmonica players who actually started playing phrases instead of using it for sound effects or wah-wahs. He taught Big Walter Horton, and later I learned from Walter Horton in Chicago. He had great tone and a real mastery of the harp—I think he was the first modern-style player. He used to tell me that Little Walter and Sonny Boy Williamson came to him for lessons. I didn't really believe him, but then I kept hearing from other people who had known Walter when he was in Memphis, and they all said it was true, that he was the king of the harmonica and everybody came around to learn from him, and Little Walter and Sonny Boy did come to him.

Walter Horton loved the harmonica; it was just part of him. I don't think anything on record compares to what he could really do. But he just wanted to have a good time, and he wasn't into being a businessman. He kind of disdained all that stuff. He'd rather be out in the alley playing with his friends than to be inside a joint doing his job.

Elwood: *Tell us about Sonny Boy Williamson...*

Musselwhite: I used to see him coming through Chicago when I played at a place called Curly's Twist City, the corner of Homan and Madison. He would put on a show that was pretty interesting—it would get pretty risqué. One night I was going in there to hear Otis Rush—Luther Tucker was playing guitar with Otis at the time. I hear the door bang like somebody kicked it open, and I looked back and here comes Sonny Boy just loping in the door. He goes up to the bar and says, "Hey, Curly, come here." And Curly comes over: "What do you want, Sonny Boy?" He said, "Man, I'm working tonight, and I want 50 bucks and I want it now." Curly said okay and gave him 50 bucks. Sonny Boy comes into the main room where the band is, and he gets himself a table and spreads his harps out and has a big bottle of gin on the floor by his feet. He didn't get on the stage, but he's got a long cord for his microphone. He sits off to the side and doesn't name the key or nothing. He just starts stomping his foot and playing. Otis and Tucker could fall in behind him; they were happy to see him there and be backing him up. The people were really knocked out. They started sending drinks over, and his whole table filled up with drinks. I believe he drank every one of them. I remember stopping by his table to say hello and I was kind of glancing at all these drinks. He said, "What are you looking at?" As if I was going to ask for one of them or something. It was like, don't think about it.

One time he was going through the audience, and he would pick out a real pretty girl and get down on his knees and be saying, [*sings*] "Oooh, Sonny Boy smells something, Mama won't you tell me where it's at?" And he'd barely turn up the hem of her dress just the tiniest little bit. Everybody would be laughing and having a great time. They thought that was the funniest thing. He was hilarious.

Elwood: *He used to play harp with his nose.*

Musselwhite: Yes, he probably got that from Walter Horton, because Walter could do that, too. Sonny Boy'd take two harmonicas and put one between his index finger and his middle finger and one between his ring finger and his little finger, and he would hold them both up to his face and play one with his nose and one with his mouth. If you were sitting in, you didn't want to use his harmonicas.

Elwood: *Sonny Boy 2 would take the whole harp in his mouth.*

Musselwhite: Like a cigar—yes, he'd just put it in his mouth. Howlin' Wolf could do that, too. I think Wolf probably learned it from Sonny Boy. Somehow they could move their tongue back and forth across the front of the harp to play different notes. It was just part of being a showman. Rick Estrin does that real good, too—he plays with Little Charlie and the Nightcats. He would put both his hands up in the air and be snapping his fingers and playing the harp at the same time. Has to be seen to be believed.

Elwood: *Was there ever a rivalry between you and Paul Butterfield when you both were playing in Chicago in the mid-'60s?*

Musselwhite: I never really felt like there was a rivalry. When I first got to Chicago, people in the clubs would call me Paul. I didn't know there was a Paul, but it didn't take long to figure out there must be some other white guy playing harmonica. Later we got to know each other and were friends. He got signed with Elektra. I had known Sam Charters for years; he was working for Vanguard and convinced them that they should have a harp player, too, and he got ahold of me.

I wasn't any sort of a threat to what Paul was doing. I don't think our styles were anything alike, but I really liked his playing. It was an inspiration for me to see somebody that's got a band and they're working and making money—I thought, "This is great. I could do this, too." I used to go over to his house, and he'd give me records. We had long talks about blues and playing and stuff. Years later his wife told me, "Paul sure did like it when you came to town, because until you came it was just him."

Elwood: *It must have been tough on you when Muddy Waters died.*

Musselwhite: Well, I hated to see him go. He gave people such a good feeling—the sound of his voice, the way he would look at you when he was talking to you. He really was an impressive person, you know. When he died I wrote a tune about it, "I Could Hear the Whole World Crying." I heard about his death from an old friend of Muddy's. After I got off the phone, I was sitting there—I was living in Richmond, California, in the Iron Triangle—just looking at the window, and I could hear a train rumbling by and a baby crying next door and a siren off in the distance. And it just seemed like the whole world was crying.

He left a real big impression on a lot of people, musically and just as a person. When he walked into a club it was like royalty—his presence just filled up the whole room. Everybody was reverent toward him. And when he was onstage, he commanded the whole stage. He was full of life and full of a kind of energy that seemed to emanate from him. When he'd be singing, his voice it was just, *wow*. People would be pinned to the walls. He was the king of the blues. Him and Wolf, they ruled Chicago. And they were sort of rivals. Wolf didn't like nobody in his band to even talk to anybody in Muddy's band. And he'd fine them, you know—"You been talking to somebody over there, I'm going to fine you 10 bucks." They were only making 15. But Muddy helped Wolf out when he first came to Chicago. It was funny that they got this rivalry going. I remember hearing about how Willie Dixon would want Wolf to do one of his tunes, and Wolf would say, "Nah, I don't like that tune," or something. So Willie would say, "Well, I got this tune for Muddy," and Wolf would say, "Let me look at that tune." So he'd get Wolf to do it, by telling him it was for Muddy.

Elwood: *When you met Willie Dixon for the first time, were you aware that he was the guy that wrote all of those great songs?*

Musselwhite: Yes; I used to see Willie all over Chicago. He'd come into the roughest little dives, and then the next time you'd see him it would be at some recording studio, being the producer, running the show. Or another time you'd see him in a jazz club or something. He really got around. Great guy. I remember Willie was starting to move out to California, maybe coming out to rent an apartment or something, and he asked me to come by his house in Chicago, and he gave me the keys to his station wagon. He knew I was going back to California, and he wanted me to drive his car out for him. That was nice to be trusted with his car full of stuff, taking it out to California for him.

Elwood: *You talked to Albert King not long before he died. Can you tell me about that?*

Musselwhite: Well, I knew that Albert was sick, and I had been asked to fill in for him on at least one date. I had sent him a couple of cards. I had his home phone number and I was thinking about calling him, but I was hesitating because I didn't know if I'd just be disturbing him, if maybe he wanted to be left alone. Then I was talking to a friend of mine who had come close to dying, and he said it had really meant a lot to him that people had called. So I thought well, that's it, I'll give him a call. We talked for awhile, and he sounded real weak. I told him that I'd hesitated to call him because I didn't want to disturb him, and he said, "Charlie, I don't care if it's four in the morning, you can call me any time." It just tugged at the old heart, you know? I was really glad I'd called him. He died on Thanksgiving eve, shortly after I had talked to him. It's hard saying goodbye to old friends and good people like Albert. We had some real good times together—he's missed today. So Albert lives, too.

Elwood: *Otis Rush is still making music. Did you ever get to know him?*

Musselwhite: Yes. We used to play at a place called the I-Spy Lounge. Otis told me that in his opinion it was the roughest club in Chicago. And it was pretty rough—I don't know if it was the roughest, but after a certain point, you can't really judge. I would work there with Johnny Young on Sundays and then in the afternoons from like four o'clock until nine o'clock, and then Otis would come in and play the rest of the night, and I'd hang out chasing women and stuff like that.

He was a great guy, and I really liked his guitar playing. He gave me my first Les Paul. He needed to go to Omaha or someplace on a gig, and he needed to borrow a car, and I happened to have a station wagon. I said, "Here, you can take this." When he came back he gave me his Les Paul. That was my first electric guitar. I had that for years till I had to get rid of it one time to pay the rent.

Elwood: *Was guitar your first instrument?*

Musselwhite: No, I'd always had harmonicas around, so it was pretty much simultaneous. But when I got up to Chicago, wherever you'd go, there would be lots of guitar players, and not that many harp players. And a lot of the guitar players were way better than me; it was easier for me to get work as a harmonica player.

Elwood: *Have you played with B.B. King much?*

Musselwhite: I've sat in with him a few times. I remember the first time I saw him; I was working at Steve Paul's Scene in New York City. I remember Steve Paul walking around in a bathrobe—it seemed like he always had a bathrobe on. But it was a great place to play. I remember doing shows with Mose Allison and Betty Carter and Johnny Winter. Sometimes my first set wouldn't start until after midnight—they went till four in the morning. One night B.B. had a night off or he got off early or something, and he came by.

He introduced himself, and we got to know each other, and we've been friends ever since. He's really a wonderful person to know. An example for us all.

Elwood: *It's interesting that you should mention Mose Allison, because you and he have a similar vocal style. Was he an influence on you?*

Musselwhite: It's hard to say. I've listened to a lot of his music, and I've recorded some of it—he's written some great tunes. But I've never consciously tried to sing like him. It seems like being from the same part of the country you're both going to kind of talk alike, but I don't have any idea what I sound like to anybody else.

Elwood: *When you were starting out, who would you try to sound like?*

Musselwhite: I don't recall trying to sound like anybody. I was just trying to get my voice to do something that sounded passable as singing—trying to hit the notes right and sing with some feeling. I never thought trying to sound like somebody was the way to go. I never tried to play like anybody, either. I just tried to learn the instrument and then play the notes that I could hear in my heart or in my head. You do come up with stuff you've heard somewhere before, but I didn't sit down and memorize styles. I know people who can say, "Well, Little Walter would play it this way, Big Walter would play it that way, and Sonny Boy would play it this way." And that's real interesting, but I never learned how to do that.

Elwood: *Do you enjoy being on the road?*

Musselwhite: I do, but sometimes I get tired of it. I like to travel where I get to actually go and see things instead of just the hotel and the club, you know. When I get a day off on the road it's a treat for me. Wherever I go, I get books about how to speak the language, and I try it out. That's a lot of fun, but sometimes it gets you in trouble. One time in Mexico City I'd finished eating and I wanted to pay my bill, and I wanted to say *pagar*, which is "to pay." But I was using *pegar*, which means I want to hit somebody. I was getting these funny looks from people, and then they started laughing because they realized I was just saying the wrong word.

Big Joe Williams used to claim he could speak Spanish. One time we went to this Mexican restaurant, and Joe told me that when we got inside, I should let him do all the talking because he spoke the language. So we go in and the waitress comes over, and he starts saying, "sylvester, sylvester." And he's getting louder and louder, as if louder would make it clear to the lady. She didn't know what he was talking about. He was trying to say *cerveza*. Finally he had to give up.

Elwood: *Did you work much with Big Joe?*

Musselwhite: Oh, yes. I first met Joe in Chicago, and we both had cots down in the basement of the Jazz Record Mart near the corner of State and Grand. We would sit up all night drinking, and he would show me things on the guitar. I'd play harmonica along with him and watch him playing guitar, and I picked up little things that he was doing. He played a 9-string guitar.

He would talk about his life and all the different people he knew—Charley Patton and Robert Johnson and a lot of other people I never heard of, people that never made records. He would tell all these tall tales about them. Gamblers, like the guy named Blue Steel—he could turn himself into a rabbit and run away when the police showed up. Joe said one time he was playing at this place and the police showed up. And Blue Steel, since he liked Joe, decided he would just go to jail with Joe and get him out later that night. And sure enough, according to Joe, when it was real quiet and everybody was asleep, Blue Steel goes over to the cell door and just blows into the lock and the door opens up and him and Joe walk away. And they left that town. It was a different world in those days. I guess he had his mojo working.

Elwood on the Air: Dragnet

HOUR: 02/24
AIRDATE: 6/15–16/02
WRITER: MERLE KESSLER

[FX: Dragnet music]

ELWOOD (as Friday): This is The House of Blues Radio Hour. I work here. I wear a badge.

[FX: Dragnet sting.]

I was turning turntables out of the utility room, waiting for the CD player to get back from the shop, when the call came in.

[FX: Phone rings. Joe picks up.]

House of Blues Radio Hour. I work here. I wear a badge.

VOICE ON PHONE (Filtered): Is this Friday?

ELWOOD: I don't know, sir. I don't have a calendar in front of me. I have a badge.

VOICE ON PHONE (Filtered): I'd like to report some criminal activity.

ELWOOD: I see. What is the nature of the criminal activity, sir? Is this a 513, or a 412?

VOICE ON PHONE (Filtered): All I know is a woman is going around breaking hearts. I believe she's a blues singer. What number is that?

ELWOOD: Sounds like a musical number, sir. Let me tell you something. It's a mean world, full of mean people, and when they step out of line, that's when I step in.

VOICE ON PHONE (Filtered): You wear a badge?

ELWOOD: I wear a badge. And I spin platters, mister, so you won't have to. I spread the word about the blues. In my book, this blues singer is presumed innocent.

VOICE ON PHONE (Filtered): You have a book?

ELWOOD: I have a badge. Now hang up the phone and do something useful.

VOICE ON PHONE (Filtered): Like what?

ELWOOD: Listen to The House of Blues Radio Hour, sir. And think about what I've said.

[FX: Phone hangs up.]

This IS The House of Blues Radio Hour. I wear a badge. And this is Koko Taylor. She sings the blues.

[Song: "Come to Mama"—Koko Taylor]

KOKO TAYLOR
True to the Blues

> "I don't call it the devil's
> music; I call it good music."

The acknowledged Queen of Chicago Blues, Koko Taylor has received 19 W.C. Handy awards, won a Grammy amid her six nominations, been inducted into the Blues Hall of Fame, and had a day named in her honor in Chicago. Through it all she has remained a messenger of the true blues, respecting the legacy of her heroes and delivering her vocals with power, honesty, and passion. Elwood caught up with Taylor in New York as she was on her way to an Alligator Records all-star show that included Lonnie Brooks and B.B. King. In their brief 1993 interview, the Memphis sharecropper's daughter recounted the archetypical story of the postwar blues migration.

Elwood Blues: *Do you remember the first blues record you heard?*

Koko Taylor: I sure do. My brother and I, we used to listen to the blues on the radio. That's all we had going back in those days. We had a disc jockey in Memphis—his name was Rufus Thomas—and, of course, B.B. King was a deejay then in West Memphis, Arkansas. So I would hear the blues played on the radio, and this record was playing by Memphis Minnie. It was called "Me and My Chauffeur Blues." I believe that was the first blues that I ever really paid attention to. Memphis Minnie, Bessie Smith, Big Mama Thornton, Muddy Waters, Howlin' Wolf, Sonny Boy Williamson, and all of these people was really my idols. They were a lot of inspiration to me because listening to them on the radio is what really got me interested in paying attention to the blues—and that's what I did. Every day I'd look for-

Koko Taylor sends her mighty voice skyward, straight from the heart.

ward to that 15 minutes on the radio listening to the blues. My dad say, "If you ain't singing gospel, then it's the devil's music." But I don't call it the devil's music; I call it good music.

After I left Memphis, my husband—everybody knew him as Pops Taylor; his name was Robert Taylor—he says, "I'm going to Chicago." I said, "Well you can't go to Chicago without taking me." Neither one of us had no money, nowhere to live, no job. He said, "I'm going to Chicago to find me a good job"—what we call a good-paying job. He found a job working at the Wilson Packing Company. We got on that Greyhound bus headed north to Chicago, and the only thing we had was 35 cents and a box of Ritz Crackers between us.

When we got to Chicago, I still loved music, I still loved the blues, and I didn't realize for a while that all of the blues people that I had been listening to on the records and hearing about, most of them was right there in Chicago. I met Howlin' Wolf and Muddy Waters. They had their band playing, and every weekend my husband and I would go out to these little blues clubs you know, local black blues clubs—it was no white audience during the years that I'm talking about. We would go to these clubs and my husband introduced the guys to me, letting them know that I really was so impressed with them and I wanted to sing—I loved to sing. So on the weekend they'd invite me up on the bandstand—"Hey, little Koke, you want to come up here and do a tune with us?" I was happy to do it because we were just jamming, you know. It was for no money, no nothing. I didn't know nothing about no records, no nothing. I was just having a good time.

That kept going on and on and on until finally I met up with Willie Dixon. Willie Dixon discovered me sitting in jamming with Howlin' Wolf. He came over to me and he says, "I never heard a woman sing the blues like you, and that's what the world needs today. We got a lot of men who sing the blues but no women." And this is when he spoke to me about recording for Chess and about contracts, and I didn't even know the meaning of the word. But under Willie Dixon's jurisdiction, we got started with my career doing "I Got What It Takes," one that he wrote especially for me. Same as he did with "Wang Dang Doodle." As the years passed, "Wang Dang Doodle" turned out to be one of the greatest hits and has become a classic today. I don't remember the exact year it was I left Chess Records. I didn't just leave Chess, Leonard Chess had a heart attack and he passed away, so I was without a recording contract. But I kept singing the blues from place to place everywhere until I met up with Bruce Iglauer at Alligator Records.

Elwood: *Some people say the people in other countries appreciate the blues better than we do in America.*

Taylor: The people in Europe love the blues, but no better than they do right here in America—I have some of the greatest fans right here. I just got home from Israel, the Holy Land. I did not think the people in Israel liked the blues, but when I got over there I found out they love the blues. They were into what I was doing, and we had a wonderful time. They're looking forward for me to come back to Israel to sing the blues.

Elwood: *Buddy Guy said, "The master blues men who passed on have left a legacy; you've got to play and carry it on." Do you feel the same way?*

Taylor: I feel the same way. We have to carry the torch because a lot of the older, real fine blues artists have passed on, like Willie Dixon, Muddy Waters, Elmore James—I could go on naming them. The few of us who are left behind, we've got to carry on, keep the blues alive. I would love to see more young people into the blues, singing the blues today. There are some, but it's not nearly as many as I would like to see into the blues.

Elwood: *Who do you see as up-and-coming young blues talent?*

Taylor: Well, you know, there's Billy Branch and Sugar Blue on harmonica. Also, there's the Kinsey Report, they are young guys—their father is Big Daddy Kinsey—I think they are one of the greatest bands around. Also, on the show with me tonight, Lonnie Brooks has his son, Ronnie Baker Brooks. He plays guitar and sings the blues, and he sounds great. Also, there's another young guy with Alligator Records called Lil' Ed. I think he's great. He plays slide guitar like his uncle [J.B. Hutto], who passed on earlier. Luther Allison has a son, Bernard Allison, who is really great, really plays the blues. I just wish there were more like them.

Elwood: *You're queen of the blues, you tour nine months a year, you're international, you've got a new album coming out—what's next?*

Taylor: Elwood, you have been one of the people who have opened the door for people like myself, so that we can keep on singing the blues, going places, doing things that we've never done before. What's next is I'm going to keep on looking up, I'm going to keep on going forward and as high as I can go, and I mean the sky is the limit. All I want to do is just keep making people happy all over the world singing the blues. When I please my fans, I've just pleased me.

Koko Taylor

RUFUS THOMAS
Workin' the Dog

> *"Every time I think I got my ends to meet, somebody come up and move the ends."*

Always an entertainer, Rufus Thomas filled his blues, funk, and soul music with an energy and a cheery humor that can be traced to his vaudeville roots. In Memphis in the '40s, his big personality fit the bill as emcee of a Beale Street amateur night that debuted future stars like B.B. King, Roscoe Gordon and Ike Turner. In the '50s Thomas began a radio career that would last until his death in 2001, and he began recording a string of hits for Sun and then Stax, including the intergalactically covered "Walking the Dog." Alone or with his daughter Carla, Thomas made it to the Top 10 every decade of his recording career, which peaked in the '70s with hits like "Do the Funky Chicken." Elwood talked with Thomas in 1995 upon the release of *Rufus Thomas Live!*

Elwood Blues: *People still talk about the Rufus and Bones comedy team back in the old days in Memphis.*

Rufus Thomas: That was with a fellow by the name of Robert Couch—they called him Bones. I had known him practically all of my life. He was in one of the first black movies, *Hallelujah*, with Nina Mae McKinney in 1928. Ooh, that sounds like a long time ago, 1928.

I was his straight man. He carried all the comedy, and he was funny as he could be. He was 4-11, and he used to wear the long ties that hung almost to the ground, the big pants and the great big shoes and the big shirts and

Tastes like funky chicken: Rufus Thomas brings his fun-loving style to a 1996 show.

the funny hats. He could walk on the stage and without saying a word, the house would go up, man, in a roar. Rufus and Bones at the Palace Theater—that's a name you'll always hear about. If you did anything in Memphis, you had to come by me first. B.B., Bobby Bland, Roscoe Gordon—these are the ones that I remember, but so many people came across there.

Elwood: *You must have crossed paths later on with a lot of those people. Did you ever say, "I remember you when I was the emcee at the Palace"?*

Thomas: They remember. They start talking about it. And when B.B. is traveling or he's being interviewed about Memphis, he always talks about amateur night on Beale Street. When he come onstage he didn't get but a dollar, and that dollar would carry him practically all the week because bus fare was about a nickel. He come up every Wednesday night, and I put him on. I said, "Well B., you were here last week." He says, "I know it, but man, I need that dollar." So I put him on again. My old buddy Bones would be mad because I put him on every Wednesday, but, well, the rest is history. B.B. is one of the most together blues singers in the country. Besides me, of course.

Elwood: *When you became a deejay at WDIA, it was one of the first black-owned stations. It must have been exciting to be involved in that.*

Thomas: It was, you know, to be a part of that kind of history. It was 1948 when WDIA went on the air, and I went there in 1951. Would you believe that I'm still there today? We have the number-one show in Memphis on Saturdays playing nothing but the blues, from six until ten Saturday morning. When I first went to WDIA I had the *House of Happiness* show, one hour on Saturday. It was a real happy show.

Elwood: *You also had a nighttime show called* Hoot and Holler, *and you had a special opening line.*

Thomas: Those days all disc jockeys—and especially black disc jockeys—had a theme song to their shows when they were coming on the air. When I come on at midnight, I opened up cold, you know. I said, "I'm young, I'm loose, I'm full of juice, I got the goose, so what's the use. We feeling gay, though we ain't got a dollar. Rufus is here so hoot and holler!" And the song I played was "Hoot and Holler" with Brownie McGhee and Sonny Terry.

Elwood: *Even though you were deejaying you didn't give up your day job.*

Thomas: Not for a long time—I stopped working at the factory in 1963. It was a textile mill, American Finishing Company. You see, the radio at that time didn't pay enough for me to let that day gig go. I'd get off at 2:30 from this textile mill and stop at home—where I lived was on the way to WDIA— and the kid was there helping me put my shoes on when I walked through the house. Then I'd go across town. If I was ever late, it was only one time. When the first record was finished, I was sitting there ready to go on the air, sitting at the microphone. And I did that for years and years. I had all kinds of jobs. I had four and five jobs at once trying to make ends meet. And every time I think I got my ends to meet, somebody come up and move the ends.

Elwood: *You worked with Sam Phillips at Sun Records. What was that like?*

Thomas: I did "Bear Cat"; that was the first hit record for Sam Phillips, and then there were others. He leased some of my stuff to Chess Records, Leonard Chess in Chicago. Sam had a stable of black entertainers at that time, and they were all good musicians, good entertainers. But while we were there, we didn't know that Sam Phillips was looking for a white boy who could sing black. In time, all of the black entertainers had to go because Sam had found somebody white who could sing black. I don't know what Sam's ideas were about that. He has talked about it, but what he has said was so flimsy that it sounded like nothing. But later on, as fate would have it, Stax came along, and I came off the street and went in there and—had the first hit record for Stax, my daughter and I—Carla and Rufus—"'Cause I Love You." It was a good, good record. From there, Carla did "Gee Whiz," which was a monster record. And after "Gee Whiz" came "The Dog."

Elwood: *How did "The Dog" get started?*

Thomas: It was a dance tune, but I didn't do the dance, I just wrote the song. We were working in a nightclub in a little place called Millington, Tennessee, which is about 15, 20 miles out of Memphis. We were playing some tune, and the bass line had the rhythm—it was just flowing. The dance "The

Dog" was already out, and this girl, she was about 5-8 and she was wearing a black leather dress and she had a long waistline, and she was just sleek in that dress. Well, if you know about how "The Dog" went, she bent over in front of the bandstand and started doing that dance, and everybody on the bandstand including me went ape. We kept the beat going, changed the bass line just a little bit, and I started to sing and the words just came right out— "Do the Dog, do the Dog . . . Do the bird dog, do the hound dog, do the bull dog . . ." Everybody all night long wanted to hear "The Dog," and it turned out to be a monster record.

Elwood: *A couple of years later you came out with "Walking the Dog." What's the story behind that?*

Thomas: I was working in this textile mill, working on boilers. I filled this big boiler about 14 feet deep with cloth, and I had to put the chemicals and stuff in there to bleach the cloth. So I'm on top, you know, lying up there while overhead was what they called a prowler that pulled the cloth down into this big boiler. I'm singing, and suddenly the words, as usual, just start coming. I don't know how they come, they just come. It was a nursery rhyme, all nursery rhymes: "Mary Mack, dressed in black, silver buttons all down her back, high hose, tippy toes; she broke a needle and she can't sew." I used to use these terms when I was playing I-Spy in the neighborhood. I do not know how "walking the dog" came at the end of the verses, but it worked like a charm. It has been one of my biggest records. More bands, white, black, blue, green play it. Even the Japanese, they're playing "Walking the Dog" until this very day. I was doing an interview in France, and this fellow said he knew 44 different versions of "Walking the Dog," some of them in foreign languages. But none of them are as good as mine, never. I defy anyone to do my material better than me.

Elwood: *How did you come to put the wedding march on the opening of "Walking the Dog"?*

Thomas: I don't know. I really don't. I didn't pick it, it just came up. All the songs I put together, other people have always gotten named for being the producer, but I have always put all of my stuff together, all of it.

Elwood: *Do you use a piano or a guitar when you're putting tunes together?*

Thomas: I don't use nothing. I get it in my head, and I hum it to the band—I can hum a full arrangement, what the horns play, bass line, guitar, the whole nine yards—and they play it. It must have worked. It comes out all right.

Elwood: *You were one of the pioneers of Southern funk. Where did that sound come from?*

Thomas: Funk is something that Memphis had that no other place in the world had. The Memphis sound was that big bass and big foot. Now, there's Motown, some of the finest music that's every been done. But it wasn't funky. They didn't have the big foot, and they didn't have the funky bass nor the strong country funk guitar. I was just about the innovator of that funky backbeat. We called that fatback. Fatback is that kind of meat you put in black-eyed peas and greens, that seasons that soul food. And when you said that fat backbeat, that funky fat backbeat, they said, "This thing is funkier than 19 yards of chitlins with onions and sardines on the side." Oh, I forgot, with pickle. Now, that's funk.

Elwood: *In the funk and disco era of the '70s you used to wear some wild outfits onstage.*

Thomas: Wild outfits? I still do it. People expect that. Two years ago I was wearing a red outfit with a cape and the tall boots. I just did a festival out in Long Beach, California, about three weeks ago, everybody went, "Where is that red suit with the cape and the gold boots?" I said, "You don't want to see me wear that red thing all the time." But when I hit the stage, there it was, the whole nine yards—Rufus is back again.

Elwood: *In the '80s you got back into the R&B sound with the album* That Woman Is Poison.

Thomas: It was an awesome album, but I feel like it fell by the wayside. I don't think that it got the push that it should have gotten.

Elwood: *I guess that's why it was re-released on Alligator years after King Snake released it.*

Thomas: You can check my record against any other thing that Alligator has ever put out. They've never had anything any better. Never. I ain't bragging, just stating facts.

Elwood: *Who are some of the people who influenced you as a writer and a performer?*

Thomas: In the beginning there were people like Louis Armstrong. I used to imitate Louis Armstrong, Fats Waller, and a fellow by the name of Gatemouth Moore, Dwight Moore. One of the songs on *That Woman Is Poison* is his—"Somebody's Got to Go." It was done back in the '40s, but can you tell that it was from the '40s? Blues is always in the now. Blues doesn't get old. Good solid blues like Muddy Waters sounds just as good today as it did 30 years ago.

Elwood: *You covered "Boom Boom"—was John Lee Hooker an influence?*

Thomas: Yes, I like him. He was on the show with us at the Long Beach. We happened to go through Nashville one day, and John Lee was in town and we all went to see him that night. He got me and Steve Cropper onstage, and oh, man, that was a big night in Nashville. John is bad. He's only man I know of who can play good blues all day and seldom rhyme his words. You ever notice that?

One of the top men that I loved was Elmore James—one of the baddest. He was the master of the slide guitar, and he could sing some blues.

Elwood: *You've been playing blues on the radio for a long time.*

Thomas: We have so much fun on our blues show, man, you wouldn't believe. We tell a few jokes, and people call up and request songs to play and jokes that we've told. I've been interviewed on some of the white stations, and they ask, "What in the world does WDIA got that they've lasted through the years and are still up there? What is it?" And I say, "Me." Hey, let's face it—I told the truth.

JUNIOR WELLS

Don't Mess with the Kid

> *"The judge said, 'Are you sure you can blow this thing?' And I said, 'I think so.'"*

Though he wielded a harp, Junior Wells was no angel. While he was still a youngster, Junior's typical boldness got him sitting in with B.B. King, landed him a gig with Muddy Waters as Little Walter's replacement, and fueled a mess of trouble with the law. Legal troubles notwithstanding, by 1957 he had cut a number of memorable sides for State Records, and the next two decades brought a wellspring of R&B classics for Chief, Profile, Delmark, and Blue Rock, including his signature "Messin' with the Kid." In the '70s Wells toured and recorded with Buddy Guy, and though his studio time dwindled in following years, his no-nonsense presence continued to command the stage and a strong following up to his death in 1998. Five years before, he talked with Elwood about his early days in Chicago.

Elwood Blues: *When was the first time you heard the blues?*

Junior Wells: It was in Whistler, Arkansas, when I used to listen to the thing from Nashville, Randy's Record Shop. They had the battery radios that you could take a clothes hanger or a piece of wire and put over it [for an antenna]. Mom sent and got me from Arkansas and brought me to Chicago where she was, then I started coming back down to Whistler, and I met B.B. King. He was playing in a club, and I asked him if I could play some harmonica with him. He says, "Well, it might be possible, but I'm not making that much to pay you, young man." I say, "I don't care about that, I just want

Junior Wells pawned his life of crime to tangle with the blues.

to play with you." So we did this particular thing—he wasn't making a lot back then, maybe $10 or $15 a night. Then he started doing that thing for Peptikon in Memphis.

Elwood: *Those radio commercials started the ball rolling for B.B. What was your first big break?*

Wells: I got a little bit of a break in Chicago with the Four Aces. They weren't the Four Aces at the time; they were called the Sceptor Three, with Louis Myers and Dave Myers—we only became to be the Four Aces after Freddy Below got out of the service. From that, I met all the other mucky-mucks, like Big Maceo and Tampa Red. They were playing down the street from my house. I had a good time, but I had a little game going and I got

Junior Wells

into a problem with that. They told my mom, "Your son a bad person, and we want to put him in the big house. It took my mom, Sunnyland Slim, Big Maceo, Tampa Red, and people like that—Muddy Waters also come over— to come to this juvenile school, and they had to sign a paper saying that they are my guardians and not to incarcerate me. It means so much to me to think that these people stood up for me, and today I'm trying to stand up for every young musician. If you want to be a thug, then that's your thing, it's not mine. But if I can help in any kind of respect at all . . .

Elwood: *There's a story that when you were a boy you got out of trouble by playing your harp in court.*

Wells: I had been playing hooky from school and working on this pop truck because Sonny Boy—not the original Sonny Boy but Rice Miller—had told me when I was in Arkansas that you had to have a Marine Band harmonica. I had a little old harp, and he took it and stomped it. So I worked on a pop truck to get this particular harmonica. It didn't cost but $2.50, but that man worked me all that week and gave me a dollar and a half, so I didn't have enough money to buy it.

I went in the pawnshop on State and Harrison and told the guy I wanted the Marine Band. He said, "Well, you don't have enough money. He showed me an old standby and said, "You can buy this." I said, "No, that's not it, and he said, "Well, you can't get no credit here because you're a kid. So some other people came in and he went to wait on them, and I left a dollar and a half and took the harmonica I wanted. I didn't think I was stealing, so I was blowing the harmonica going out the door. Going down the street, here comes squad cars with guns and everything like that. They made like I had stole it but not in my mind.

I went up before the judge, and the judge asked me did I steal the harmonica? I said, "No I didn't." He said, "Well, did you pay for it? I said no. I told him what I did, and he said, "Is this a thing that you do all the time?" I said no, I'd never done that before. He said, "Did he give you permission to leave the premises with this harmonica?" I said no. He said, "Well now, don't you know if he didn't give you permission to leave the premises with this harmonica, that you stole it? I said, no, I didn't think I was stealing it. I said I told him I would bring his money the next week, and I told him about cutting school.

So he asked the pawnbroker, "Do you have any objections about who gives your other dollar?" He said, "No, I just want my dollar." The judge said, "Are you sure you can blow this thing?" And I said, "I think so," and I went to blow the harmonica and everybody jumped up in the courtroom. He said, "All right, sit down. The first record you have, I have to get it first because you owe me my money. I said, "I'm going to give it to you," but he passed away. I did send it to his family.

Elwood: *That was your first paying gig, in court.*

Wells: You got that right!

Elwood: *You became a student and friend of Little Walter. Talk about how you got together with him?*

Wells: I thought I was doing a thing until I heard Walter. When I heard Walter, I said I know I can do this. So I'm in the bathroom in my house and I've got the door locked, and Mom says, "Open the door, your sister is trying to get in there," but I wouldn't open it. She said, "I'm going to kill you if you don't open the door." So I opened the door, and she started smacking me. My older sister was going with a police officer, and he said, "You're beating him up." She said, "He ain't never going to learn nothing, just get out of here. Take him anyplace you want."

That's when I met Little Walter. I went over to the Ebony Lounge in North Chicago, and I met Muddy and Walter at the Saturday matinee. The owner got on my case because I'm too young to be in there, but my sister's boyfriend flashes the badge and says, "I'm responsible for him." He asked Muddy when he came in, would it be possible if I could come up and jam some? Muddy said, "Well, I guess so. Young man, do you know your time?" I said, I think so. He said, "I have no problem about him coming up and playing, but I have a problem with Walter because this is Walter's amplifier and his microphone, and I have to ask Walter." Walter looked at me and said, "That little old pipsqueak? Let him go ahead, man; let him kick himself out."

So I went up there and we got into it, and I made about $60 or $70. Walter asked me if I had ever played saxophone, I said, "No, do you have one?" He said, "No, but you've got a good thing together." He gave me a couple of dollars and said, "Go and get yourself a gin." I said, "No, I can't do that, because you called me a pipsqueak. So my sister's old man said, "Are you going to say that to the man that you're blowing into his microphone?" I said, "Oh, I'm sorry." So Walter went and got a gin. We stepped out the back door in the alley. He said, "Come on," and I said, "No, I can't do that. I don't drink. He says, "You don't drink now, but sooner or later you're going to have a drink. He gave me a little taste, I thought it was the terriblist thing I ever had in my life.

Elwood: *How old were you then?*

Wells: Thirteen. Then Walter got sick, and Muddy was doing a thing in the Apollo Theater, so he picked me for the tour.

Elwood: *What was your first show like?*

Wells: When we went out there and I turned around and saw those people, I fell over my amplifier, and everybody was laughing and hollering. So Muddy say, "Excuse us, but we've got a young man here, he never did the thing like this before. He's trying to get himself together. Would ya'll excuse us for a few minutes?" He say, "Go back and do a taste of that gin." That's what I did. I went back and got it. Settled my nerves. We had a good time.

Elwood: *Junior, what advice would you give to a young kid with a harp who wants to get into the blues and make it a career?*

Wells: I would tell them one thing—you're not going to just do it by yourself. You need somebody to give you a little helping hand like they did with me. I could have been in detention for the rest of my life, you know, but I'm not a criminal now, and it means so much.

Rock
Royalty

STEVE TYLER, JOE PERRY & TOM HAMILTON OF AEROSMITH

Talking the Talk, Walking the Walk

> *"It's all about taking almost crude musicianship and raw talent and using that as a channel to express an emotion."*

Boston-based Aerosmith helped define hard rock with its mix of gritty, riff-based rockers like "Walk This Way" and stadium-swaying power ballads like "Dream On." The quintet stood at the top of charts in the '70s, but the band's popularity wavered in the early '80s amid personal problems and shifting personnel. In the late '80s, however, the original members— vocalist Steve Tyler, guitarists Joe Perry and Brad Whitford, bassist Tom Hamilton, and drummer Joey Kramer—regrouped for a comeback. That lineup was still going strong when Tyler, Perry, and Hamilton talked to Elwood in 1993 about the band's history and its roots in the blues, which Aerosmith would return to on 2004's *Honkin' on Bobo*.

Elwood Blues: *Some people see blues as limiting because of its structure. But there are some people who can, within that structure, create all kinds of variety. The same seems to be true with your music.*

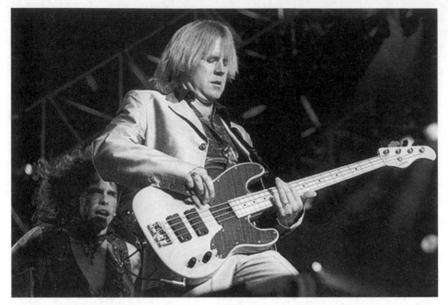

Influenced by Delta blues, Tom Hamilton and his band were playing Elmore James tunes the first time Steve Tyler saw him.

Tom Hamilton: It's just a springboard that lets something else happen—having a good time and letting emotion come out. You can say funny things or cool things or sad things through melody or lyrics or guitar riffs, or even rhythms. But you need to take it into another realm.

Elwood: *It's great that you're back together and writing again. How does that work?*

Steve Tyler: It's like if I said to you, "Hey, man, we're all here because we're not all there," and you go, "Great, take that, keep it, write it down, wrap a song around it—'We're all here because we're not all there.'" Or Joe will come with a lick that sounds melodically just as cool as that statement. And I'll wrap something around it.

When you're a touring band, you want to have something behind you—like you're in a rocket ship going to the moon, you want to know you got something in your retro-rockets so you can make it back. And when you do an album, you want to have a bunch of little gems in there to keep you going. So when we're writing together, we'll come up with something and go, Oh, that's so good. That's what I'd like to stand in front of 35,000 people and play—that's the kind of feeling that will keep me out there for a year and a half going from South America to Boston.

Elwood: *Before you wrote your own songs, what music were you playing?*

Hamilton: Yardbirds, Ten Years After, old Jeff Beck songs—stuff that was

The blues brought Aerosmith together, and the blues keeps them going: Original members Joe Perry and Steve Tyler onstage at RFK Stadium in Washington, D.C., in 2001.

based on Mississippi Delta music but played through much bigger amplifiers.

Joe Perry: We were hearing the blues secondhand, coming from guys like Clapton and Beck and Page, and we'd see it was written by Willie Dixon, and we'd go, "Oh, that's interesting." I can remember hearing Chuck Berry songs done by the Beatles and the Stones, and my friend going, "Check this out," and playing me a Chuck Berry record—it was the real deal. So I started looking back.

Elwood: *Joe, what's so important about Chuck Berry? What still sounds good today?*

Perry: He's got the massive backbeat that just kills.

Hamilton: And it's not refined music. It's all about taking almost crude musicianship and raw talent and using that as a channel to express an emotion. That's what rock 'n' roll is all about. It's not about being polished and perfectly presented.

Perry: It tells a nice, concise story—it's really easy to get. It's all wrapped around that rhythm, and that's what scares a lot of people. It did back in those days.

Tyler: The media back then said it was the devil's music and black music. But Chuck Berry wanted to bring it to the masses, so he commercialized it a little bit.

Elwood: *Do you remember the first R&B or blues record you bought?*

Tyler: No, I don't think I can. I was kind of stuck in the Everly Brothers and Johnny Horton. It might have been something along the lines of Taj Mahal, which was early '60s. I got some tapes, and then I kind of delved backwards into the early scratchy stuff.

Elwood: *That's interesting, because the Allman Brothers' big tune, "Statesboro Blues," is by Blind Willie McTell. But they told me that Taj Mahal turned them on to it. As a matter of fact, there's a very similar "Linin' Track" you guys did. Sounds like the Taj Mahal tune.*

Tyler: That's where I got it from. In doing my research, I found out that it was an old field holler, which was public domain, but someone came along by the name of Huddie Ledbetter [a.k.a. Leadbelly] and scooped up all that stuff and put it under his name so he could get the money from it. So when I borrowed that lick, we had to pay royalties.

Perry: And we went back a long way, past where he got it. I bet you can trace the themes of all these songs to way back.

Elwood: *Right. Recording really only started in the turn of the 19th century, in the teens, but these themes probably go back to the Civil War.*

Tyler: But some lawyer came in and said, "Hey, you could own that. Just put it under your name."

Elwood: *What about you, Joe? Do you remember your first R&B record?*

Perry: I think the first blues record I got was the John Mayall, *A Hard Road* with Eric Clapton. [*A Hard Road*, 1967, featured Peter Green; Mayall's 1966 *Blues Breakers with Eric Clapton* featured EC.] My parents went crazy because of the length of their hair on the cover, which was really not too radical. Also a Chuck Berry greatest hits record with 14 songs on it—I forgot which. Those were the first ones I remember wearing out, playing a lot.

Elwood: *That how you started to get your chops together?*

Perry: I think so. I first bought all the fake books, the Beatles books, and played all the chords and stuff. And then I started listening to the English blues guitar players and Jeff Beck on his first record [*Truth*, 1968]. You know, '67, '68, '69 was a great era because there was so much music coming out. Fleetwood Mac with Peter Green was a really big influence—Beck might come through twice a year, but Fleetwood Mac, they were always in Boston. I remember them rehearsing there a lot, and I would go in and see them. They were playing Elmore James songs and all that.

Hamilton: I probably bought a lot of British rock albums before I bought my first blues album. Then, through a guy we were in a band with, Joe and I got turned on to the origins of what we were listening to. So the first blues album I ever bought was *Electric Mud* [Muddy Waters, 1968]. The purists think it's a pretty crappy album, but to me it was so cool. "Hoochie Coochie Man" is really sloppy and out of control, but to me it's great.

With Fleetwood Mac most people think about Stevie Nicks and that kind of stuff. But Fleetwood Mac started out as a completely different kind of band—it was a rocking blues band. Joe and I used to go see them at this place called the Boston Tea Party. They would come in with this wall of Fender amps, and they just cooked. You couldn't believe how great they played these R&B and blues songs. When we say Fleetwood Mac, that's what we mean, not "Rhiannon." I'm not implying that there wasn't some good quality in that later stuff. I'm just staying the stuff that we're based on goes back to a different kind of band.

Elwood: *Tell me about Aerosmith's early days.*

Tyler: Out in Long Island in the '60s I was doing all those clubs—I went out there as the house band and I finally just threw my hands in the air and said, "I'm getting nowhere fast." A couple of guys were doing speed, as I was too, trying to write songs, and everybody was yawning and getting up at all hours of the morning, just going nowhere. So I jumped over the drums I was playing at the time and I hitch-hiked home. Joe Perry was in a band with Tom and all of them, playing at a little club in George's Mills, New Hampshire. I went to see them, and they were doing Elmore James and "All Your Love" (Otis Rush/John Mayall) and all that good stuff.

Hamilton: "Going Home"—that was our big song.

Perry: And "Train Kept a Rollin'," which was the one song we had in common—we played it and they played it, and it was like, sad jamming.

Tyler: And "Rattlesnake Shake"—that was the kind of stuff I thought, Wow. They were out of tune, they really couldn't play, but they had the magic. None of those bands that were playing the clubs over and over and were getting good and polished had that magic. Any manager can put ties on a bunch of guys, just like the Beatles in the beginning, but the Beatles had that something that no one else had, the capability to play. That's what these guys had. Even though they were out of tune, they made "Rattlesnake Shake" rock like a mofo. That's what caught my eye.

Elwood: *Now, "Rattlesnake Shake" was Fleetwood Mac, and "Train Kept a Rollin'" was Yardbirds, obviously, but before that wasn't that a Rock 'N Roll Trio song?*

Tyler: Yes, Johnny Burnette, right.

Elwood: *That's where the Yardbirds got it.*

Tyler: It is, positively. We've been paying royalties all these years.

Perry: I've heard it in a different form, like big bands doing that song even earlier than that. That's another one of those old holler songs that picked up various writers as it went along.

Elwood: *Do you ever yearn for the old days when you could play the clubs?*

Hamilton: No, because we didn't really play the clubs. We avoided the clubs like the plague because we wanted to be the kind of band we are now. The idea was to get gigs that in some way simulated a concert. A lot of times that would mean playing at a high school dance, because it would be in the auditorium where the stage was up at one end and we'd be up there on it. Instead of playing five sets of Top 40, we'd play three sets of cuts from our favorite albums.

Perry: We wanted to avoid having to play a whole bunch of other people's songs and not having enough time to develop our own stuff. A lot of our friends who were playing in bands ended up playing Top 40 so much that they didn't have time to rehearse. They were making good money and always had new amps and stuff, but we wanted to develop our own music. So we would end up working on the weekends, playing one-nighters in clubs and high school dances. We'd rehearse during the day and try not to drink so much. These days we jump into a club once in a while and play, and we also leave room in our set to throw in a couple of songs that we used to play in those days.

Elwood: *Like what?*

Perry: Well, "Train Kept a Rollin'" we always play, and we're always digging up an old blues song from here or there.

Tyler: We played "All Your Love" the other night with Ry Cooder in L.A. at the Forum. We invited Ry up onstage—man, oh, man.

Perry: We played "Hangman Jury" and "All Your Love"—it was great. But the sound check was really great because we played for like 45 minutes with him.

Elwood: *What did you play at the sound check?*

Perry: Well, those songs and . . .

Hamilton: "Honky Tonk Women."

Perry: I thought he was going to get flipped out because I heard stories that he and the Stones—to put it nicely—don't have a relationship anymore. So we just said, "Well, what about 'Honky Tonk Women,'" and he said, "Well, I haven't played it in a while, let's give it a try." And it sounded great.

Tyler: That style of fingerpicking the two strings that Keith got ahold of—it's clearly Ry's. It felt really good to play onstage with that sound.

Elwood: *What's the relationship between blues and rock 'n' roll?*

Tyler: Well, the blues had a baby, as a very wonderful man once said, and they called it rock 'n' roll. It's all about expression. The best stuff is the most obvious.

Perry: I think it's the rhythms and the simplicity of the chord structures. When it got electric and there was a little more adrenaline pumped in there, it got a little faster. But it's still the same music and the same feeling.

Hamilton: It's like tribal stories that get passed down through the generations and never get written down. There's something about the feeling of the blues that you can't put into a book and teach in college. To some extent you can explain the style and the chords and the scales and stuff, but as far as putting across the feeling—that's something else altogether.

Elwood on the Air: Who Wants to Marry a Blues Man

HOUR: 00/17
AIRDATE: 4/22–23/00
WRITER: AARON MACHADO

HOST: Welcome back to "Who Wants to Marry a Blues Man"! Our eligible blues musician is Elwood Blues. Elwood, what inspired you to participate in this? Are you a hopeless romantic—someone who believes in soul mates?

ELWOOD: Uh, yeah . . . sure . . . as well as the cash prize and the free honeymoon trip.

HOST: We have an interested bachelorette from Maine. What's your question.

LADY #1: Yeah, hi Elwood! Since you are a blues man, should I assume that you are gainfully employed as a blues musician?

ELWOOD: Well ma'am, I think "occasionally" employed would be more accurate terminology.

HOST: Okay! Glad to hear the word "employed" in there somewhere! Next question . . . the young lady from Nevada.

LADY #2: Hi Elwood. Since you are so ready to be married, you must have already experienced some great relationships.

ELWOOD: Oh yeah!

LADY #2: What was the longest relationship you ever had?

ELWOOD: Oh, the longest? Well, it is hard to determine the quality of a relationship by the amount of time it . . .

HOST: Please answer the question

ELWOOD: Three weeks

HOST: You know what that means ladies—whoever marries him will be the first to win his heart! Sounds romantic. Next question.

LADY #3: Yeah . . . so this guy is a flaky musician, who is out of work half the time, and can't commit to a relationship. Why are we competing to marry him?!

ELWOOD: Have you heard about the free honeymoon trip?

[FX: chaos as the women voice their anger]

What a scam!

This is an embarrassment!!

I should have been on last week for "Who Wants to Marry a Short Order Cook"!

HOST: Okay, why don't we take a break and calm everyone down a bit. We'll be back with more "Who Wants to Marry a Blues Man!"

ELWOOD: If this falls apart . . . I still get my trip, right?

[Song: "Don't Let Me Be Misunderstood"—Eric Burdon & the Animals]

ERIC BURDON
Finally Understood

> "He said, 'How do I get in there?' So I said, 'Well, let me just kick the doors in for you.'"

I n the 1960s Eric Burdon was one of the talented British musicians who nurtured a revival of American blues and R&B. Burdon's raw, passionate vocals on songs such as "We've Got to Get Out of This Place" and "House of Rising Sun" made stars of the Animals, a group whose name the hard-working singer continues to keep alive. Elwood talked to Eric in 2001, when he had just completed his memoir, *Don't Let Me Be Misunderstood*, and shortly after the death of John Lee Hooker.

Elwood Blues: *We've had John Lee Hooker on this radio program of course many times and we're all devastated to see him go, but, wow, what a time we had with him.*

Eric Burdon: Yeah, he was for me blues personified and very gentle, sweet guy.

Elwood: *Did John Lee originally inspire you to start playing the blues?*

Burdon: Who originally inspired me? Muddy Waters, Big Bill Broonzy, and in the singing department Jimmy Witherspoon, Jimmy Rushing, Big Joe Turner, Sister Rosetta Tharpe . . . the list is endless. I was able as a teenager to meet every one of these people, including Louis Armstrong, when I was 15, 16. There was a venue in my hometown of Newcastle called City Hall, and I knew that if I stood in that doorway long enough I would meet every-

*From back alleys to the Hall of Fame: Hardworking Animals
leader Eric Burdon belts a tune onstage in the 1970s.*

body and anybody who played there. So I just made that doorway my territory—I'd go there after school with my haversack full of school notes and
stand there in the freezing cold, in the rain, and wait for people.

I remember Big Bill Broonzy came ambling up the street with his guitar
over his back and wearing a big heavy greatcoat and a winter hat, looking
around like he was lost—in those days, those guys traveled without any
road assistants at all, no road manager, nothing. I said, "You looking for the
City Hall? Well, this is the door." He said, "How do I get in there?" So I said,
"Well, let me just kick the doors in for you." Which I did—just gave the
doors a hefty kick and they swung open and he walked in.

Lots of times I couldn't afford to go to the shows. By just hanging in
there—plus the fact that I knew all the lyrics to all the songs—the night
Louis Armstrong was there somehow word got backstage to him that there

was this young white kid outside who was singing along with every song, knew all the lyrics. Jack Teagarden, who was Armstrong's trombone player at the time, came out to the street, and I was invited into Armstrong's dressing room. I felt like I'd walked through the gates of heaven.

Elwood: *I can understand. Over the years you have befriended many other legendary musicians. In your book you talk about your relationship with Jimi Hendrix. How did you first meet him?*

Burdon: The first time I met Jimi Hendrix I had no idea it was him. It was after a show at the Paramount in New York where the Animals were topping the bill with Little Richard. Little Richard was infamous and probably still is for always going overtime—if there's an audience there to entertain, Little Richard will stay on stage. We were in a huge industrial elevator, and Little Richard was talking with the promoters. They were telling him, "Look, the New York unions are going to fine you, they're going to fine us, the Paramount Theater, $10,000 if you go overtime." A huge argument erupted, and there was this young black kid who was trying to get between the promoters and Richard to cool things out. I didn't realize until somebody told me recently that it was Jimi Hendrix. That was the first time we actually were in the same room together.

Elwood: *What other memories of Hendrix you can share with us?*

Burdon: It may not sound like an exciting story, but one New Year's Eve I didn't join any of the typical parties going on in town; I stayed in my apartment just listening to music. There was a knock at the door, and it was Hendrix. He said, "I can't deal with all of that stuff, man. I just want to listen to some blues." So we cracked open a bottle of wine and listened to Jimmy Reed records all night. That was the way we spent our New Year's.

Elwood: *What was it like for you when the Animals first came to America?*

Burdon: Before the Animals became a commercial success I was ready to join the Merchant Navy to make my way to America to search for the source of the music that I loved so much. And I was just about to sign on in the navy when the Animals got popular, and all of a sudden we were on our way to the United States. I made sure that in every town that we visited, I crossed the tracks and found the local black blues club. And by doing that I ran into and saw some of the greatest performers in their home environment. I spent a lot of time up in Harlem—that was my escape from the white fans because they wouldn't follow me there. I made close friends with Honey Coles, the manager of the Apollo, and I had an ongoing pass backstage. That was a great feeling for me to be invited into that family of performers. I met Big Maybelle, B.B. King, Joe Tex, James Brown—the list is endless.

Elwood: *I understand that in New Orleans they recently found the actual location of the House of the Rising Sun.*

Burdon: It's owned by a well-known lady attorney who owns lots of properties throughout the French Quarter. After buying the house she had a feeling when she was refurbishing it that it was the Rising Sun, due to murals that she found on the walls. Because she's an attorney she was able to get the city police records that go back to before 1900; she started to investigate and was able to discern that it actually is the House of the Rising Sun. She invited me there for a very special night; her guests were city dignitaries including high-ranking police officers and two high-court judges, and 40 Catholic nuns. That was quite an exciting evening. I've been back several times since and made good friends with the owner of the house.

Over the years, every time I've visited New Orleans, I've been approached by people who have told me, "You want to know where the real Rising Sun is—I know where it is." I've been invited to men's prisons, insane asylums, women's prisons, drug dealers' houses, Mafia kingpins' houses—that strange, eclectic mix of people who live down there in Louisiana, just using the lure of "we're going to show you the real House of the Rising Sun." When I saw this house, I instantly knew in my bones that it was the real place. For me that's the completion of a circle.

Elwood: *I guess the next completion was being inducted into the Rock & Roll Hall of Fame. Was that a good night for you?*

Burdon: I wasn't there—I was on the road working in Germany. I know that's hard for people to swallow, and I think that the people at the Hall of Fame were slightly cheesed off at me. They thought I was rebuffing them or something. But you know, I am a hard-working performer, and I spend my life on the road. So the chances are that I would be in a different location the night that they wanted me to be inducted into the Hall of Fame. Life goes on, you know. I couldn't say to a promoter in Germany, "Look, I have to get on a plane and fly to America because I've been inducted into the Hall of Fame and I can't do your next three shows.

Elwood: *As long as you're not sitting on a beach in Hawaii—you're out there working, right?*

Burdon: Yeah, of course. But since then I got invited back to do the mega-TV HBO special they did, and I performed there along with many other great artists. So I guess they figured it out and they've forgiven me or something. It's a great honor to be recognized by one's peers and know that the Animals name is a part of that museum.

ROBERT PLANT
The Songs Remain the Same

> *"It was absolutely amazing
> to hear this music which
> had nothing to do with the
> English consciousness."*

The line from blues to heavy metal and its dozens of permutations is no more clear than in the music of Led Zeppelin. Formed in 1968 from the remnants of the Yardbirds, Led Zeppelin modeled many of its songs—for all their sonic bombast and hippie-era lyrical mysticism—after the work of Muddy Waters, Otis Rush, Howlin' Wolf, and Willie Dixon. Former Zeppelin singer Robert Plant is quick to acknowledge the debt, noting in this mid-'90s interview that his own blues roots go back to his childhood in Birmingham, England.

Elwood Blues: *In the 1960s blues seemed to come back to America by way of British artists such as the Rolling Stones, the Yardbirds, John Mayall, and Led Zeppelin. How did that link come about?*

Robert Plant: In 1968, when I arrived on the West Coast with Jimmy Page and the re-formed Yardbirds that had changed their name to Led Zeppelin, we were virtually a blues band. Page and I and John Bonham, who had played with me before, built most of our repertoire around Chicago blues or even earlier, country blues. And apart from some activities taking place around the Newport Jazz Festival, with George Wein bringing Chuck Berry, Skip James, Son House, awareness in America of this music was confined to largely a kind of folk-club/university-campus scene. The guys who were

He can't quit the blues: Led Zeppelin's Robert Plant was heavily influenced by greats like Otis Rush.

playing in groups were either ripoffs of the Beatles, or there was a lot of garage punk coming out of New York and the East Coast, like the Electric Prunes and Count Five. Mike Bloomfield and Elvin Bishop were very lively, and John Hammond Jr. was playing a lot, but we came over with a kind of continuation of the Howlin' Wolf sexual swagger of blues. We'd gotten a complete history of this, not by chance, not by mystery, but because in Britain there was a whole totally different awareness of blues.

Now how can it be that working class white kids in England who had never encountered the black American, who were much more acquainted with Asians and Indians, how come we suddenly got turned onto this plain, beautiful music? I was 14, working in Woolworth's clearing out the elevator shaft for three bucks a day or whatever it was, and I was ordering Blind Boy Fuller LPs and I got the first Robert Johnson album, which had been issued in about 1962—there's this great story about how Johnson's record never sold anything, but when it was seen on a Bob Dylan album cover, suddenly people started listening to it. Well, in England, Johnson and his whole vibe was legendary stuff. When I was 15 two German promoters brought blues festivals through Europe, introducing instead Bukka White, Son House, Skip James, Sleepy John Estes, Hammie Nixon . . . Willie Dixon was part of the backing trio with Sunnyland Slim and Clifton James on drums—you just can't imagine what it was like for us. It was absolutely amazing to hear this music which had nothing to do with the English consciousness.

Elwood: *What was the connection then?*

Plant: The connection was relief because Presley was wailing the blues, you see. He was the catalyst for a whole generation of people who are my age and a little younger, because Presley took the blues and he took the hillbilly shit and he mixed it up like Carl Perkins and Jerry Lee Lewis, and they were wailing. Jerry Lee Lewis used to crawl under the juke joints and hear that stompin' left hand of the boogie-woogie piano player, and he brought it through to us. Little Richard, in his camp sort of way, was doing the same thing, and Ray Charles was giving us some kind of slick city stuff which was right there in the pocket. The stuff that he did with Tom Dowd, Jerry Wexler, and Ahmet Ertegun at Atlantic Records was unbelievable. I've been with Atlantic for 25 years and I know all the stories—I know Wilson Pickett's negotiations for his record deal with a gun on the counter. . . .

When bands clone Led Zeppelin, they've got to understand where Zep came from. Listen to *The Rocking Chair Album* by Howlin' Wolf, with "You'll Be Mine" and all that, and you can hear every T. Rex lick, you can hear bits of David Bowie, you can hear everything.

Those blues guys were troubadours; they were gypsies. They didn't want to pull cotton or work in a gas station—it would be much better to be with some chick on a Friday who belonged to somebody else and then be gone. That whole kind of romance of wailing the blue notes—because that's what rock 'n' roll is, it's the blues—you've got to get the blue notes in.

Everybody who is good, whether it's Faith No More or Stone Temple Pilots, they got the blue note.

Elwood: *So the blue note is the connection?*

Plant: Well, it's the wail. When women come to me and say, "Man, you moan better than anybody else," I say, "No, listen to James Brown, or check Robert Johnson's 'Preaching Blues.'" But I moan because you can't say everything with lyrics; the whole thing about the blues is that it transmits emotion even if it's secondhand and even if it's repetitious. The moaning makes it work. "Howlin' for my baby," said the Wolf. You know, there are a lot of lyrics from Blind Boy Fuller or Sleepy John Estes—I still don't know what they're talking about. But it's not just words, it's delivery. That's why

Zep triumphed, because we delivered. It wasn't just the same song every night. It's the way you tell them.

Elwood: *Do you remember the first blues record you got turned on to?*

Plant: The first blues record I ever got, I came in top of my year at school, and my parents said, "We'll buy you a record, son," and I had "Help Me," by Sonny Boy Williamson.

Elwood: *What appealed to you about that record?*

Plant: It's got a cool rhythm, but it was the way he was growling, "You gotta help me baby, I can't do it all by myself." It's sort of ambiguous. He's talking about everything, you know. About the sexuality, the reliance, the need, and I was a young man. I had pain in the loins, I got some fire down below, and I was diggin' this old guy wailing. When my parents bought me the record and I put it on the record player, they immediately cut the plug off. They said, "This is the devil's music." I said, "No, it's the blue note." Now my mom loves Sonny Boy Williamson—isn't that great? She's 73 and she really thinks he's cool.

Elwood: *You met Sonny Boy, right?*

Plant: Oh yeah. I went to one of the blues festivals that was traveling through Europe. There was a whole vibe about them being some kind of mass howling experience with these guys from Mississippi or Chicago coming to Birmingham, England. They didn't really want to be there, especially playing to a bunch of squeaky white kids, you know.

I was in the bathroom taking a leak when Sonny Boy came in. He was about eight inches taller than me and he was wearing a harlequin suit. Now, Sonny Boy was so big and so daunting a character—one of his tricks was playing the harmonica by just sliding it into his mouth without using his hands; he also unfortunately used to play it with his rather large nose. But he's taking a leak, I'm taking a leak, and I'm saying, as a million people have said to me, "Mr. Williamson, I want to thank you, you've been such a great influence and inspiration and can I have your autograph?" He looked down at me with those big eyes and opened his mouth with one tooth in it and he said, "Get lost, son," and I said, "Thank you." A great moment for me. I learned a lot from that—I was heartbroken. I would never do that to anybody.

Elwood: *Did you see him perform on his own, or was that with the Yardbirds?*

Plant: No, the Yardbirds thing was later, but it was also more of a studio thing. Sonny Boy didn't think the Yardbirds were any good, and he didn't think the Animals were much good. He was sort of drawn into those record dates by a guy named Giorgio Golmelsky. He really was at his best when he was rockin' on his Trumpet Records stuff in the early '50s or the stuff he did at Chess, *Down and Out Blues* with "Fattenin' Frog for Snakes," that sort of stuff. When he came to Europe he just used a bass player—Ransom Knowling or Willie Dixon—and S.P. Leary or Clifton James on drums, and Hubert

Sumlin on guitar, who is stunning. When you get a nice, uncomplicated combination of people and you listen to Sonny Boy, really rockin' . . . the Yardbirds couldn't do a thing for him.

Elwood: *When you started playing, what songs were you doing?*

Plant: I started in blues bands—I was in several blues bands in my area. At the time we were into "Got My Mojo Working," Muddy Waters stuff, which was mostly acoustic. I was playing washboard and harmonica, so it was a bit like Sonny Terry. They let me take a verse of "Got My Mojo Working," and then I'd take two verses and sing a bit louder. And then I got it— I realized I could sing the blue note, too.

My father used to pick me up from these clubs, and he would sit in his car wondering what in God's name was going on. Once he peeked in through a chink in the curtain and saw this wailing, howling, sort of post-Kerouac beatnik scene with black men with stiletto knives and college kids and all that sort of thing. He was as heartbroken as I was elated, because I loved it.

The unfortunate thing is that a lot of blues has become a bit designer. I guess it would be unfair to want people to be in such dire situations that they really howl, but I don't like the fact that the blues sometimes becomes sort of cabaret.

Elwood: *What do you mean designer or cabaret?*

Plant: The blues that we talk about, the blues that had that sound, that kind of plaintive mood, came from an environment and a location and a set of standards and lifestyle and expectancy that are all but gone in many respects. Therefore, the actual language of the blues has changed. Things get tempered down. It becomes a bit diluted.

I played at a big blues festival near Florence about three months ago, and I was absolutely stunned when I heard James Cotton leading 14,000 Italians in a perfectly anglicized version of "Sweet Home Chicago." The Italians were singing it with great gusto—the Italians know this song like they know "Stairway to Heaven," and I think that's really, really funny. Robert Johnson sang "Sweet Home Chicago," and it was this beautiful cry from the heart, getting away from the Delta and that sort of thing. But now you've got Italian hippies clapping their hands and girls in beautiful dresses fanning their bodies singing "Sweet Home Chicago."

Elwood: *What blues songs were really influential to you?*

Plant: I would say "So Many Roads" by Otis Rush is one of the most moving adventures in the blues. The whole thing about his voice, the guitar playing—on *Led Zeppelin I* we did "I Can't Quit You Baby," which is an Otis Rush song.

Elwood: *Some people have slagged you guys for taking that music. Why?*

Plant: Because they didn't take it. Maybe we fucked it up, but I don't think we did. I think we brought it back in another form, rather like Cream did with Skip James's stuff—"I'm So Glad," that sort of thing. Maybe because it was too white and the sexuality of it was obvious. I don't have any complaints about that. It's the way I wanted to express it vocally. I think Page played from God on those early cuts, "You Shook Me," "I Can't Quit You Baby." Nobody can complain, because by doing that we got a lot of kids way back into the blues. They had already got a finger on the Yardbirds, who were playing this kind of amoebic blues, but we had Bonham and Jones behind us who really gave it something else.

Elwood on the Air: Sugar Daddy

HOUR: 00/26
AIRDATE: 6/24–25/00
WRITER: ANDY VALVUR

[FX: doorbell]

[FX: door opening]

WOMAN: [sexy, sultry] Well hello . . . you must be Elwood. Come in.

ELWOOD: Yes ma'am. And may I just say—wow!

WOMAN: Why thank you.

ELWOOD: This place is great. And the views. I can see all of Chicago! What do you do?

WOMAN: I'm a model. Can I get you something to drink?

ELWOOD: Sure. A coke, no ice. Boy, the modeling business must be real good.

WOMAN: I do OK. Do you want to take off your hat . . . or your sunglasses?

ELWOOD: Uh . . . that's OK. Now about the sugar daddy thing . . . your ad says.

WOMAN: Let's not talk about business just yet. Come here and sit down. Tell me what do you do for a living?

ELWOOD: A little of this, a little of that . . . I have a band . . .

WOMAN: You're a musician?! [coos] oooooo

ELWOOD: Yeah, and I do a little thing called The House of Blues Radio Hour. It is a part of The House of Blues.

WOMAN: Wow. You own restaurants and radio stations. I'm very impressed.

ELWOOD: Uh well . . . I don't exactly. . .

WOMAN: So. . .what sort of an arrangement are you looking for?

ELWOOD: Uh. . .a pretty simple one. You know, no strings. I am on the road a lot, so I need to be flexible.

WOMAN: I totally understand. That's the way I want it too.

ELWOOD: Well great.

WOMAN: So, you want to talk money?

ELWOOD: Might as well . . .uh . . .how does a thousand a month sound?

WOMAN: [petulant, coy] Oh Elwood . . . you can do better than that . . . can't you?

ELWOOD: I can?? [confused] um . . . I mean . . . yeah . . . I can. How about three thousand?

WOMAN: Elwood . . . look at me. Does this look like three thousand a month to you?

ELWOOD: No ma'am. YOU look like ten thousand a month. But I don't want to take advantage of you. Three thousand a month is more than I need.

WOMAN: [shocked] Excuse me??

ELWOOD: Three thou . . .

WOMAN: I think you're a little confused. You are the sugar daddy.

ELWOOD: Me??!! I make two-fifty a week. When I'm working.

WOMAN: Didn't you read the ad?

[FX: paper rustle]

ELWOOD: Yeah. It says right here, I can be your sugar daddy. Call Bambi at . . .

WOMAN: [irritated] The ad says: I can be yours . . . with an S . . . I can be yours, sugar daddy. You spilled mustard on the paper.

ELWOOD: Does this mean you won't be my sugar daddy?

WOMAN: OUT!!!! NOW!!

[Song: "Evil Ways"—Santana]

CARLOS SANTANA
A Different Kind of Church

> *"Blues can put a mirror on you and make you ask, 'Are you satisfied with the life you're living?'"*

Fusing blues, rock, and Latin sounds, Carlos Santana led a musical revolution in the '60s whose influence is still strong today. Since the Santana band's emergence at the 1969 Woodstock festival, the Mexican-born guitarist has lent his talent and vision to a kaleidoscopic succession of bands and side projects, through it all staying true to a belief in the spiritual power of music. While nurturing a worldwide legion of devoted fans, Carlos continues to honor his music heroes. Elwood spoke to Santana shortly before the 25th anniversary of Woodstock '69.

Elwood Blues: *What does the blues mean to you?*

Carlos Santana: The blues consciousness to me has been a healing force and a force of hope. The blues is the first foundation of all music, because it deals with the human element, which is passion and compassion. Pavarotti sings the blues. It's Italian and it's opera, but it's still the blues. It's the same with Ravi Shankar or some cat in Japan playing Koto with those big old picks. It's still the blues.

Elwood: *A lot of people see the blues as down, sad music, but that's not really the case, is it?*

Santana: No—they only see a reflection of their own miserable lives. It's kind of like taking mescaline—don't take mescaline if you're not happy with

*Carlos Santana drawing on his five elements—soul, heart,
mind, body, and cojones.*

life man, 'cause you're gonna hurt yourself and hurt somebody. Blues is a
reflection of yourself. If people could see the blues for what it is, they'll see
the beautiful side of their lives. It's like racism: If you've already made up
your mind what that person in front of you is like, you've already put a lid
on him, like you've bound his legs and his arms and asked him to swim to
Alcatraz—he's just not gonna do it. So you have to unbind that person and
unbind your mind, and do the same thing with the blues.

One of the real masters of blues is Miles Davis. I love the way he broke
the stereotype. Miles Davis said, "My mother's good looking, my daddy's
rich, I have never suffered or intend to suffer, and I can play some blues. So
don't put me on that stereotype that you gotta be pickin' cotton or that BS."

If you can articulate your passion and your compassion, you can play some blues.

Elwood: *Can you remember the first time you heard a guitar?*

Santana: It was in Tijuana—a man named Javier Batiz. He was a combination of B.B. King, Little Richard, with the Little Richard hairdo and the khaki print pants pressed like jackknives, man—so sharp, you know.

Elwood: *Did you hear the blues in Tijuana?*

Santana: Yeah. There were some radio stations that would play the Pat Boone stuff, and the other stations would play the gutbucket—we call it "cut and shoot" because it you don't play it right, they cut or shoot you. Some blues audiences in the real funky side of Tijuana or Juarez or the South Side of Chicago, if you put in too many fancy chords, man, they gonna know it.

I heard B.B. King's music in Tijuana and John Lee Hooker's. That was my supreme fascination, just like today for the kids would be Metallica. At that time, that was it—very little anything else.

Elwood: *When you started in the mid-'60s in San Francisco it was the Santana Blues Band.*

Santana: I'm really grateful I was in the era of the '60s when it was like putting a huge microscope to the blues for the first time. Then it went from microscopic to cosmic because of Jimi Hendrix, the way he did the blues. I'm spoiled because I heard the blues before they were using monitors or PA's, or speakers, just about. You know, I heard it coming out right out of the bone into the steel and the wood in the guitar—*bam*, right to your heart.

I saw B.B. King here in '66. He got a standing ovation before he hit the first note, and he started crying—I mean, he just lost it. I remember he went to wipe his tears and all you could see were the diamonds shining from his hand and the tears. It gets to you, you know. But when he hit the note to bring the band in, my whole life was changed again.

Elwood: *Were you influenced by the British invasion?*

Santana: What British invasion? The Rolling Stones were playing Muddy Waters, John Mayall was playing Otis Rush . . . they were playing our stuff, and second-generation at that. Fleetwood Mac, they were all blues, just a little louder.

Elwood: *Most people don't know that "Black Magic Woman" was a Fleetwood Mac song—a Peter Green tune. How did you get turned on to that?*

Santana: By Gregg Rolie, the keyboard player [with the band Santana and later Journey]. If you take the words from "Black Magic Woman" and just leave the rhythm, it's "All Your Love"—it's Otis Rush. We all borrow from everybody; the beautiful thing is that there is room in the blues to get your own fingerprints, the way Stevie Ray Vaughan got his own fingerprints the last three years of his life. Before that, all the blues players used to criticize him: "Man, you sound like Albert King or somebody, but you don't sound like yourself." Before he passed he had found his fingerprints—huge fingerprints. Jimi also has huge fingerprints on the blues. Your fingerprints are your tone and the way you phrase. That's what we encourage the young people to do—learn from B.B. King, use your tape recorder, but after a while, put all that stuff away and just play by yourself in the dark.

Elwood: *In one of his last interviews Stevie talked about how he can't think about it—it's not like you're playing the guitar, you are the guitar. How do you find that zone for yourself?*

Santana: All you can do is try. It's like the movie *Ghost*, when after the guy dies he finds another ghost in the subway, and this ghost is able to kick a can, which the other guy can't. So he says, "Man, teach me how to do that." And the guy says, "You accumulate all your anger, all your joy, all your horniness, your passion, everything, you just put it into one thing, and *bam*." Same thing when you play one note of the blues—you have to hit that note with five elements: soul, heart, mind, body, and your *cajones*. You do that, you will create some kind of impact on the listener.

Elwood: *I witnessed Bob Marley's first performance in New York City, Central Park. There were black people, white people, Latinos, all these people coming together, and they were all looking at each other going, "What the hell, what are you doing here?"—because New York has that vibe. Then the band was late for the show, so everybody was lined up outside waiting for the doors to open. But when the band did their sound check and all of a sudden the drums kicked in with that backwards beat, everybody was going, "Yeah, that's why we're here—I get it." It was spiritual.*

Santana: It's a different kind of church. It's not the other kind of church that they thrive on making you feel like a turkey so they can tax you. Music—especially the blues—it liberates you. Blues can put a mirror on you and make you ask you the same question Bob Marley asks you: "Are you satisfied with the life you're living?" When you can do that with music— whether it's blues or reggae—when you question the listener so the listener will go to the closet and get rid of stuff that is not him or her anymore, you've made some progress. That's when art is not wasted and musician's lives are not wasted, because if we listen to the best sum of what they do for us, they make us better human beings. Don't look at their personal lives, because that's incidental—it's like looking at the shell. Don't look at the shell, look at the black pearl.

I'll give you a good story about Muddy Waters. He opened up for us at Notre Dame University, and the last song was gonna be "Got My Mojo Working." But before he played it, they called him up for an ovation, and he says, "Before I play my last song, I want you all to give a nice hand to my granddaughter." So this beautiful lady goes up on stage—she's in her 20s and it's his granddaughter. Then he says, "I want you to give a nice hand to my daughter," and we're thinking it's going the girl's mom, right? Wrong. It's a little three-year-old girl. And Muddy says, "Now you know I still got my mojo working"—and the band just went into it.

God created Muddy Waters and Howlin' Wolf and all those rascals—I want to grow to be like these kooks. What did Slim Harpo say? "Come here baby, let your hair down, let your hair roll down, 'cause we ain't gonna go to heaven anyhow, so let's burn." God really loves these people because they're loose, they're not so uptight. Some of those people will go into heaven faster than somebody who carries the Bible all the time but he's always messing with people.

Elwood: *Your father-in-law, Saunders King, is a great blues player. Can you tell me about him?*

Santana: B.B. King called me around '85 and he says, "Carlos, why didn't you tell me that Saunders King was your father-in-law? I just saw Saunders King on your video. When I was just a young man, Saunders King and T-Bone Walker were my gods." So I told that to my father-in-law, and he says, "Yeah, I remember the boy when he couldn't play his guitar."

My wife and I discovered all these posters, like Saunders King and Billie Holiday at the Savoy here in San Francisco, Art Tatum and Saunders King, and Charlie Mingus, Lester Young . . . all those incredible musicians went through his band. To me he's a great fountain of information; I asked him, "Did you ever meet Charlie Parker?" "Oh, yeah, I saw him in Kansas City." So time freezes—I'm there.

Elwood: *Michael Bloomfield was big in your life, wasn't he?*

Santana: Yeah, Michael Bloomfield and Peter Green. They used to make B.B. King sweat, man. You know, Eric Clapton created a big impact on musicians. Here in Santa Cruz there was a guitar player who just played Eric Clapton from '67—just three months of Eric Clapton—that's his whole thing. Michael Bloomfield was like that, only he had something that Peter Green and everybody else didn't have—an individual fingerprint. By the time he got to [Paul Butterfield's] *East–West* album, because he was living in San Francisco, he started picking up Ravi Shankar's music and John Coltrane's and Cannonball Adderley's. So all of a sudden, instead of playing the three minutes of blues, it became like a seven-and-a-half-minute overture. Paul Butterfield with Bloomfield, Jimi Hendrix, Cream—I saw all three bands at their peak. When Paul Butterfield used to go into "Born in Chicago" and "Got My Mojo Working," it was just as strong as "All Along the Watchtower" or "Voodoo Child" or "Crossroads."

Elwood: *The 25th anniversary of Woodstock is coming up. Woodstock is where the world stopped to hear what Santana, the band, was putting down. How do you feel looking back on that with 25 years of perspective?*

Santana: I feel great, man. I feel I learned a lot from it. I still feel that we need to keep pressing forward with the values that we learned, the positive values. If another Woodstock is going to happen, it should be in the hands of people like American Indians, aborigines from Australia . . . Nelson Mandela should be there, and then you bring the bands to represent a cross-rainbow section of what America is doing. Bring the best of America. Don't just bring squares or hips, loud or soft. Bring all of it. American Indian, reggae, blues. Bring three kinds of blues—Louisiana, Mississippi, and Chicago or Texas. Most of all, don't let the corporations run it. What I learned from Bill Graham is that you have to guard the real principles, the first fountains. A lot of time we spend too much money on the Pat Boones and then forget about Little Richards. Mariah Carey or whatever is fine, but don't forget about Aretha and Patti LaBelle.

BOB WEIR
Workingman's Blues

> *"The idiom has so much integrity that if you approach it correctly, it draws you to it rather than you drawing it to whatever you're working with."*

A singularly creative guitarist and accomplished songwriter, Grateful Dead founding member Bob Weir provided the rhythmic counterpoint to Jerry Garcia's probing solos during the band's fabled 30-year history. Though the Grateful Dead gained fame and adulation through its freeform musical explorations, the band's roots—and especially Weir's—lead straight back to the blues. Now fronting the musical incarnation known as The Dead, Weir talked about the early days in this Greatful Dead–era interview with Elwood.

Elwood Blues: *I don't think a lot of people use "blues" and "Grateful Dead" in the same sentence. But maybe they're mistaken.*

Bob Weir: Well, we started out playing not exactly as a blues band but as blues and rock 'n' roll, and we always included some blues numbers in our shows. We have a featured blues song early on in the set, and then often we later get back into it. Blues was one of the cornerstones of our little musical edification.

Elwood: *You guys started out as a jug band . . .*

Weir: . . . which is country blues.

Grateful for the blues: Bob Weir started playing Chuck Berry tunes at age 16.

Elwood: *How did it evolve into an electric blues band?*

Weir: We were all working in a music store. I was teaching beginning and intermediate students, Jerry Garcia had the advanced students, and Pigpen [keyboardist Ron McKernan] was basically sweeping the floor and stuff like that. The son of the store owner decided he wanted to start a band, and seeing that he had the electric instruments right there—well, hell yeah, we'll play. As it turned out, he couldn't go on with us so we replaced him with [bassist] Phil Lesh and brought in [drummer] Billy Kreutzmann—that was the nucleus of the Grateful Dead.

Elwood: *Did you get to keep the instruments?*

Weir: We had to pay them off, but yeah.

Elwood: *What blues songs were you playing?*

Weir: We were playing a fair number of tunes by Willie Dixon, like "Little Red Rooster"; Freddie King, who was popular back then; and Slim Harpo. They were playing that on the black AM stations here. We also listened to Bobby Bland, Jimmy McCracklin—the old R&B guys.

Elwood: *When did you personally first hear the blues?*

Weir: I was about 16. I was a folk guitarist, and that was wearing a little thin for me. I sort of stumbled into the blues scenes in the [San Francisco] Bay Area, in Palo Alto and Berkeley, where there were little groups of folk guitarists who were drifting into blues. One of my teachers was Reverend Gary Davis. He was from Atlanta through New York, and his stuff was acoustic guitar music, but it was way different from anything else that was going on.

Elwood: *I didn't realize you took lessons directly from the Reverend. What was that like?*

Weir: He was wonderful. He used to have us sneak in cigars, and he liked me to bring in a cute bit of fluff. He was blind, but he could more or less sense whether he liked what he "saw." And that would keep him going—you'd get a much better lesson that way.

Elwood: *Now, when you say fluff . . .*

Weir: Oh, a girl. Just to sort of hang out and be pretty.

Elwood: *[Laughs.] That's great. And what was he like as a teacher?*

Weir: He was a good teacher. I was pretty familiar with his stuff; I knew the songs, I had the records, but I couldn't pick it off of the records. So I watched him play, and he would have me play it back to him until I got it right, with the proper authority and all that stuff. It wasn't so much the fingering as how much "thump" I was getting out of the guitar—how much intent, how much noise I was making.

Elwood: *What a great teacher to have. Who were some of your earliest teachers?*

Weir: Well, unbeknownst to him, Jorma Kaukonen [of the Jefferson Airplane]. I used to watch him whenever he would play around Palo Alto, and I would steal like crazy from him. On record I would listen to a lot of Chuck Berry, of course. I also spent a little time with Lightnin' Hopkins way back when, and Mance Lipscomb.

Elwood: *There's a name that doesn't come up a lot.*

Weir: He was a Delta blues player who had a singular style—he played in standard tuning, and his style was more reflective of ragtime than of other Delta blues styles.

Elwood: *Did you get a chance to play with any of those people?*

Weir: Yeah, all of them.

Elwood: *That must have been a trip!*

Weir: Yeah, it was. They were getting on in years but they weren't hoary with age yet—they still had a lot of vitality.

Elwood: *Do you remember the first blues record you ever bought?*

Weir: It had to be Gary Davis. After that, the floodgates opened.

Elwood: *You're still playing tunes like "Little Red Rooster." How do you decide to keep something like that in your repertoire?*

Weir: That just organically emerged within the contour of our show—there's gonna be a spot that it's gonna want to taper down to a blues number. It's kind of like if you're playing football, you want to establish your running game so you can pass and stuff like that, and in music you want to establish your blues idiom so that—well, at least the way we play, so that we can draw from it later on.

Elwood: *You wrote a song with Willie Dixon. How did that come about?*

Weir: It was a tune called "Eternity"—I believe it might have been the last tune he ever wrote. Rob Wasserman, the bass player, was working on his *Trios* record and he was talking to Willie Dixon. I had played with Willie a number of years earlier and he remembered me, so Rob said, "Why don't we get together and see if we can punch out a tune or two?" And we did, and it worked out very well. We became good friends—I lit the candles on his 75th birthday cake.

Elwood: *That's great—the man who* was *the blues. In the early days a lot of the Dead stuff came straight out of the blues. On the first record there was "Sitting on Top of the World," "Good Morning Little School Girl"—where did you learn these tunes?*

Weir: We got "Good Morning Little School Girl" from Junior Wells's rendition. We were in a record shop in L.A. when we were living down there during the first few months of the band, and they were playing this record that had just come in, and it was just glorious. You know, Buddy Guy, Junior Wells—just a little quartet, very, very lean, very spare. We all wigged over it and bought the record, and we learned that and a few other tunes from it.

Elwood: *It's funny how "Good Morning Little School Girl" has all of a sudden had this incredible resurgence—everybody recording this song.*

Weir: The lyric is so preposterous—it's blues humor at its very finest.

Elwood: *Yeah. What are some other examples of that blues humor?*

Weir: Well, you can go into "I'm a Man" and the ridiculous claims in that tune. B.B King has always got a couple of cute tunes. And there's Howlin' Wolf you know, "Three hundred pounds of heavenly joy, built for comfort not for speed," all that kind of stuff.

I never met the Wolf. I revere him, but I don't think he ever got the recognition he rightly deserved. During the Nixon years, they were having National Negro's Week or something like that, and Tricia Nixon told her dad

Surviving Woodstock

"Woodstock was three days of intense partying," Bob Weir recalls of the epochal 1969 music fair/tribal gathering. "I had a great time except for when we played. Our soundman at the time, Augustus Owsley Stanley, decided everything was wired wrong and that he should wire everything basically backwards. Well, this didn't work—every time I touched my instrument I got a shock. Everyone had this problem except for Billy [Kreutzmann], who wasn't plugged into anything. Once I touched my instrument and my microphone at the same time, and I got a big, bright baseball-sized blue spark that lifted me off my feet and sent me about eight or nine feet back against my amplifier. I wasn't knocked cold—I don't know why—but I kept a cautious distance from my microphone from then on. Meanwhile it was raining—that didn't help matters—and we put in probably our worst show for several years in either direction. But the rest of the Woodstock experience was just fine."

[*voice changes*], "Oh, Daddy, we have to get somebody authentic . . ." for a White House breakfast or a Sunday brunch, and they ended up getting the Wolf. It didn't work out all that well for them. The Wolf did his standard show—he was down on the floor crawling around doing "Crawling King Snake Blues," and all that kind of stuff, and I think some of the stuffed shirts were just a touch horrified. I would have loved to have been there.

Elwood: [*Laughs.*] *People have difficulty listening to the Wolf. They go, "That song was really, like, kind of distorted," but I say, "Yeah, but it's supposed to be that way!"*

Weir: It's supposed to be funky; it was made on funky equipment. Two bits says the engineer's meter wasn't working, and he missed the distortion. Besides that, you don't tell the Wolf, "We had a little distortion here—we have to cut that one again. He'll probably take your head off. So you play it back—"sounds great"—and if he doesn't hear the distortion you'll live to record another tune.

Elwood: *One of the folk tales says that Wolf and Muddy Waters were always at each others throats, claiming that Willie Dixon was giving the other one the better songs. What made Muddy Waters such a special performer?*

Weir: It was all a matter of delivery, just like the Wolf. The Wolf had his style, not to mention the fact that he was a good singer. On his records there's some scary stuff he was doing with his voice, and he was a decent guitar player, as was Muddy. Muddy had that delivery that really bawls out in your face. No one else has ever come close to it

Elwood: *Yeah, yeah. Is there anybody you're familiar with today who's making music like that?*

Weir: Well, I was in Kansas City last week, and I saw Koko Taylor. Her backup band is a pretty good little blues ensemble—they're all young black kids from Chicago. It's good to see black kids playing the blues again and not ashamed of it, because for the longest time the blues was passé in the black community. Now it seems that black kids are starting to realize that they have a rich cultural heritage and they're starting to dive into it.

Elwood: *Did it seem strange to you that in the '60s the blues had to go to England and then come back?*

Weir: Nobody takes it seriously in your own backyard, I guess. The blues was really news in Europe, just as jazz was, and here, if you can turn on the radio and it's there, people take it for granted. For years you had to go to Europe to get a lot of blues recordings. The selection here was nowhere near as good as the average music store in Amsterdam.

Elwood: *Do you find that Deadheads are hip to the blues?*

Weir: A lot of them are, yeah. I ran into some of our fans in Kansas City at a blues club. No one knew I was in town so they weren't coming to see me, they were coming to see Koko Taylor.

Elwood: *That's great. You get a little scared that this music is not going to be appreciated.*

Weir: All you have to do is catch a good blues performance and you're hooked for life.

Elwood: *When does a performance click for you?*

Weir: There's a point when the song falls together; it might be from the first note or it might be a verse or two into it. The blues is a repetitive sort of medium. Twelve-bar blues—especially if there is no bridge—is just verse after verse after verse. So you treat each verse specially; each one has its own little theme, and then the song has an overall theme as well. When all that comes together, starts locking together, you know that you are playing this song, that you're playing "Little Red Rooster" and it's fresh and it's new and it's alive. The song lives on the stage with you. That's when you know you're doing it.

Elwood: *Where is the line between rock 'n' roll and blues?*

Weir: It's a fuzzy line at best. It's tough to describe, but when it's the blues it really *feels* like the blues. When it's rock 'n' roll there's more white influence—rock 'n' roll is half white in its derivation, and there's a different feel that that influence brought to rock 'n' roll—a little more country.

Elwood: *Right. So what blues songs in particular influenced rock 'n' roll?*

Weir: I'm not sure how much blues tunes have changed rock 'n' roll so much as supported it and gave it deeper roots. But certainly "Dust My Broom," and "I'm a Man" came up a lot when we were younger. But the thing is, when a rock 'n' roll band does a blues number, suddenly it becomes a blues band for a moment or two. So I don't think the blues numbers or the blues idiom has melded into rock 'n' roll. It still stands separate. The idiom has so much integrity that if you approach it correctly, it draws you to it rather than you drawing it to whatever you're working with.

It takes years to learn to do correctly—if there is such a thing—how to deliver a blues number. There's a style of performance that's separate from the rock 'n' roll style, and you can bring that style of performance—that attitude, I guess—into your own medium. But it takes years to do.

Elwood: *What do you mean when you say that it takes time to perfect knowing how to do it?*

Weir: It's a feel thing. But I think I can describe it in a story. When I was working with Willie Dixon on "Eternity," we just got together and I came up with some chord changes and ran them down to Rob and played them; I was sort of scatting a provisional melody. And Willie's sitting there and he's listening and he's smiling and he's got a pad of paper, and he just starts dashing down these thoughts. And I kept going over and over these chord changes, this provisional melody. So he hands me this piece of paper, and the lyrics seem awfully simplistic. I was a little deflated, but, still, here's my chance to work with the great Willie Dixon. You gotta at least give it a try; you'll have to just take what you get from him—maybe he's getting a little old and not everything he cranks out is quite what it was when he was in his prime. But nonetheless, I gotta honor the guy. He's saying, "Well, go ahead, sing 'em." So I get through the first verse, and it's okay. And I get about halfway into the second verse and everything went *ding*. Yeah, it's simple— it's supposed to be simple, stupid. There was something really elemental about it, something intrinsically wonderful—the message is simply loving someone through eternity. You can say that, but you can't feel that, or at least I can't. I never did really grasp what that meant and really can't even to this day unless I'm singing the song. Then it comes clear to me. There's something magical about it. So I have this little flash, this little awakening—the light goes on. I understand. And Willie's sitting back and he's laughing, "Now you see it, now you see it. That's the wisdom of the blues."

BILL WYMAN
Stone Freed

> *"Pretty much every original blues record has something that's worth learning from."*

Instrumental in bringing the sound of the blues back to America in the '60s and '70s, the Rolling Stones have long acknowledged their debt to the music of Muddy Waters, Howlin' Wolf, and other greats. None of the Stones, however, has championed the blues more than Bill Wyman, the stoic bassist who—along with drummer Charlie Watts—laid the foundation that allowed Mick Jagger and Co. to become a rock 'n' roll phenomenon. After Wyman left the band in 1993 he pursued blues-based projects such as the Rhythm Kings, and in 2001 he released the 46-track CD set *Bill Wyman's Blues Odyssey*—an enlightening 46-track collection of his favorite music from the 1920s to the '40s—as well as the book *Bill Wyman's Blues Odyssey: A Journey to Music's Heart and Soul*. Elwood talked to Wyman shortly before the debut of the book and CD set.

Elwood Blues: *How did you get introduced to the blues?*
Bill Wyman: The '60s British invasion came from the blues without any of us realizing it. Just about every band that came out in the '60s in England and went all around the world—the Beatles, the Stones, the Who, Kinks, Zeppelin, and many, many more—we all started off playing skiffle music, which was done by a guy called Lonnie Donegan, who had a hit with a Leadbelly song called "Rock Island Line" around 1956. We all found that

*Continuing the tradition: Rolling Stones founding bassist Bill
Wyman has rambled back to his blues roots.*

you could play skiffle with three or four guitars—you didn't need a bass,
you didn't need drums, you didn't need a lead singer. You all sang along to
these songs. And then we discovered they were all songs from Leadbelly
and Woody Guthrie, basically—Woody Guthrie, as we know, inspired people like Bob Dylan later on. So we were playing versions of blues without
realizing it.

Blues was not on sale in England in those days, and it wasn't when I
joined the beginnings of the Stones in late '62. You had to send away to
America, if you knew what to ask for, and most people didn't. Blues records
were never played on the radio. The only blues people who had been in England were Muddy Waters and Big Bill Broonzy; they came in and toured
with jazz bands. So the jazz fraternity saw them, but the public didn't. So
blues was a new music when the Stones started playing it. We brought it
back to America 18 months later and played it freshly—or our version of it—
to a white audience who were also mostly unaware of it.

Elwood: *Do you remember the first blues performance you saw?*

Wyman: John Lee Hooker came over to England in early '64, before we
came to America, and we did some gigs with him on the bill. I knew about
Chuck Berry, who isn't really a blues artist, but he did the occasional thing
like "Confessing the Blues." Bo Diddley was doing his form of the blues,
which we knew. We toured with him and did his records right from the very
beginning, when we were a pure blues band. And then when we came to

America, we started to meet people. I met John Hammond Jr. in Greenwich Village, and I recorded with him on his first album. I met Lonnie Johnson, the great jazz-blues guitarist from the '30 s right to the '60s. He played with people like Duke Ellington and Louis Armstrong as well as with all the blues artists. I met him on the street in the Village and talked to him. It was those kinds of meetings. You'd go to the Ashgrove in Los Angeles you'd sit among 25 people and watch John Lee Hooker. And Jesse Fuller, 72 years old, the guy who wrote "San Francisco Bay Blues." He tap-danced his way through the end of the song. It was fantastic. It was all those kinds of moments. Of course, later in '69 we toured America and got Chuck Berry and B.B. King and his band on tour with us, which was great. And in 1970 in Europe we had Buddy Guy, Junior Wells, and a very young Bonnie Raitt traveling with us through Europe and England. And so it went on.

Elwood: *One of the things I appreciate about bands like the Stones is that you promoted these artists who may not otherwise have been appreciated.*

Wyman: Certainly. The black kids knew them, but the white kids on the other side of town didn't. They'd say, "Who is Muddy Waters? Where can we hear him?" And you'd say, "Just go across town." But it was a bit difficult in those days. There was violence going on in some of the towns. So I can understand why the kids didn't go over there, but we used to. We didn't hang out in the clubs—we'd go over there very quickly and back, and buy records in a little record store in some street just to find some stuff that maybe we'd never heard before. We'd zoom in on a taxi and jump out and run in the place and just grab handfuls of records and pay for them, and then jump in the taxi and go tearing off back to our hotel on the other side of town.

Elwood: *Do you still have those records?*

Wyman: Every one of them, of course.

Elwood: *Are there any gems that stand out for you?*

Wyman: For me they're all gems. Pretty much every original blues record has something that's worth learning from or hearing, whether it's a little bit of a lyric, a little riff, an introduction line, or just the atmosphere of the way the song was sung and what it was sung about. If it was a great fire in Natchez or the flood of Tupelo, Mississippi, you learned about that. The songs were about true-life events, and that's why I love the blues. It's the most sincere and honest music of any you hear, maybe apart from jazz. You believe pretty much everything they said because the songs were about something that happened in their lives. It was always sung more from the heart than any other music, and certainly much more honestly than popular music was.

Those smarmy pop songs about lipstick on your collar and that kind of stuff, it was just laughable. It was nice for some parts of the population, but I couldn't relate to any of that. But when someone sang about working on the railroad at a dollar a day, hammering stakes into wood and all that, you could appreciate it, because he probably did it. It wasn't as romantic, it wasn't much fun, but it was true to life.

Elwood: *John Lee Hooker recently passed away. Did you ever get a chance to play with him?*

Wyman: He did shows with us, and I went to his shows and went backstage and chatted with him. When we'd tour in America, if he was around he'd come backstage and hang out in the dressing room. So he was kind of a friend, but I never physically performed with him except when he came onstage with the Stones in '89 on a pay-per-view in Atlantic City. Eric Clapton was up there as well—that was a bit of fun.

There are other people I played with much more, like Muddy Waters. I put a rhythm section together for him in the Montreux Jazz Festival. I played the whole night there with Muddy, Buddy Guy, Junior Wells, and Pinetop Perkins. And three years later I played three numbers with his whole Chicago band in the same place. Muddy was always very pro-Stones; he always said, "They's the boys that put me back on the road, you know, when people had forgotten me. And they used my name, my song, 'Rolling Stone Blues.'"

When we first came to Chicago in '64 and recorded at Chess Studios, Muddy helped us carry our guitars in from the van and bring the equipment into the studio. That was a bit of a shock; there was our idol, and he said, "You guys want help?" We looked around and it was Muddy Waters—we nearly fell over.

Elwood: *What was he like as a person?*

Wyman: A very sweet man. I went to festivals where he was playing with people like Cab Calloway and Bonnie Raitt, and was in his band when they were traveling or played alongside with him when he didn't have his own band with him. We remained very good friends right through to the end of his life. The Stones did a lot of his songs, of course. I also did an album with Howlin' Wolf in 1970 with Eric Clapton, Charlie Watts, and Hubert Sumlin [*The London Howlin' Wolf Sessions*]. That was wonderful. I got to know Wolf even better. I had dinner with his family and spent the night just rapping about music and life.

Elwood: *What was he like?*

Wyman: Well, this guy looked like a giant bear. I mean, he had size-20 shoes. He was very frightening onstage. But when you got to talk to him, he was a really sweet man, very gentle and very considerate. I'm very fond of the moments I spent with him. We got him on *Shindig*, the American pop show, in 1965 when we were going to feature our new single, "Satisfaction"—it was the first time we played it live on American television. We insisted that if they wanted us on the show, they'd have Howlin' Wolf on with us, which was totally alien to their concept, because it was a pop show for kids. But they agreed. So, he came on and we sat around the bandstand while he sang. It was wonderful.

Elwood: *Once I heard that voice it was all over for me.*

Wyman: When he sang that song "Evil," it really was. You believed every word of it. That voice was wonderful, he played great harmonica, and he always had a great band. But there's a lot of close seconds to Wolf—Muddy, B.B. King, Buddy Guy, there's loads of them. But if I had to choose one as the most inspiring it would be Wolf. He was a farmer who didn't record until he was past 40.

Elwood: *It was same thing with John Lee Hooker—he worked picking cotton.*

Wyman: And he worked in a car factory in Detroit. Some of them ended up working as porters and things like that in hotels and apartment buildings. But that was a lot better than the guys in the '20s and '30, most of them had no other means of support. They just went out and sang on street corners and were discovered, made a few records, and vanished forever. But there were some great ones back then. Blind Lemon Jefferson must have been so inspirational to Robert Johnson, because you can hear very similar things. And Blind Willie McTell in the '30s, who did all those fantastic songs with a soft voice and beautiful lyrics. His "Statesboro Blues" was carried on by the Allman Brothers and Taj Mahal. Canned Heat based all their songs on a guy from the '30 s called Little Son Jackson. When you hear him, you hear them.

I don't want those people to be forgotten, because they were wonderful, wonderful artists who did great songs. And they weren't all sad songs, because the blues isn't always sad. A lot of it is very humorous. There's a guy I love from the late 30's, Tommy McClennan, who was quite an aggressive player and singer. He cracks me up every time he sings, "I got a brown-skin woman, her front tooth crowned with gold, and she's got a lien on my body and a mortgage on my soul," and then he plays a lick and says, "Do that again, 'cause it's the best one you've got." Those little moments are lovely.

Elwood: *Then there were people like Papa Charlie Jackson and Frankie Jackson . . .*

Wyman: Half-pint Jackson—he used to sing like a woman and dress up like a woman. People thought he was a woman until they actually saw him play. He made some really good records. There's lots of people who just made four records and then vanished forever. So there must be thousands out there that were also brilliant and had great songs and great lyrics and great voices, and could play beautifully, who were never recorded in those days. Because it was only by pure chance you were discovered by a field unit going from town to town. I've got some wonderful stuff by a guy from 1927 called Luke Jordan, who only did 10 songs, four of which are lost forever. He wrote a song called "Pick a Poor Robin Clean"—"I ate his head and ate his feet, but I couldn't eat his body 'cause it wasn't good to eat, but I picked poor robin clean." They obviously caught little birds to feed on because they were hungry. Then you had all the '30s guys and the women, of course, who wrote all those saucy songs.

Elwood: *I'm impressed at how many lyrics you know from these songs.*

Wyman: Well, 'cause I've been listening to them. They're in my collection and I love blues music, so I know them all. They're very humorous, a lot of them. Bo Carter sings "Warm My Wiener" or "Banana in Your Fruit Basket" or "Ram Rod Daddy" and all these saucy songs—"my lead's all gone, my pencil don't write no more." You can't help laughing. They talk about automobiles and they're really talking about their girlfriend.

Elwood: *Is there anybody now who is carrying on the spirit of those old tunes?*

Wyman: Oh, yeah. One of my favorites of the new breed is Keb' Mo'. We've played three or four festivals that Keb's been on, so we've made friends and I find him very good. There's another guy on Blind Pig, John Mooney, who does some tracks that sound just like Son House. Then there's Muddy's son, Big Bill Morganfield. He sounds a bit like his dad, and he's writing good songs.

When we recorded that album with Howlin' Wolf we were trying to do "Red Rooster," not the way the Stones did it, but the way Wolf did it. Wolf's trying to teach Eric Clapton to play the slide and he's not quite getting in there properly, so Eric says, "Well, Wolf, it's your song, you did it, you know exactly how it goes. Why don't you do it and then we'll cut the track and it will be perfect." And Wolf says, "No, man, no, no. You've got to do it, because when I'm gone somebody got to carry it on." That's the essence of it. It gets carried on. Howlin' Wolf and Son House used to sit and watch Charley Patton as 13-year-olds, and they learned from him and traveled with him. In the '20s Charley Patton was renowned for playing a guitar behind his head and through his legs, and gyrating all over the stage on his knees and on the floor. And that's exactly what T-Bone Walker did 20 years later, and what Jimi Hendrix was doing in the late '60s. It's not stealing. It's just continuing a tradition. That's the way I see it anyway.

Elwood: *Some of the new crop of players sound like they've skipped the whole '60s and '70s and have drawn directly from the originators.*

Wyman: That's what I like. There are quite a lot of them out there. But there are also the ones who think that blues started with the Rolling Stones and Eric Clapton, the Freddie King/Albert King/Albert Collins sort of thing, and Johnny Winter. So someone says there's a great blues band at this pub, so you go out and all you hear all night is like heavy metal almost. That ain't blues to me. There's no feeling, there's no emotion, there's no honesty in it. It's just bashed out, and I can do without that.

Elwood: *Your new band, the Rhythm Kings, seems like a more relaxed outfit than the Stones.*

Wyman: No pressures, just fun in this band. Whereas with the other one you had to always do a better album, a better tour, a better set. And stage lighting had to be better. So it got bigger, and bigger, and bigger, and bigger, and bigger. Somewhere along the line the music gets affected, because you're distracted. But that wasn't the reason I left. I left after 31 years because in my mind there was nothing else to do in the band except repeat what we'd already done. There was nothing more to aim for, nothing to achieve that you hadn't already achieved. I didn't want to play all those records and those songs for another ten years—"Jumpin' Jack Flash," "Under My Thumb," "Satisfaction," "Honky Tonk Women." I didn't want to keep going just for the sake of picking up a pile of money. I see Mick and Charlie almost weekly when I'm in England. We go to lunches, we go to each other's houses, when we're on holiday sometimes in the south of France we hang out together. I'm very proud of what I did in the Stones. But I had to move on.

ZZ TOP
Texas Three-Step

> *"Blues is always gonna be the backbone of this band."*

ZZ Top's durability pays tribute to the strength of its solid blues base. Guitarist Billy Gibbons, bass player Dusty Hill, and drummer Frank Beard have been touring and recording together for more than three decades, mixing the Texas blues tradition with their own brand of riff-heavy, humor-laced rock 'n' roll. Formed in Houston in 1970, the trio built a fervent following in the '70s with boogiefied albums such as *Tres Hombres* before taking a hiatus and then re-emerging with classics like *Deguello* and *Eliminator*, and embracing the MTV age with their videos for "Legs" and "Sharp Dressed Man." They've carried on their hard-working ways through the new millennium, pausing briefly to talk to Elwood after the release of 1994's *Antenna*.

Elwood Blues: *So how did you guys get into the blues?*

Dusty Hill: My mother listened to a lot of blues, so there were a lot of blues records around the house. You know, Lightnin' Hopkins, on down the list, I can remember being very young and assuming everyone had these records. People would come over to the house and I'd play these records, and all of a sudden their parents wouldn't let them come over anymore. I'd like to think it was because of the records. My brother, Rocky, started playing guitar, and we would listen to late-night radio and occasionally we'd be fortunate enough to catch a blues show along with early rock 'n' roll. It seemed a natural thing. In later years when I was playing bass around Dallas, I was

Sharp-dressed blues men (from left) Billy Gibbons, Frank Beard, and Dusty Hill bring their Texas boogie to a 2002 show.

fortunate enough to play with Freddie King a number of times, which was a great experience, and it just went on from there.

Billy Gibbons: When he says "fortunate enough to play with Freddie King," he's obviously remembering the nights when he was in the right key at the right time and seemed to be pleasing to Freddie.

Hill: Yeah, because if you weren't, it was not pleasing. Freddie wasn't all that vocal to the band because he didn't have to be. He would look over his shoulder at you, and you knew you were doing something wrong—correct it now.

Elwood: *He was a big guy, wasn't he?*

Hill: Very large. I remember I showed up at a place called the Ascot Ballroom in Dallas with my big bass guitar in tow, and the doorman stopped me and said, "Where do you think you're going, kid?" You know, I was 13, maybe 14. I said, "I'm with the band," and he went, "Yeah, right." All of a sudden the seas just parted and Freddie—I think he was in his pink suit or his yellow one—Freddie walked up and grabbed me and said, "Come on." He was a very imposing figure. Real nice guy, though.

Elwood: *What are some other things you remember about Freddie?*

Frank Beard: The best story that I can think of is when ZZ first got together, and it was kind of a blues tour. We were the only white band, and we were opening the show for all of these great players. Freddie was on that show, so we'd do our bit and we'd hang around the stage and watch all the rest of them. One night Freddie was up there playing, and he wasn't too happy with the way things were going. He ended his last song and the curtains closed, and we're on the side so we can still see the band. He walked back and booted the drummer right in the butt, and then the curtains reopened and he went into his encore and he was cooking. Freddie had an idea how he wanted his band to sound.

Hill: We're talking about a guy that's from Texas, went to Chicago, had some of the most definitive and successful blues recordings, including "Hide Away," but Freddie King was personable and genuinely interested if you were a musician who showed an interest in what he was doing. He had no hesitation whatsoever to invite you in to interface with what he was doing. And as long as you did it right, if you didn't want to get the boot . . .

Gibbons: The lineup on that tour was just almost unbelievable— Freddie King, Muddy Waters, Furry Lewis. Freddie said, "So, you want to meet Muddy Waters, come on downstairs after the show," and we actually went downstairs before the show. So Freddie stops us about ten feet back of the main body of bands because we had walked in on a card game taking place on a Fender bass-guitar case that had been suspended between a couple of deck chairs. The money was flying, the cards were flying, everything was going quite well, and to get attention without saying anything, Freddie produced a coffee-can–sized wad of bills and laid it gingerly on the case and said, "I'm in, and these are my friends." We were just ready to start shaking hands, and Muddy Waters looked up and saw Dusty and Frank and myself. He smiled and said, "Pleased to meet ya," and that's all that was required. Then it was game time and there was no more talking.

Hill: Freddie demanded perfection onstage but in another way he was very easygoing. For a long time he didn't have an actual band; he would hire musicians to play shows. In '68, I think it was, my brother and myself were hired to do two weeks with him at the Fillmore. Freddie was not big on rehearsals, you know, but everything we had planned were Freddie's songs—we would do one and then introduce Freddie. It's about show time, but there's no Freddie. Well, Bill Graham says time to play, so we hit the stage and do our one song—no Freddie. So Rocky and I started doing material that we had done for years. We did three or four songs, and the crowd likes it okay, but they didn't come to see us. I'm in the middle of this one song that we stretched out twice as long as it should be, and I look to the side of the stage and there stands Freddie with his guitar, this huge smile, and I'm going,

"Come on Freddie," and he goes, "Just take it easy." He slapped that strap over one shoulder, hit the stage, and just knocked them out. It didn't bother him in the slightest.

Elwood: *Getting back to our first question, what about you, Frank? How did you get into the blues?*

Beard: I had an older sister, and in the middle '50s, when I five or six, she got into Elvis. The whole family got into him really, and we started buying records—the first record I ever bought was Chuck Berry's "Maybelline." So from about '55 to '58 everybody was on the same wavelength, and then Jerry Lee Lewis got in trouble for having a young wife, and Chuck got put in jail, and there was a split in the family. My sister went along with Frankie Avalon, Bobby Vee, Bobby Vinton and Paul Anka, but I discovered there were certain radio stations that at certain times of certain days, the radio stations down South would throw out some good blues. That's when I got into listening to that kind of music. That sustained me up until the time of the English thing. So when I heard Cream doing "Crossroads," I would go, "Damn, listen how they're doing that song," rather than thinking that they wrote that song. But for people getting into the blues now, it might be easier to ease backwards through that than to throw the Robert Johnson box set to somebody and say, "Dig it"—because that might be too far from where they're living.

Elwood: *Who was the first blues drummer who caught your attention?*

Beard: Sonny Freeman was great, and I also liked Lightnin' Hopkins's drummer, Spider Kilpatrick, down in Houston when we were forming. He must have been in his 70s by then, and he was a total character. His floor tom had no legs; it just sat on the ground, and that was his table where his drink and porkchop sandwich was. He was so fine to watch. He'd start a roll, and something would go wrong with it and it would just disintegrate, but it would always end up at the right place and he'd be right with Lightnin'.

Gibbons: The Spider roll.

Beard: Yeah. I mean, you'd be like amazed at like, how did he do that? It's like he almost fell off the stool, it's what it sounded like, but than at the very end, he'd pull it all together and it was just superiorly funky.

Gibbons: Those with a sharp eye will take note that at any live ZZ Top performance, there is a rather odd-looking drum arrangement, which Frank acknowledges is from the influence of Spider Kilpatrick—always one drum that has drinks, ashtrays, sandwiches, photographs.

Beard: Yeah, it's the third floor tom, and it has no other function—it's a table. I'm going to put a little doily on it.

Elwood: *So what about you Billy? How did you get into blues?*

Gibbons: Pretty much the same way. The discussion that's taking place now is the same discussion that led toward the naming of the most recent

ZZ Top recording *Antenna*, because before we played drums, bass, and guitar, we played the radio.

Elwood: *Frank, you seem to have that connection to rock 'n' roll and Elvis. Can you think of an artist or song that really affected rock 'n' roll?*

Beard: It ain't a blues song, but the rock 'n' roll song of all times was Bill Haley in "Rock Around the Clock." That was the one that broke that thing open. Clearly we don't sit around and listen to blues music all the time, we listen to all kinds. But I do know that when it's time to make a ZZ Top record, there's always a two-week span before we start writing and we've been apart for a while, that we get back together and just play, and it's always the old blues songs that we play. We do that for a couple of weeks, and that puts us in the mood to write our songs. Blues is always gonna be the backbone of this band.

Elwood: *What tunes do you play to get into the groove?*

Beard: Oh, we like to do Muddy's "Two Trains Running" a whole lot. We also like to do a lot of Freddie King songs because Dusty knows all the words.

Elwood: *People talk a lot about Muddy Waters, Howlin' Wolf, Freddie King, but who are some of the lesser-known blues musicians who influenced rock 'n' roll?*

Gibbons: One of the artists who was always a frontline performer in our opinion is Houston Stackhouse. He's one of the enigmatic figures, of which there are many, I guess—we could do a whole show on every blues man that you've never heard and once heard, will be the blues men that you will never hear again. Perhaps of more prominence would be Robert Junior Lockwood, but I'm constantly amazed at the number of people who may not have heard his name. If you ever go into New Orleans and say "Professor Longhair," they say it's okay to come in—that's another guy who is just now starting to enjoy some kind of renowned success that you would assume would have always been there. So, it's peculiar to find out there's always more.

Our recording career has such deep roots in Memphis—having worked there for the last 15 records—and the "King Biscuit Time" [radio program] comes into Memphis clearly if you're lucky enough to be close to a radio at the noon hour. One of the high points for us was hearing the host, Sonny Payne, say, "We got a special request to play this song by Houston Stackhouse. The request goes out to his daughter." It was a great moment to hear this thing is still going strong.

Elwood: *Getting back to Muddy Waters one more time, tell us about Muddywood.*

Gibbons: The blues is in an upbeat mode right now, and we've always enjoyed a certain amount of blueness in our musical endeavor—that has really been the cornerstone of what we've done, and it's been even deepened by our association in Texas, Memphis, Mississippi, and now even in California, New York, South America, Japan. It's everywhere. And we were reminded by a number of people that the blues never does really ever go away, it's just lower and higher. This kind of proved itself when a friend of ours passed through Mississippi on his way back to Tennessee and spotted a sign that said "Blues Museum." He asked us if we knew anything about a blues museum, which we did not at the time. So on our day off we decided to drive to Mississippi, and sure enough, not only did we find a blues museum, we found the curator, and Jim O'Neal, who was the founder of *Living Blues* magazine, gathered us up to go take a look at the cabin that Muddy Waters grew up in, maybe nine miles from the museum.

The purpose of the visit was to inspect the cabin because it was under threat of being taken down. But it was such a significant landmark that the community said, "Let's take a second look before we just do away with this thing." We were fortunately given a souvenir chunk of wood that had been blown off the roof by a recent tornado. On our way back to Memphis we said, "Wouldn't it be fine if . . . 'What's your guitar made of?' 'Muddy Water's house.'" The return trip took us straight to Pyramid Guitar Shop in Memphis, and six or eight weeks later we had this piece of Muddy Waters's house fashioned into a guitar. And that's Muddywood. You can see it in the Delta Blues Museum in Clarksdale, Mississippi, and follow the construction of the instrument and the presentation to the museum. It was our humble way of paying back for so much that had come our way in helping us play the stuff that we play. We all wish we hadn't played the guitar, because it plays so good we didn't want to give it up.

Keepers
of the
Flame

MARCIA BALL
Borderline Case

> *"Texas is a guitar state . . .*
> *whereas lots of pianos,*
> *lots of keyboards came out*
> *Louisiana."*

Growing up in Vinton, Louisiana, Marcia Ball was nurtured in the east Texas–southwest Louisiana music scene that has produced such distinctive artists as Janis Joplin, Johnny and Edgar Winter, Clifton Chenier, and Gatemouth Brown. Formally trained on piano, Ball carries on the funky keyboard tradition of Professor Longhair and Allen Toussaint with a style that mixes blues, R&B, rock 'n' roll, gospel, and boogie-woogie. Recordings like *Presumed Innocent* and *Gatorhythms* also highlight her songwriting and vocal skills. Elwood talked to Marcia in 2002, shortly before *Presumed Innocent* won a W.C. Handy best-album award.

Elwood Blues: *What was it like growing up along the Louisiana-Texas border?*
Marcia Ball: That was really important in the way I developed. Everybody in our part of the country has a certain amount of music in them. Part of that is the Cajun influence, which pervades that area no matter what side of the state line you live on. It happened that I lived on the Louisiana side, which was the looser side. That's where all the honky-tonks were, because you could always drink a little younger and a little easier down in Louisiana. The bands on both sides of the line reflected influences from both sides. Johnny and Edgar Winter and Janis Joplin were in Beaumont and Port Arthur, and Lonnie Brooks and Gatemouth Brown were running both sides

At the crossroads: Marcia Ball's eclectic style comes from both sides of the border town she grew up in.

of the line. Mose Allison did some time down there around Lake Charles, playing in those places when he was living in Baton Rouge, and all of the Cajun bands and Clifton Chenier and Lazy Lester were recording in Crowley at J.D. Miller's studio and at Gold Band and Khoury's in Lake Charles, where Phil Phillips recorded "Sea of Love." That was all going on in the '50s. I was little and getting immersed in this music.

Elwood: *What would you say is the difference musically between Louisiana and Texas?*

Ball: There are regional differences in every area: the Houston influence, the Duke/Peacock records influence—Don Robey and those guys—the Starday Records influence, which was more country and Western swing. Starday actually preceded the Duke Peacock guys and created an interesting body of work that Albert Collins and Bobby Bland would be good examples of: big-horn-band Texas, what they call a Texas shuffle. But I've always found that Texas is a guitar state—although there are great keyboard players, and of course, the Texas tenor saxophone players—whereas lots of pianos, lots of keyboards came out Louisiana, including the accordions. That would be a big difference.

Elwood: *Why are New Orleans—and Louisiana in general—such big areas for keyboards?*

Ball: I'm not sure, except that on both sides of the line there was a strong barrelhouse piano tradition, whorehouse pianos, and then just plain honky-tonk pianos. There were lumber camps along the Gulf Coast on both sides—east Texas and southwestern Louisiana—and guys would ride the rails and hop off and play in a lumber camp for a while. I knew some of those guys in Austin and had the pleasure of working with them in their later years. One was Roosevelt Williams, known as Gray Ghost, who was in his 90s when he died just a couple of years ago and was still playing incredibly. They called him Ghost because he would ghost into town on the rails with a jumpsuit or something over his nice clothes—this is how the story goes—and then pull that off and go in and play in the barrelhouse, and then disappear as quickly and as completely as he had arrived. Erbie Bowser was another, and there was a great piano player, Lavada Durst, who was also a preacher and an early black deejay who crossed the color line and performed on white radio in central Texas.

Elwood: *You mentioned some piano styles I'd like to talk about. How did barrelhouse, stride, and boogie-woogie come about?*

Ball: Barrelhouse, stride, and boogie-woogie all emanate from the same place and they all crisscross back and forth. They're maybe descended from ragtime, or maybe ragtime—formal ragtime, which Scott Joplin annotated—was descended from the barrelhouse music that he was hearing. Probably a lot of that came out of church. Down on the Gulf Coast they called it barrel-house because of the lumber camps, work camps, and railroad camps that people worked in, but in New Orleans in Storyville, those guys were playing ragtime. There are distinct differences, and there are many boogie-woogie patterns, and of course, there are the New York boogie-woogie giants and the Kansas City boogie-woogie players, so it was a national phenomenon.

Elwood: *Who are some of the great boogie-woogie and stride players who influenced you?*

Ball: Eubie Blake was amazing all of his life, into his 90s and 100 years old. The New York giants—Meade Lux Lewis, Albert Ammons, and Pete Johnson—would be three. Then there are Roosevelt Sykes and Champion Jack Dupree, in terms of the broad range of piano players. Of course, the

New Orleans guys—Professor Longhair and Tuts Washington—were enormous influences on me. My son loves boogie-woogie piano, so he and I are racing to collect records by Crippled Clarence Lofton and people like that. I also loved the Western swing piano players like Moon Mullican and Al Strickland, who played with Bob Wills and the Texas Playboys. Those guys had an incredible style based on big-band jazz. I've got old LPs from down on the Gulf Coast recorded in the '30s and '40s by people that no one has ever heard of, obscure records that are amazing.

Elwood: *One of my current favorites is Henry Butler.*

Ball: Oh, Henry Butler is a monster, my friend.

Elwood: *Do you play the accordion?*

Ball: Poorly, and I really don't play button accordion at all. The button accordion is the Cajun accordion, also sometimes called the German accordion or the conjunto accordion. It's diatonic the way a harmonica is diatonic—when you blow you get one note, when you suck you get another. Instead of a keyboard on one side, the button accordion has a single, double, or triple row of buttons. And to my mind, those buttons have absolutely no linear arrangement at all, so I'm completely lost on them. Usually on the other hand, the left hand, there is an "in" chord and an "out" chord, also like a harmonica, so that's why when you see somebody playing a button accordion—especially a single-row Cajun accordion—they'll have several accordions on stage, because each one is only functional in two keys. The three-row accordions are a lot more versatile. When you hear somebody like Flaco Jimenez or Joel Guzman or Steve Jordan play one of those, you realize that there's nothing that they can't do.

Elwood: *Those three are Texas guys; who are some Louisiana button accordion players?*

Ball: It's getting so that's everybody goes every which way, and that's a fun thing about what's happening in Cajun and zydeco right now. Steve Riley—he plays both kinds—Wayne Toups, Gino Delafose—Gino's black, so you want to throw him into the zydeco school, but he is descended from a more traditional Cajun style. His daddy was very traditional; he played button accordion and played Cajun music rather than zydeco music. Gino, being young and adventurous, is taking it a little bit farther.

Elwood: *In your opinion, what's the difference between Cajun and zydeco?*

Ball: When it started out there was a color line: Cajun was white, French music, *chanky-chank* music, and zydeco was blues-influenced, and, as invented by Clifton Chenier, was played on a big keyboard accordion that really had a lot more relationship to a Hammond B-3 organ. If you ever hear Buckwheat Zydeco play B-3, you'll know what I mean. But now all of those lines are blurred, thank goodness, and they're all playing together.

Elwood: *You moved to Austin, Texas, in the '70s, when Antone's became a hot* *spot for blues and roots music. Do you have any special memories from the Antone's days?*

Ball: In particular at the very beginning—they opened in July of 1975. I know this because I was eight months' pregnant and he opened with Clifton Chenier on a several-day stand over the Fourth of July weekend—I was there dancing, of course—and my son was born a month later, on August 5, 1975. We played with Junior Walker there, back when my band was practically still a country band. I saw many, many great bands at the original Sixth Street location. They briefly moved to a north Austin location, and I remember seeing Jake Andrews when he was about 12 playing with Jimmie Vaughan. The heyday was probably the Guadalupe Street years, when they started having anniversary parties there in the summertime, that week in July with every living guitar player, every living musician that they could round up. Eddie Taylor, Jimmy Johnson, and Muddy Waters and Buddy Guy and Junior Wells and Pinetop Perkins would come, and Willy "Big Eyes" Smith would be playing. Both Jimmy and Stevie Ray were there playing, and Hubert Sumlin and Mel Brown and Lazy Lester and people that I didn't even know were still alive were all there at the same time and all playing.

Elwood: *In Austin did you ever get a chance to meet Janis Joplin?*

Ball: I didn't meet her, but I saw her play several times. She was a big influence on me. When I first started singing in bands, her music was current, and I did several of her songs. One of her big influences and her help along the way was an older man, a musician in Austin named Kenneth Threadgill. He was first in line for the first liquor license in Travis County after prohibition was repealed. He had a filling station with a beer bar, and he would open up early in the morning, catch guys on their way to work, serve them a few beers, close up in the middle of the day, and open up in the afternoon and serve them their beers on the way home. By the late '60s the hippies were hanging out in his bar at night. He was a silver-haired daddy with kind of long, real pretty hair, which all us hippies could relate to. He had met Jimmie Rodgers in his youth, and he was a blues yodeler. He had a little string band that would play there, and a couple of times a night he would come from around the bar in his little bartender's white apron and grab that microphone in both hands and cock his head up and yodel and sing "All Along the Watchtower." He was just wonderful. He was an influence, a help to Janis when she lived there, when she was still running around playing her autoharp and singing folk music. That's where they would hang out. He had a birthday—it would have been 1970—and they had a reunion, and she flew in from Hawaii and came and played. She came alone, and she sat down with a guitar and played "Me and Bobby McGee" and "Help Me Make It Through the Night," which was great. I think that's the first time I'd heard those songs.

Elwood: *Speaking of great female artists, you're involved in a tribute to Sister Rosetta Tharpe. Can you tell us a little about her?*

Ball: Well, in the '30s and '40s she was a very successful gospel singer, but she was a guitar player at a time when gospel was played on the piano, and she was also a walking, moving, dancing singer—she had Chuck Berry–type moves before Chuck. She had a great body of material, and then she crossed over and was a pop star—she sang with Lucky Millinder's band—and that was a real hard line to walk at that time. You really would lose your gospel crowd if you crossed over, but for many years she managed to hang onto both types of music.

Elwood: *It's often said that blues came out of the gospel tradition, but all of a sudden it got this label of "devil's music." How did that happen?*

Ball: I would say that in the day when someone started out playing in church, they would be drawn away from their church and find themselves on the other side of the tracks playing in the honky-tonks where the liquor flowed and the gambling and the wild side of life were the thing. That definitely was a falling away, and I think that probably a lot of people fell away, thank goodness.

Elwood: *There are also folks who straddled the line.*

Ball: Yes, well, I think you can. I also know a lot of people who went back to church—in some cases it probably saved their lives. I know people whose families and husbands, wives, or children drew the line in the dirt and said, "You're not going playing in those honky-tonks anymore."

JOHN POPPER &
CHAN KINCHLA OF
BLUES TRAVELER

Back on the Road

> *"If we can play honestly,*
> *then it will sound like some*
> *reflection of the blues."*

Fronted by incendiary harmonica player/singer/guitarist John Popper, Blues Traveler has been a major force in the jam band movement—Popper himself originated the idea for the HORDE tour. Formed in 1988, the band has found success onstage and on record while overcoming a string of hardships, culminating in the death of bassist Bob Sheehan in 1999. Through it all they've kept their sense of humor, as this 2001 interview with Popper and bassist Chan Kinchla shows.

Elwood Blues: *Could you please share with the listeners how it was to be a friend and a bandmate of Bob Sheehan?*

John Popper: The song "Pretty Angry" [from *Bridge*] was medicinal for me. I was going through a really rough time—I was 420 pounds at that point and Bobby just left. The song is about his little brother John and me at his house in New Orleans right after the funeral in New York. We're packing up his boxes; I looked at John and he looked at me, and I was like, here we are cleaning up his crap again. That song is about the anger—it surprised me how angry I felt. You try and put sense to losing someone, and there really

177

Suitcase full of blues: Chan Kinchla and John Popper play Colorado's 2002 Blues & Brews Festival.

isn't any certainly on the short term. In the long term, it reminded me how fragile life is and made me want to live. I just lost 180 pounds because I intend to stay here. I'm not going down that road.

Elwood: *And I know the feeling of losing a very dear friend.*

Popper: Yes, you miss him every day, and what you try to do is make that a good thing, not some sort of regret. You have to live your life, and the band has its own life and you have to allow it to grow and become what it is.

Elwood: *How is the band doing now?*

Chan Kinchla: We're just finding our identity with these new players. I think doing the record with them really helped us feel out where we fit sonically. But you don't really know how it's going to work with all the intangibles of band chemistry until you start taking it out live. We're in the process of discovering our new identity, and it's an exciting time.

Popper: It's sounding really good. We're really pleased. I'm psyched I don't have to do so many frenetic harmonica solos; I get to relax and take a breath once in a while.

Kinchla: And I have somebody [keyboardist Ben Wilson] who can actually play full chords to comp with me.

Popper: This poor bastard has been using a harp as an accompanist for ten years.

Kinchla: And John's been blowing as hard as he can to try and make it sound like a piano.

Popper: As you know, Elwood, there are about three or four chords that you can maybe squeeze out of a harp, and you just need more than that when you're really comping behind somebody, like doing a James Brown/Maceo Parker kind of a groove. When you listen to James Brown, those sparse guitar riffs that sit in the exact right spot make you just have to move. Maceo says he puts the beat on *one* and *three* instead of *two* and *four*— he claims that's a natural beat. I'm not sure about it; I go back and forth. Some beboppers say the upbeat of *four* is the only beat you should count. That's how you're cool if you're a bebopper—you snap your fingers every upbeat of *four*.

Elwood: *What does the blues mean to you?*

Popper: For us the blues is just playing as honestly as we can. If we can play honestly, then it will sound like some reflection of the blues. I always feel a little like we're perpetrating when we get next to B.B. King or someone like that, because that is a traditional blues style. We like the blues, but we don't rely on the tradition so much.

Kinchla: I think what's great about the blues and the reason blues reaches everybody on such a gut level is because it gets rid of a lot of the gobblygook of theory and complex chord structures. It's very simple music, but it speaks in such a deep way and it reaches such an emotional level because it's so simple.

Popper: And it's accessible to everyone.

Kinchla: Everyone, can play it and everyone can be involved in it—it's people music.

Elwood: *Who are some of the people who influenced you?*

Popper: Yes. As you know, Elwood, you are the reason I got into playing the harmonica. To start from *The Blues Brothers* movie being your inspiration to being in *Blues Brothers 2000* is a very "Twilight Zone" kind of experience for me.

Elwood: *The pleasure is truly all mine. You've said you were influenced by Jimi Hendrix. I was surprised to hear that.*

Popper: You might have got me into pulling the harp, but when I heard Jimi Hendrix play *Voodoo Child* I knew I had to play music for a living. That sound that he made, that noise got up in my toes and hasn't left. He played like a storm. He played like a force of nature. When somebody cuts through because they are so talented. It makes things clear to you. It's like how I got into basketball watching Michael Jordan play. When he would fade through the opposing team it was like everyone was standing still and everyone's breath kind of just goes *haaa*. And suddenly basketball became clear to me. I understood the beauty of it. After Jimi Hendrix, I could get into jazz and I could get into classical. He opened up my head.

Elwood: *What about you, Chan?*

Kinchla: Well, Jimi Hendrix for all those same reasons. Just a month ago I got the new live Jim Hendrix compilation—I'm still listening to Hendrix and I know I will until the day I die. And for good, indignant energy, the music that still rocks my world is punk rock.

Popper: Don't forget Zeppelin. This guy was a big drunken Zeppelin brawler when I met him.

Kinchla: And I'm still a big drunk Zeppelin brawler.

Popper: As far as live influences, the Allman Brothers really helped us see how to be a jam band. They took us under their wing early on.

Elwood: *Do you remember a specific Allman Brothers performance?*

Popper: When Dickey Betts got arrested for punching out some cops up in Stowe, Vermont, they asked me to sit in with them. We did "Elizabeth Reed," and I was creaming in my pants. I couldn't believe I was up there and, oh, my God, I'm playing with the Allman Brothers.

Kinchla: I remember the first tour we opened with the Allman Brothers. We were just 19 and we hadn't done an album; Bill Graham got us on the show. We played for their crowd and came offstage—it was a pivotal period for us; we were just learning our power onstage. Dickey Betts is walking across the stage—I didn't even make it off the stage—and he gives me a big hug, slaps me on the butt, and says how much he loved it. That kind of support from somebody who didn't have to take the time to do that, or even show how much he liked it, pushes you a long way. Those guys were always open to that.

Popper: Another big moment was Carlos Santana doing "Mountain Cry" with us. We couldn't believe it—he was playing a song we wrote and we were trading solos with him. All of us were trying to duel with him; he's taking Chan on, he's taking me on, back and forth. It was fun.

Kinchla: It was probably kind of humorous to him. He's like, ah, these kids.

Popper: We were freaking out, going, oh, my God, we played with Carlos Santana. And Bill Graham says, "I remember when Carlos was saying that about Muddy Waters," and we felt part of the tradition. That wound up being the last day that I saw Bill alive. And that was the day Miles Davis died, so that was a very heavy day for music.

Elwood: *Any other influences you'd like to talk about?*

Popper: Coming from New Jersey, I was in high school when *Born in the USA* came out, so I hated Bruce Springsteen. I was like, ugh, who's this butt with the little hat sticking out of it that I have to see on every billboard? You know, that stupid '80s dance and the "Dancing in the Dark" video where he brings Courteney Cox up there like she's in the audience. That's what I thought Springsteen was about. It took me about ten years to realize that he'd been influencing me all along. People always said, "Listen to the early stuff. Listen to *Greetings from Asbury Park*." There is a poetic term for cramming too many lyrics into a line, and I just love the way he does that. "Just for Me" was my homage to Springsteen—that kind of reckless abandon to just throw on lyrics. I think I set a world speed record in the third verse for most words per second.

Elwood: *It's not often you hear musicians like you guys give credit to all these other people.*

Kinchla: Being creative is not just having an original thought. It's having your eyes open and letting a lot of things in and then reinterpreting them so that people get a new perspective. It's coming from all around you; you have to keep your eyes open and be influenced to be creative.

Popper: That was a profoundly deep statement, Obi-Wan.

Kinchla: Thank you. I think I've just summed it up—I might have just found the secret of creativity right here in this room.

Popper: Now we can quit.

Kinchla: I think it might come from being in the presence of Elwood.

Elwood: *How is touring going for you guys?*

Popper: We're getting boobs flashed at us a lot more. It's kind of cool. We've skewed cuter, you know—the new guys in the band are little hotties. We were thinking of making them wear collars or something onstage.

Kinchla: So when you see us go looking for tight clothes and lots of dance moves and boobs. And bras onstage and, oh, and we play music too.

Popper: We're thinking of skewing to the original boy-band kind of thing, like the N'Sync. We feel they were directly ripping off our style, so we're bringing back a lot of the choreography, a lot of the Spandex.

Kinchla: We want to be known as the band that brought on the Boy Band Jam Band era.

Popper: Yeah, we're going to write a new song called "Oh Girl, Girl, Oh. You Do It to Me Girl, Girl You Do."

Kinchla: "Man."

Popper: It's probably a little long. We might lose the "man."

Elwood: *Any advice for folks who want to be in this business?*

Popper: I am a rare exception in that I got into rock 'n' roll not for the chicks but for the musical integrity—and I was wrong. It's about the chicks. You guys were all right. I remember thinking everyone was really stupid— "Oh, they're just doing this for girls." Elwood, that's the reason—just do it for that. If you can't get laid, you're doing something wrong with the music.

Kinchla: Exactly. That's a sure sign that you're not playing well.

Elwood on the Air: Lowered Expectations

HOUR: 03/35
AIRDATE: 8/30–31/03
WRITER: MERLE KESSLER

ELWOOD: This is Elwood Blues. This is The House of Blues Radio Hour.

[FX: Doorbell.]

Hang on. Somebody at the door.

[FX: Door opens.]

Can I help you?

MAN: (Way Eeyore) It won't take much.

ELWOOD: Are you selling something?

MAN: I represent a new concept in religion.

ELWOOD: Uh-oh.

MAN: Our brochure.

ELWOOD: There's nothing on it.

MAN: Exactly.

ELWOOD: You offer nothing?

MAN: The First Church of Lowered Expectations. Do you want to be happy?

ELWOOD: Of course.

MAN: Don't come running to us. Do you want inner peace?

ELWOOD: That would be nice.

MAN: Can't help you there either.

ELWOOD: What exactly does the First Church of Lowered Expectations have to offer?

MAN: An opportunity to gather with morose people who have given up hope. You have to bring your own coffee, though.

ELWOOD: And then—?

MAN: That's about it really. Our credo? Get used to it.

ELWOOD: I am closing the door now.

[FX: Door shuts.]

MAN: (Muffled): I'm used to it.

ELWOOD: Sometimes lowered expectations can work out for you. Just ask Popa Chubby.

[Song: "Looking for One Kiss"—Popa Chubby]

POPA CHUBBY
Playing from the Heart

> *"People like Muddy and Howlin' Wolf and Freddie King . . . they all put their own stamp on it. That's what I'm trying to do."*

Blame it on Chuck Berry. It was his New York show that diverted a young Ted Horowitz from the Bronx to the blues. Raised in a music-loving family, the future Popa Chubby experienced the London-to-Chicago learning process familiar to budding blues guitarists in the '70s. A 1992 talent contest brought him a new-artist award and an opening set at the Long Beach Blues Festival. That opened the door to tours and recordings, including his major-label debut, *Booty and the Beast*, which set the tone for his ongoing experiment of mixing pop, jazz, and Southern rock flavors into his solid blues base. Elwood talked to Chubby after the release of his 2001 album, *How'd a White Boy Get the Blues?*

Elwood Blues: *How did a New York guy like you get into the blues?*
Popa Chubby: I was pretty much raised with the blues, you know. My mom and dad were big music fans. They were native New Yorkers, and when they were young they went out every night to see jazz and blues. That's when 52nd Street was alive with bebop, and my dad was into Muddy Waters and Elmore James and Chuck Berry. When I was about eight years old he took me to see Chuck Berry play, and that changed my life. I said, that's what I want to do when I get big.
Elwood: *What impressed you about Chuck Berry?*

Popa Chubby, bringing new meaning to blues licks.

Chubby: It was at Madison Square Garden, and I guess it was an oldies revival. Chuck Berry, Fats Domino, so many great people were on the bill. One thing I remember is Chuck being up there and being huge. I was just a little kid, and he was such a big man—his hands were enormous, and he was jumping around playing his guitar. I could see a big wad of money in his back pocket, and I thought, "Man, that's for me."

Elwood: *So you started playing music right after that?*

Chubby: Yes. I started out playing the drum kit, but that didn't work out too well because they all complained about the noise. So then I picked up the electric guitar, much to everybody's chagrin—from the minute I started playing the guitar, people started telling me to turn it down. That's still going on, but I never listen to them—I'm still playing loud and proud, and that's what it's all about, man. Playing the music for the people and bringing some joy into the world.

Elwood: *How did you go about learning the instrument?*

Chubby: Like a lot of kids did. I picked up my Rolling Stones records and played along with them. From Chuck Berry I got into Keith Richards and Jeff Beck and Jimmy Page and Led Zeppelin. And from them I started seeing a name on all the records—Willie Dixon. On the first Led Zeppelin record I heard their cover of Otis Rush's version of the Willie Dixon song "I Can't Quit You Baby," and my life was changed forever. Then somebody gave me Otis Rush's record, and I realized that Led Zeppelin had played his version verbatim, note for note. I was very impressed by that.

When I was about 19, somebody played me a Freddie King record. That was like being hit by a cannonball—a Texas cannonball, to be exact. It floored me. I realized that if I ever got to that point, I'd be doing okay. Day by day it's been a path to try and follow and play that kind of music and play it right. At the same time, I want to add my own creativity to it, which is I think important in blues. That's what the great blues men all did. People like Muddy and Howlin' Wolf and Freddie King and B.B. and Albert and so many others, they all put their own stamp on it. That's what I'm trying to do: borrow from the masters and put my own stamp on the music.

Elwood: *What is it about Freddie King hit you so hard?*

Chubby: It was just pure unadulterated emotion. The man played from every ounce of his heart and really didn't know any other way. Freddie wasn't the most technical guitar player. He wasn't the most technical singer. But when he played, it was 110 percent feeling, and that's what the blues is all about. The blues ain't nothing but a feeling, and Freddie had that.

Freddie did so much great stuff, and he was far ahead of his time. All the later stuff he did with Leon Russell on Shelter Records, it was so ground-breaking. Nobody has ever crossed boundaries like that in the blues since.

Elwood: *People divide up the blues into categories like the Chicago sound and the Texas sound. What's the New York sound?*

Chubby: It borrows from a lot of different influences. It's hard and visceral, and it makes no apologies. The New York sound of blues and the New York sound of music is in your face—it is what it is. It's like riding a subway at rush hour—people get along because they have to.

Elwood: *You spend a lot of time touring overseas. What's that like for you?*

Chubby: I tour over in Europe, a good six months out of the year, which is great because the European audiences are really good, and the music has a lot of importance over there. So that's been really rewarding, but I've always felt a kind of vacancy that I'm not doing it as much as I should be in my own home. Now I'm doing that, and I'm starting to feel that fulfillment, which is such a beautiful thing as an artist, where you feel like you're actually covering all the bases and doing what you're supposed to do, and people are responding to it.

Elwood: *You wrote every song on your new record, which is great because you see so many records these days are half cover songs and half special guests and things like that.*

Chubby: It's kind of sad because either you get records like that or you get really good blues artists who have decided that in order to succeed they need to play rock music. And they're not playing rock music because it's from their heart, they're playing it because they think they'll cross over. So instead of writing good blues songs, they write bad rock songs. Willie Dixon is my idol, and he was the best songwriter in rock 'n' roll, plain and simple. That's what it's all about for me. It always comes down to the song. You should try to write songs that express where you're at as a human being. If you can do that, everything else is going to fall into place.

Elwood: *You have a song where you talk about guys you knew growing up who didn't make, that aren't here anymore. Did playing the blues keep that from happening to you?*

Chubby: Absolutely. Music has saved my life, and it's given me so much. Music is sacred—to me it's the closest thing I'll ever get to religion. Music has given me not only a way to make a living but a way to live and a way to feel good about myself and a way to survive. And I feel like I owe my audience everything. If somebody has the inclination to plop down their hard-earned money to buy my record or see my show, I feel like I'd better deliver for them. I got no time for rock stars. To me, a rock star is somebody who doesn't care—it's more about their ego than what they're doing. To me, it's all about connecting with the people. When you get that, you get a true musical experience.

Elwood: *Early in your career you worked with Tom Dowd, the legendary Atlantic Records engineer and producer. What did you learn from him?*

Chubby: When I worked with Tom he was 72 years old, and this man showed up for work every day. I thought, Man, that's how you do it. You show up like as if you were a carpenter. And if I were a carpenter, I'd show up and I'd work eight hours a day. That's what I do as a musician. I work every day. That causes the creative process to not be put on a pedestal, which I think is dangerous. I think the best way to make good records is to just make them part of your life, make your expression of your creativity a normal part of your life instead of something that's a special thing. Because then you're relaxed and you're able to express your true feelings without that other stuff getting in the way.

Elwood: *What's your advice to musicians who are trying to make it, trying to play and record.*

Chubby: Play because you love to play. Don't go looking for a record deal. If you go looking for a record deal, you'll never find one. Do what you do because you love to do it.

Elwood: *To take a cue from the title of your album, how does a white boy get the blues?*

Chubby: The blues ain't about being white or black or yellow or green or anything else. When you think about it, the least important part of your body is the pigment of your skin—you could lose the pigment in your skin, and you'd still be 100 percent intact. The bigger question is, how does anybody get the blues? And the real question is, how does anybody get through life?

Elwood: *If the pigment in your skin is the least important part of your body, what's the most important?*

Chubby: Your heart, my brother, your heart. And the part you can't see, your soul.

SHEMEKIA COPELAND
Make Room for Daughter

> *"When I first heard Robert Plant I thought that Led Zeppelin was a big black gospel singer."*

Though she grew up in the shadow of her father, Johnny Clyde Copeland, Shemekia Copeland has since claimed her own territory on the blues map, firing up audiences with her searing vocals and powerful stage presence. Born in Harlem in 1979, she infused her father's Texas-flavored blues with the street sounds of her childhood to create her own energetic style. Elwood talked to Copeland in 2000, right after the release of her album *Wicked*, which brought her a Grammy nomination and the first of her four W.C. Handy awards.

Elwood Blues: *You started touring with your father when you were in your teens. When did you start thinking that was something you wanted to do for a living?*

Shemekia Copeland: I was 16. I always told everybody I got a calling, except I didn't get a calling to become a nun, I got a calling to become a blues singer. It was almost overnight and it was a good thing. I'm happy that it happened the way it did. I thought I started too late, but I think everything worked out great.

Elwood: *What did you imagine you would do if you couldn't make a living singing the blues?*

Copeland: I thought that I was going to be a psychiatrist and help peo-

Just warming up: Blues scion Shemekia Copeland says she's still perfecting her vocal style.

ple and things like that, but that didn't work out. It turns out I need a psychiatrist, but I won't ever be one. I think I'll stick to the blues.

Elwood: *When you were growing up did you realize how important your father was in the blues world?*

Copeland: When I was 9 years old and then when I was 12, I went to Spain with my dad, and it was such an eye-opener for me because I did not realize how well-known he was and how many people loved him. And it all just clicked why he was away for two months at a time. He was very much a part of my life because he called me every day. But when I went with him and saw thousands of people out there that loved him so much, it just all clicked. Even now in my travels, I run into people who say, "Your father changed my life. He is the reason why I married my wife." Or they tell me great stories like, "I saw him in New York and there were 15 people in the audience, and he played like he was playing at Madison Square Garden. And the second set, there were three people in the audience and he played even better than the first set." So I just love listening to these stories and collecting photos that people give me. If there is anybody out there who has photos of my dad, just keep on bringing them.

Elwood: *You grew up in Harlem and then you were schooled in Texas. How did that affect your music?*

Copeland: My dad was from Texas, and he always was Texas blues, Texas blues. That was important to him, but I think it is more important for people to know where I came from. I really didn't go to Texas until I was 16 years old. So any Texas blues that I have is all from my father. Most of my influences came from growing up in Harlem and the struggles that I had. It was a tough time.

Elwood: *Who are some of the singers that have influenced you?*

Copeland: Oh God, there's tons of ladies that have influenced my style. I love Ruth Brown and Koko Taylor and Etta James and Bessie Smith, Big Mama Thornton. But when I grew up, I never really wanted to sound like them. I wanted to sound more like Otis Redding. I like those strong, masculine, rough voices—Otis, Sam Cooke, Sam Moore, O.V. Wright. That is what I wanted to sound like. I'm still working on that. That is why I like Tina Turner so much; she's got that rough sound. But I have many different types of influences. It is strange, but I like a lot of rock 'n' rollers. The Rolling Stones and the Beatles I loved. Led Zeppelin I just got into—when I first heard Robert Plant I thought that Led Zeppelin was a big black gospel singer. I met him recently in Europe and I told him that, and he didn't slap me or anything. People in the hotel were saying, "Robert Plant is looking for you." And I'm thinking, Robert Plant is looking for me? I got all weirded out, and then I finally met him and he was the sweetest guy. I met Bill Wyman during the same time. We were on an elevator in Belgium and Bill Wyman said, "Oh, I know you." And I said, "Oh, I know you too." He started laughing, and we had the best conversation.

I respect those guys so much—Led Zeppelin and the Who and the Stones—because they got people listening to the blues. They did a lot for a lot of blues artists, and I appreciate that.

Elwood: *Otis is one of my favorites. What is it about him that people love so much?*

Copeland: He was amazing. What was so great about those guys—Otis Redding, Sam Cooke, any of them—is that when they opened their mouths, you knew it was them. Even the groups—the Temptations, the Four Tops, the Persuasions—you knew who you were listening to. Now people all sound alike. I don't listen to the radio anymore except when I listen to blues shows.

I met Carla Thomas; she walked up to me and said, "Hi, Shemekia, my name is Carla Thomas." And I said, "Oh, Carla Thomas, I love you so much. Then I said, "I'm so mad at you," because she got to sing with Otis and be with him. He died when he was 26 years old. I wish he hadn't gone so soon, because he'd still be very young and I could be singing with him.

Elwood: *How were the audiences in Europe when you toured over there?*

Copeland: Great. Europe is a really great place for the blues. People just love it—if you have 5,000 people in a city, 3,500 are going to be at the show. You're in Germany and you're singing in English, and they are singing along with you. I was there for about five weeks and I did like 11 countries, and every country was better than the last.

Elwood: *You're only 21, but you're already on your way to a great career. What advice do you have for other young women who want to follow that same kind of road?*

Copeland: I always say that 99.5% of everything I've ever learned in my life comes from listening. When I talk to Ruth Brown, I take in every word that she says and live my life by it, and I did the same thing when my father was alive. And you shouldn't let things get to your head, because you can come down that ladder just as fast as you go up. I was talking to Keb' Mo' yesterday, and through all of his accomplishments and however long he's been doing this, he is just a great guy. Ruth Brown has won a Tony Award and Grammy, and she is the most down-to-earth person you'll ever want to meet. But you have all of these people walking around with chips on their shoulders being all bitter and cruel—I figure, why? You can get so much further just being a decent person, a real person.

Elwood on the Air: Mississippi

HOUR: 00/25
AIRDATE: 6/17–18/00
WRITER: ANDY VALVUR

[FX: Car on the highway, blues tune in the background]

[FX: Police siren in the distance]

ELWOOD: Oh, man . . .

[FX: Knocking on plastic]

That is the last time I buy a radar detector from Billy the Bargain. Man I bet this is going to be a shake down. Uh . . . hi officer . . . I was . . .

COP: [southern accent]: License and registration please.

ELWOOD: Uh . . . yes sir . . . you see I was . . .

COP: You know how fast you were going?

ELWOOD: Uh gee . . . well . . .

COP: This license is expired, Mr. Blues.

ELWOOD: Yea well . . . you see I was gonna renew it before I left.

COP: It expired last year.

ELWOOD: I've been kinda busy.

COP: Mmm hmm.

ELWOOD: Look, I'm in kind of a hurry . . . so if you could just give me the ticket . . .

COP: What's in the trunk?

ELWOOD: [quickly] Nothing. Spare tire . . . CD's, recording equipment.

COP: I see you've been shopping at Billy the Bargain's.

ELWOOD: Excuse me? You know Billy the Bargain?

COP: Heck Elwood, I used to be a cop on the South Side.

ELWOOD: Of Chicago?

COP: Is there another South Side? What are you doing in Mississippi son?

ELWOOD: I'm going to the hill country to interview the North Mississippi Allstars.

COP: For The House of Blues Radio Hour?

ELWOOD: Why . . . uh . . . yeah? You know the show?

COP: Heck, Elwood. I wouldn't miss it. You're going to love the Allstars. Fine bunch of boys. We're real proud of 'em down here.

ELWOOD: I know, I got 'em on my CD player.

COP: Well, you best not be late.

ELWOOD: [relieved] Yes sir. Oh, man . . . I thought this was gonna be a shake down.

COP: Aww, Elwood, you got us Mississippi folks all wrong.

ELWOOD: I sure do.

COP: Now git. And do me a favor . . .

ELWOOD: Yes sir?

COP: Get your license renewed.

ELWOOD: You bet.

COP: And one more thing . . .

ELWOOD: Name it.

COP: Turn up the CD. Let me hear some o' them Allstars.

ELWOOD: My pleasure!

[Song: "Shake 'Em On Down"—North Mississippi Allstars]

LUTHER DICKINSON
Honor Thy Fathers

> *"The boogie's in and it's got to come out."*

Blues is a family affair for Luther Dickinson. His father is an important player and producer in the Memphis music scene, and with brother Cody he leads the North Mississippi Allstars, a band that includes scions of the region's blues royalty. Equally at home in juke joints and on the jam-band circuit, the brothers carry on a unique blues tradition while cultivating the Allstars' kaleidoscopic blend of roots and modern styles. Hailed as one of his generation's best guitarists, Luther talked with Elwood in 1999 after the release of the Allstars' debut album, *Shake Hands with Shorty*.

Elwood Blues: *Your band has a different take on the blues. Where does that come from?*

Luther Dickinson: The North Mississippi Allstars come from that special little place in Mississippi just south of Memphis, east of the Delta. It's the hill country, and up in the hills they've got a different type of blues that's just been coming up in the last 60 years or so. You got Mississippi Fred McDowell—he goes further back—but these days you got Mr. R.L. Burnside and Junior Kimbrough, just recently passed, and Othar Turner. [Turner died in 2003.] Those guys got this style of blues that's different than the Delta or Chicago blues. And we grew up influenced by that. My brother and I were just playing whatever type of crazy rock 'n' roll we would play as we were growing up, and we still do, man. We'd play that style of blues, and it turns into rock 'n' roll with me.

Luther Dickinson and his best friend catch up on old times.

Elwood: *How'd you get into the blues?*

Dickinson: Our father, Jim Dickinson, played with a lot of great musicians and grew up checking out the blues resurgence in Memphis, with people like Furry Lewis and Bukka White and Sleepy John Estes. And there was Mississippi John and Mississippi Fred McDowell. We grew up listening to our father's record collection. He had a band, Mud Boy and the Neutrons, and they did the same thing we do—played rock and psychedelic harmonized versions of old blues songs that they liked. And then we got older and became friends with Cedric Burnside and Garry Burnside and some of the musical families around the hills. It's been a natural progression for us.

Elwood: *Do you remember the first time you heard the blues?*

Dickinson: Wow, we grew up hearing the stuff. The first music that really struck home to me was watching our father's band in Memphis. Our dad was playing piano and singing. Lee Baker, the guitar player, was a great idol of mine. I wanted to play like him so I could play with my dad.

Elwood: *Other than your dad, who's the first blues musician you saw live?*

Dickinson: It would be Furry Lewis. Oh, man, he was great. Furry Lewis influenced everybody in the Memphis scene from the '60s on. We're still influenced by him. He was proud of being from Memphis. He lived on Beale Street, and that was his scene.

Elwood: *Tell us more about the Burnsides.*

Dickinson: We live about 15 minutes apart—we live in Independence, they live out in Chulahoma. R.L., he's the living king of the north Mississippi guitar. He's got those old songs—he and Junior and Fred would all do the same songs, just different versions. And R.L., he's got the whole family—he's got Wayne, an awesome guitar player, and he's got Cedric playing drums with him, and Garry Burnside, who's a great bass and guitar player. Junior Kimbrough taught him by hand. Garry played on all of Junior's records, and he plays in our band a lot.

Kenny Brown, the great Mississippi guitar player who plays with R.L. Burnside, we owe a lot to him—well, I do. He took me out on my first road trip, and Kenny and Cedric and I would open for R.L.—I got to sit in with R.L. in the second set. I was about 22, and that was a life changer. I learned how to survive on the road and take care of business, and I saw the great potential for our music for the audiences in other parts of the country. We said, man, there's something going on down here.

Elwood: *When you go home do you sit in at the clubs?*

Dickinson: Junior Kimbrough's son still keeps his famous juke joint open. Whenever we're home and get a chance, we go down there and sit in and hang out and shoot pool and drink beer. It's happening, man. And the cool thing is, you've got all the Ole Miss girls coming in there. These are girls who can't even get into clubs, they're like 18 and they're all rolling into Junior's. He'd love it.

Elwood: *What was it like growing up around the studio with your dad?*

Dickinson: It's been great growing up around him and watching him and all his friends and different people he works with play and interact. That's how we learned to be musicians. The older guys like our father were the first-generation rock 'n' rollers, and they're still rocking—the Allman Brothers are still out there doing it. It's like Louis Armstrong—you can do it all your life. You get better with age.

Our dad grew up in Memphis, and he remembers before rock 'n' roll, when people were searching for something, a sound that they would hear in R&B or whatever. And then he watched the whole Elvis thing. He saw Howlin' Wolf in person and the Memphis Jug Band, and Stax Records and that whole thing. He led an incredible musical rock 'n' roll life. He plays piano and guitar and produces a lot. He played piano on Dylan's last record, *Time Out of Mind*. That was a dream come true for him.

Elwood: *You've done some producing yourself.*

Dickinson: I produced two records on Othar Turner and the Rising Star Fife and Drum Band, the first being *Everybody Hollerin' Goat*, which *Rolling Stone* declared in the top five blues records of the '90s. That was great for Othar; he was like 91 at the time and it was his debut record. The new one is Othar Turner and the Afrosippi All Stars, *From Senegal to Senatobia*. It's a group of Senegalese musicians with Othar and his family—African folk primitive modernism. It's bad. We've got Morikeba—he's a true griot from Senegal—playing the kora, a 22-string harp instrument.

Elwood: *How does that mix with American blues?*

Dickinson: The only key was to get the harp tuned to the fife. Othar plays a cane fife, and each fife's a different key. And Morikeba tunes to open G naturally. So we had to get him tuned down, and once we did that, the party was on. We had bottleneck guitar, cane fife, and kora with 11 percussionists behind us, and then all of Othar's daughters and granddaughters singing gospel harmony.

Elwood: *Tell me about the North Mississippi Allstars' first album.*

Dickinson: Let me see if I can describe a little something of the vibe we try to capture. Imagine a Sunday night in Mississippi, and you're driving down the highway and you're going to the juke joint. You don't know quite where it is, but then you see the cars and you get out, and you hear the bugs and you feel that white grass at your feet. You're walking in, you hear the music, you're coming closer, and you pay your bucks. Then you get in there, get you a cold beer, sit back, and the music's just grooving. You've got a couple of drummers kicking it, and everybody's dancing, just swinging to the music. Elwood, you know how it goes. There's a guitar, they'll be playing a Junior Kimbrough song, and they'll be keeping it right, old-fashioned old-school style, and then towards the end of the song, they might break out, like, Jimi Hendrix feedback. It's just modern Mississippi boogie, man. The boogie's in and it's got to come out.

Elwood: *Did you write the songs on the album?*

Dickinson: No, those are all old traditional hill country songs. It's a tribute to this tradition—a combination of oral tradition and musical tradition. Say a song like "Po Black Maddie"—Fred McDowell did it in the '60s and '70s, Junior Kimbrough did it, R.L. Burnside does it, Othar Turner does it. Everybody does it, each with his same variations on the same lyrical theme. It's like a folk oral tradition with different music and different arrangements and styles underneath it. We just took that and did our own version. It goes back to Elvis. When the white boys play the blues it turns into rock 'n' roll. But those older lyrics are really hard to beat. People don't talk like that anymore.

Elwood: *Who are your favorites on guitar, your main inspirations?*

Dickinson: Man, I listened to everybody over the years. I've taken a lot from the class guys from the '60 s like Duane Allman and Jimi Hendrix, and then taken stuff from Mississippi Fred McDowell, Mississippi John Hurt, and R.L. Burnside. I've learned a lot from Memphis guitar players, too, like Charlie Freeman and [Mabon] "Teenie" Hodges and Roland James—all those classic Memphis guys. And I just rolled it all up into my vocabulary.

But like Duane says, you've got to get out there and hit that note. I just try to put everything together and play my best every night.

Elwood: *What's your main guitar? Do you have one?*

Dickinson: I've got over 20 guitars, man. I've got a lot of old Harmonys and Kays and Silvertones. But I got this great Gibson new, an ES-175, that's one of my main guitars. I play in three different tunings: standard tuning, open Spanish *G*, and natural open *B*. So I keep three guitars with me at all times, because we'll be switching up.

Elwood: *Do you have any advice for young musicians?*

Dickinson: Man, you've got to play, play, play. Practice, practice. And listen and be sympathetic to the music and learn what other people have to teach you, as opposed to trying to push your own thing. It's great now, because you can go to the record store and get some of the oldest, most obscure, primitive stuff. If a young cat was going to study the blues, I'd say go back to the beginnings, way back: Elmore James, Jimmy Reed, early Chess recordings, Muddy Waters, Howlin' Wolf, Bo Diddley, and further back to Blind Willie Johnson, Robert Johnson, the classics. Because it just doesn't get any better than that old stuff. Just stay with it and give it all you've got. I always tell cats, the guitar will be their best friend. It's like Fred McDowell says, you might be feeling bad or lonesome, and you pick up your guitar and play a piece, and it will pacify your mind.

MICHAEL HILL
New York State of Mind

> *"You can't escape from the blues whether you listen to the music or not."*

Michael Hill's solo career blossomed with 1994's *Bloodlines*, but the roots of his rock-inspired blues style had been planted in the '70s during sessions for acts like Little Richard and Carla Thomas. Hill's guitar idols Jimi Hendrix, B.B. King, and Buddy Guy deeply influence his sound, as does the socially consciousness songwriting of Bob Marley. The Bronx-born Hill helped establish the Black Rock Coalition, a New York collective of musicians and artists. Elwood talked to Hill right before the 2001 release of his fourth album, *Larger Than Life*, which features Living Colour guitarist Vernon Reid.

Elwood Blues: *Tell us about your background. How did you get into music and the blues?*

Michael Hill: I grew up with a lot of music around me. My mother played piano and sang, and her mother did, too. My father had a great record collection, and I have two sisters and a brother with whom I started a band in '73. We were playing funk and R&B and all kinds of stuff. But ultimately I started playing the guitar because of Jimi Hendrix, and that led me to the blues. So my deepest connection to the instrument has always been through the blues.

Elwood: *A lot of guys your age point to Hendrix as their main influence.*

Hill: For me, Hendrix was a magical but organic culmination of R&B,

One part Hendrix, one part Marley, two parts B.B. King,
Michael Hill's blues blend is 100% original.

rock, and blues, and he embodied the combination of those influences. He was an amazing player and performer, but it was his songwriting that made him so special. I was fortunate to see him play five times, so he's where it all started for me with the guitar.

Elwood: *How did Hendrix lead you to the blues.*

Hill: During the late '60 s and early '70s we got to see all the people who Bill Graham brought into the Fillmore East. Around that time he was mixing shows up—you'd have the Jefferson Airplane and Albert King and that kind of thing. My classmates and I liked Hendrix and Clapton, and they always talked about Buddy Guy and B.B. King and those folks. So of course we wanted to know about that.

Elwood: *For all those people who never got to see Hendrix play, tell us about your experience at the Fillmore East.*

Hill: It was really exciting. Paul, my best friend at the time, and I went both nights to the Band of Gypsys' late shows. The first night my date and I were in the second balcony, and there was a guy in the aisle having a bad trip. She got really upset, and she wanted to leave—they're playing "Them Changes" as we're walking out of the Fillmore East. I was a little annoyed. The next night Paul and I wound up getting down to about the seventh row. The music was new at the time, and Hendrix also did his classics. He was playing with Buddy Miles, and Miles had the big foot—the groove was so deep. Hendrix's playing on the *Band of Gypsys* album is different than on his other stuff, largely because of the funk and the groove. Powerful night—the intensity and the energy were just amazing.

Afterward, Paul and I stood outside the door of the Fillmore East—it was freezing cold. Eventually Hendrix came out. He had on this really light shirt, but he stood there signing autographs for everybody. He was such a humble and generous guy. He signed my program, and it came out kind of light. So he said, "Is that all right?" And I'm like speechless. Needless to say, I'll never forget that.

Elwood: *After you saw Hendrix, who are some the other players you saw and who influenced you?*

Hill: I saw Buddy Guy pretty early on in a club, and I saw B.B. King at a concert at Hunter College. At the Fillmore East I saw Jeff Beck with his original group with Rod Stewart. All three of those guys are really deep influences on my playing and my love of the guitar, especially B.B. and Buddy—you have the singing and the whole thing. Guitar playing is nice, but the singing and writing are crucial, and you have to take all of it seriously. Serious fun, I guess it is.

Elwood: *You've recorded with B.B. How did that come about?*

Hill: I was blessed. Two friends of mine, Jon Tiven and Vernon Reid, produced some songs for B.B. King, and I was invited to be the rhythm guitarist on this session. We did four songs, and one of them wound up on his box set. Then we were invited to the session where he came and did his guitar and vocal parts, and he was exactly what you would hope one of your heroes would be like. He was so gracious and eloquent. He's telling stories and it was amazing. It was really a blessing to be in his company.

One year my band was the house band for the press conference for a blues festival in New York, and B.B. King and Buddy Guy both sat in with us. Hey, that's absolute heaven. It was intimidating, but they're both so gracious we had a great time. It's something you never forget.

Elwood: *You've also opened for another legendary blues man, Luther Allison.*

Hill: That was another one of those blessings, and I actually had the opportunity to meet him for a few minutes. This was not very long before he passed away. We just got to speak briefly, and what he said to me was so inspiring, just his one sentence. He was a very intense guy. Bruce Iglauer [of Alligator Records] took me up to meet him in his dressing room. You know, Luther was very intense, and he's getting ready for the show, and he doesn't like to meet people, maybe. Luther came out and said he had heard our set, and he looked at me dead in the eye and said, "Keep on doing what you're doing—let them know where we're coming from." I was like, whoa—you got it. That's one of the things that keeps me doing this, regardless of the ups and downs.

Elwood: *We're at a time when so many players are passing on, not only the guys who laid the foundation, but second-generation blues men like Luther Allison.*

Hill: Yes, you've got to get out there and see folks. They're coming right to your neighborhood, but no one on TV is necessarily telling you that they're there. It's worthwhile to seek them out.

Elwood: *People talk about a Chicago sound and Mississippi sound. Is there a New York sound?*

Hill: There's a certain energy that is typical of New York, and there's also a blending of flavors in our music, the different rhythms that we've all grown up with because everybody in my band has played in funk bands and reggae bands and rock bands and wedding bands and everything. All the music that we love is connected to the blues fusion bands. I try to write in a way that those seasonings are a part of the music and part of the spirit of the blues.

Elwood: *You mentioned reggae; did you ever get a chance to see Bob Marley?*

Hill: Oh, yeah. I was walking through Central Park one day on the way to a vocal lesson after work. They used to have concerts there, and I asked someone, "Who's playing tonight?" and the guy said, "Bob Marley and the Wailers." I had been reading about reggae and Bob Marley, but I didn't know what reggae was, really. There are certain places in the park where you could stand on a rock and see into the venue. They happened to be doing their sound check at the time, and they went into "Slave Driver." I was like, whoa. I went to the phone, called my vocal coach, and said, "I've got to work late. I won't be able to come." Then I grabbed a ticket and saw Bob Marley for the first time. A powerful, powerful performer, great songwriter. He's one of my inspirations in terms of lyrics and just as a band—their dynamics, their whole thing.

Elwood: *There's a serious connection between blues and reggae.*

Hill: Absolutely. Reggae has roots in R&B, and R&B has roots in the blues. So all of this stuff is so connected. The blues is one of the foundations of American culture and definitely of African-American culture. To be African-American, the blues are in your blood, but besides blues music there's also literature, there's poetry. You can't escape from the blues whether you listen to the music or not.

Elwood: *You're involved in the Black Rock Coalition. Tell us about that.*

Hill: It started out as an advocacy group for black musicians who wanted to play original music that didn't necessarily fit into the music-industry pigeonholes. Vernon Reid was one of the founders. It encourages people to play what's in their hearts. It didn't have to be smooth R&B—though that's great and hip-hop is great—but even if it doesn't sound like what's on the radio, you still should be playing music from your heart. In all the music that we really love and is the foundation of music we love, people were playing from the heart. So that's what the Black Rock Coalition is all about. We would do shows in schools, and we had seminars and meetings on aspects of the industry. The BRC has also done two compilation albums that each had ten bands doing original music. Everybody in my band actually now I've met through the Black Rock Coalition. And it's not just black folks and not just musicians either—it's all kinds of people and writers and poets—it's a good thing.

RICK HOLMSTROM

L. A. Stories

> *"I was green as a pool table*
> *and twice as square."*

Growing up in Fairbanks, Alaska, Rick Holmstrom lived about as far away as is possible from the Delta, Chicago, Austin, or any other U.S. locale associated with the blues. But after he landed in Southern California, Holmstrom dived into a blues scene that included players like Johnny Dyer, whose roots go right to the Delta. In addition to playing with the likes of Dyer, harp man William Clarke, he ultimately became an integral part of Rod Piazza and the Mighty Flyers. Holmstrom brought his purist yet creative guitar style to two well-received albums. When Elwood talked to Holmstrom in 2002, he had gone in a new direction by using hip-hop sampling techniques to create the engagingly eclectic *Hydraulic Groove*.

Elwood Blues: *You grew up in Fairbanks, Alaska, which is not exactly known as a hotbed of blues. How did you get into this music?*

Rick Holmstrom: My father was a deejay. He was a real big roots-rock fan and a little bit of a blues and R&B fan, so I was always around the music. As a kid I listened to all the rock bands that were popular, the Rolling Stones, Led Zeppelin. And my father would always point out, hey, that's nothing but a Chuck Berry lick, or that's just Muddy Waters regurgitated by some long-haired guys. And then my dad took me to see Chuck Berry when I was about 12 years old, and that really twisted my head around. Chuck was on fire, and he had a great band backing him.

I bought a little Silvertone Les Paul copy in the mid-'70s—it was terrible. I was probably 10, 12 years. I knew a few chords here and there, but I wasn't

Musical time machine: Rick Holmstrom is taking the blues of the past into the digital age.

all that accomplished at it. When I moved down to California to go to college, some school friends had a band that basically played beer parties, and they convinced me to get into the band. That's when it really all started.

Elwood: *Who did you listen to when you were getting into the blues?*

Holmstrom: I was constantly going back further and further and further. I remember buying my first T-Bone Walker cassette tape and listening to it on the way home and realizing, man this is where Chuck Berry got his stuff. Then you realize T-Bone Walker was influenced by people like Blind Lemon Jefferson or Count Basie's band, and you start piecing it all together, what it all means, how it happened. One of the things that I learned about all of these people who are originals and who had their own identifiable sound, was that they mixed and matched old things and new things. And at the time, what they were doing was unusual, maybe even odd. T-Bone was the guy who jumped out in front with the guitar and did splits and played behind his head way before Jimi Hendrix was even a gleam in his father's eye. He totally tore the whole scene apart.

Elwood: *What T-Bone Walker tunes jumped out at you?*

Holmstrom: Just about anything that he did early on, because here was this guy bending strings and playing the guitar as the lead instrument. And he's playing and singing at the same time. I don't think there was anybody that was doing it quite like that. Lonnie Johnson, Big Bill Broonzy maybe were starting to mess around with it. But T-Bone really solidified it. I just love songs like "Party Girl" or "Two Bones and a Pick" or "Strollin' with Bones."

Elwood: *When did things start happening for you in your music career?*

Holmstrom: My big break happened when I met William Clarke—he was a harmonica player and singer who eventually recorded numerous albums for Alligator. He passed away a few years ago. I met Bill in 1987 and started going out to see him and sitting in with his band, and then in late 1988 or early 1989 I started touring with him. I'm telling you, I could barely play—I was green as a pool table and twice as square. I was a good rhythm guitar player, and I think that's why he hired me. It took me a year or so before I was up to speed. I joined the band right before he signed with Alligator, and then things really took off for us. We were on the road a lot, and I learned a lot about playing.

Elwood: *What kind of things did you learn from him?*

Holmstrom: I think the biggest thing I learned from Bill Clarke came about because he never rehearsed. It was always seat-of-the-pants, so you couldn't fall back on some stock arrangement or just say, "Hey, I played my part." You had to listen to what he was playing and react to it, and that's the way I learned how to play. Looking back on it now, it was incredibly stressful. I was trying to keep up with him, and I didn't know what he was going to do, and he wasn't always the easiest guy to communicate with about what he was thinking. But that taught me how to think on my feet. By the time I left his band in 1991 I was on my way—I had learned in a super-quick time how to play this music.

Other people that mentored me were Junior Watson, the original guitar player in Rod Piazza's Mighty Flyers, and Smokey Wilson. I played and recorded with him. I learned an awful lot, of course, from Johnny Dyer, who I did two records with.

Elwood: *Johnny Dyer grew up in Muddy Waters's hometown of Rolling Fork, Mississippi, on the Stovall plantation.*

Holmstrom: Right. He grew up around Muddy and Muddy's family. To me he's the closest living thing we have, especially vocally, to Muddy. He moved out here to Los Angeles when he was 18 or 19 and played on the scene for a while. Then he had a family and started driving trucks—he drove a truck for 30, 35 years to put his kids through school. When I met up with him in the early '90s he was just getting ready to retire from this truck-driving job, so it all worked out perfect for us. I played with him for a few years and recorded two records on Black Top. Johnny is still one of my best friends.

Elwood: *It's great to be able to connect with the older generation of players.*

Holmstrom: It is amazing. When I played with William Clarke, we went over to Holland to the Utrecht Festival and we got to back up Jimmy Rogers, who played with Muddy and was an architect of the Chicago blues sound. He's the guy that played all of the cool stuff under Muddy and on his own records. He played a lot of low-note bass lines; Muddy and Jimmy Rogers had this intertwining thing going where two guitars would sound like one giant guitar. It wasn't necessarily a worked-out thing. They played together so long that they just weaved in and out. Jimmy turned out to be a great friend and a great mentor, too. He passed away just a couple of years ago.

Elwood: *What was Jimmy Rogers like?*

Holmstrom: He is the anti-stereotype of what you would think a grizzled old Chicago blues guy would be like. You would think maybe they'd be gruff and drunk all the time or cynical or something like that. Jimmy liked to have a little nip here and there, no doubt about that. But he was a very warm, generous fellow. When I first played with him he took so much time and answered all my questions. I wish I'd had a tape recorder going then, because I probably talked to him for hours before this one gig and then a few gigs after that, too. I don't know how many times that guy must have answered all of these same questions from some young white blues guitar player—you know: "Tell me about Little Walter, tell me about Muddy. How did you record this?" But it never phased him, and he always answered them thoroughly.

The second time I played with him was when I was with Rod Piazza and the Mighty Flyers and we backed him up. I thought I did a good job backing him up, but then Rod came up to me on the break and said, "Hey, Jimmy wants you to play more guitar, man. He wants you to really let loose." I had been playing understated and thinking I had to stay out of his way. What I realized is that those guys want the people in their band playing strong, because it makes them look better. But he was so nice and considerate of a guy that he wasn't going to turn around and yell at me onstage or anything like that. He was going to go through the proper channels. On the next set I got up there and let loose a little bit, and Jimmy's asking me to come over to his room the next day and hang out.

It's a sad thing that so many of the guys are passing away. You really have to wonder what we're going to have, what we're going to be left with, because even the next generation of players is watered down another notch from the original thing.

Elwood: *In addition to Jimmy Rogers and Johnny Dyer, when you went to Los Angeles, there were other players of that generation who had gone out West.*

Holmstrom: I don't know if it's the weather or the economy—maybe it was the defense industry jobs in the '40s and '50s that pulled a lot of guys from Texas and even Chicago. By the time I came around, a lot of them had already left us. But some of them were still around. Willie Dixon was living out here, and you could see Lowell Fulson and Johnny Guitar Watson driving around town in a big Cadillac with JGTRW on the license plate. People don't realize how vibrant a scene Los Angeles has had for years, and how important it was to this music. When people think of blues, a lot of times they're force-fed what some New York City writer tells them is blues—Mississippi stuff, and maybe a little Chicago and a little Texas/Louisiana-type thing. But there's Piedmont blues in the hills of the Carolinas, there's Los Angeles blues, there's great stuff that happened in the Bay Area, and Gulf Coast stuff that was amazing. People owe it to themselves to search that stuff out.

Elwood: *Speaking of Mississippi, a couple of years ago you and your band did a record with R.L. Burnside,* Wish I Was in Heaven Sitting Down.

Holmstrom: Right. We basically went into the studio and recorded the way we normally do, which is all in one room, live, with a lot of funky old little amps and guitars and lots of room ambience. And then they loaded that music into a computer and twisted it around and edited it and monkeyed with it, and turned it into something that still has that funky, greasy edge but sounds a little bit more dance-oriented.

From the day that we recorded that record, I never heard it until the day it came out. And when it came out it just blew my mind. Just the other day we played a set, and then a DJ came on and started playing dance music, and he played "Two Many Ups" by R.L. Burnside. That was great because here you have this music that has the tones and the approach and the feel of blues but has the beat and the drive of a modern dance record. If you can turn people on to blues that way, twist their ear just enough to make them go, I think I'm going to check out R.L. Burnside's new record, then you've done something.

Elwood: *You take that approach on your new album, with loops and samples and various kinds of studio processing, and lots of funky grooves.*

Holmstrom: I'm as big a blues Nazi as anybody. I didn't want to listen to any music that came after Magic Sam died, and that was 1969. I had years where I didn't want to listen to the Meters, didn't want to listen to any funk or soul—I wanted to be so pure in what I was doing.

But I went through that phase, I learned a lot from it, and then I started getting interested in other stuff. If people don't dig it, that's fine. But for every one person who doesn't dig it, I might be able to bring in five who never would have listened to a traditional blues record of mine.

Elwood: *People tend to forget that there was a lot of experimenting on some of the old records they love.*

Holmstrom: I come from a music scene where "retro" is the word. Myself and my peers love this old music so much that sometimes we get a little too caught up in trying to play it so authentically and so correctly, like the last 50 years of modern music never happened. But if you listen to great stuff from Stax or HI Records out of Memphis in the late '60s, early '70s, the bands were twisting it around and getting funky with it. To me, that's still blues.

Elwood on the Air: Thanksgiving

HOUR: 99/48
AIRDATE: 11/27–28/99
WRITER: ANDY VALVUR

[medium office]

FEMALE: Mr. Anderson will see you now, Mr. Blues

ELWOOD: Thank you, ma'am.

[FX footsteps/door opening]

MR. ANDERSON: Good afternoon.

ELWOOD: Good afternoon to you. I'm Elwood Blues.

MR. ANDERSON: Hello Mr. Blues. As you know I am personnel director of this shopping mall, what exactly can I do for you today?

ELWOOD: Well sir, I would like the opportunity to increase the level of Thanksgiving spirit at this fine shopping establishment.

MR. ANDERSON: Thanksgiving spirit?

ELWOOD: Exactly. Have you ever asked yourself why Thanksgiving, as a holiday, simply does not create the excitement that your other major holidays do?

MR. ANDERSON: It hadn't really crossed my mind.

ELWOOD: Think about it. Christmas. Easter. Halloween. They all seem to have a little more magic than Thanksgiving.

MR. ANDERSON: I guess I can see that.

ELWOOD: I believe I know why. Characters.

MR. ANDERSON: Characters?

ELWOOD: Characters. Mascots. Spokes-creatures. I'm talking about your Santa Claus, your Easter Bunny, your Halloween ghosts and goblins.

MR. ANDERSON: And Thanksgiving has no . . . "character"?

ELWOOD: Exactly. That is why I am offering my services to you as the new Thanksgiving character—"Elwood the Thanksgiving Blues Man."

MR. ANDERSON: Thanksgiving Blues Man?

ELWOOD: A lovable holiday mascot that spreads joy and excitement every Thanksgiving. I could wander your mall greeting customers, posing for pictures, and singing Thanksgiving carols.

MR. ANDERSON: And you think this will increase Thanksgiving excitement?

ELWOOD: With all due respect sir—if the Tooth Fairy can get children excited about their teeth falling out of their heads, I believe the Thanksgiving Blues Man can get people excited about Thanksgiving.

MR. ANDERSON: You're serious, aren't you?

ELWOOD: All I ask in return is 50 percent of the profits and full ownership of my name and likeness.

MR. ANDERSON: And these "Thanksgiving carols"—would you write them yourself?

ELWOOD: I would not have to. There are already countless blues songs about food—which is really what Thanksgiving is all about, right? These could be the carols. In fact, I have a small cassette player right here in my briefcase.

MR. ANDERSON: I should have known.

ELWOOD: Take a listen to some of these food songs and see if they put the Thanksgiving sprit in you. Come on, Mr. Anderson, get down with your bad self.

MR. ANDERSON: Well, I don't know . . .

ELWOOD: C'mon. Shake what mama gave ya. That's it. I can see you getting that holiday spirit big time.

[Song: "200 Lbs of Fun"—Candye Kane]

CANDYE KANE
Larger Than Life

> *"You won't see Big Bad*
> *Voodoo Daddy singing*
> *'I'm in love with a boy.'"*

Carrying on the blues-belting tradition of Bessie Smith, former sex worker Candye Kane backs up her bawdy shtick with a powerful voice and a solid feeling for swing and jump blues. The Los Angeles native overcame a tumultuous youth and a failed attempt at country music to emerge as a blues singer in the early '90s, and she has since bolstered her credentials with several well-regarded CDs. Elwood talked with Kane in 1999 after the release of the House of Blues compilation *Essential Women in Blues*.

Elwood Blues: *What's it like to be on a CD with some of the most important names in blues?*

Candye Kane: It's a huge honor. Etta James, Big Maybelle, Big Mama Thornton, Bessie Smith are all idols of mine because they were all big women who sang about sexuality and weren't afraid of being large and sexy. It's a misconception in our culture that you have to be thin and look a certain way to be sexy—or sexually active, even. So it's nice to see strong women like that; it's what brought me to the blues in the first place. I'm proud to be on the CD with all those women.

Elwood: *What was it about Bessie Smith that attracted you to her?*

Kane: Her being a bisexual blues singer was the biggest thing. The way that she was unafraid to have affairs with women and men was pretty

Living large: Candye Kane was seduced by the sound of the blues' biggest and sexiest vocalists.

incredible. Plus her barrelhouse style. She was a big woman but she wasn't afraid to sing songs about being sexy and provocative. I love her version of "You've Been a Good Ole Wagon," which I cover on my new record, *Swango*. It's the same thing with Etta James. I've had the privilege of opening for her probably ten times, and she's been so supportive and wonderful to me. But more than that she just has this wonderful and sexy way of being. And she's a big, big woman. She gets up there and straddles that stool and shakes her butt around and does these things with her mouth that are nasty. My god, I'm no virgin, but when I saw her do some of those things onstage with her tongue it blew me away. She's incredible.

    Elwood: *What about Big Maybelle?*

Kane: I love Big Maybelle, again because of her size and that she was provocative being a big woman. But also her voice is so gripping and incredible. The first time I heard her I was just blown away by the sheer power and energy of her performance. I started thinking about all the things I wasn't and all the things she was—ballsy and brash and huge. So I try to emulate that as much as possible. I didn't want to do her song "Candy" at first because I thought it was too egotistical. But my mother used to sing it to me a different way, more like the Limeliters or something. So when I did it I felt like it was a tribute to my mother and to Big Maybelle, and that was pretty perfect for me.

Elwood: *What was your path into the blues?*

Kane: I was really a country singer because that's what I grew up with. In my household, my parents had a lot of different kinds of music like soundtracks, Bobby Darin, Nat King Cole, and stuff like that. But I grew up singing country because country had a lot of beautiful ballads and that was what I was used to. But it's hard to make a living playing country music at my level, and there's not a huge circuit that you can go and play your own original material in country bars. If you play country music you often have to play covers of the latest Garth Brooks songs. So that was a dilemma for me. Over time I discovered a lot of wonderful singers who were either white and sang blues or who were black and sort of sounded white, like Sarah Vaughan, whose diction was so wonderful. So I started to think that singing the blues wasn't as much of a race issue. I had thought that because I was a white girl singing the blues, it would be an insult to black people, and I didn't know any blues singers that I could ask, "Hey what do you think about this theory."

So when I found singers like Kay Starr and Patti Page who did blues records, I started thinking that it was actually okay. And I think country and blues have a lot in common. Country music was a way for people to sing about heartbreak and have fun on the porch when they couldn't go out and see live music or hear it on a record player. While the blues certainly has much more of a legacy steeped in heartbreak and oppression, it still was a means of entertainment and a means of having a good time with people expressing what they felt. So I think the two are kind of related.

Elwood: *Were your parents musical?*

Kane: Yeah, my dad is a guitar player and he plays flute, and my mom is a music lover—she had a lot of nice records. They were really beatnik parents. My dad was a body painter in the '60s, so I was around a lot of arty people and music and bongo-playing parties and stuff. And like a lot of people I got involved in singing in church and I used to direct the kids choir. So I had a lot of stage experience by the time I started being a real singer.

Elwood: *I understand your stage show is wild and large.*

Kane: I think it's a big show. We do blues and swing, we do some boogie, some Western swing even, some polkas, but the core of it all is at swing, so we try to keep it all really swingin' and colorful and exciting and flamboyant. I would hope that if someone is going to spend ten dollars to see me on a Friday night that I'm not going to be dressed in an old sweater and stretch pants or something—I try to give the people something exciting to look at if they're not dancing.

Elwood: *Swing music lets you sing provocative, racy lyrics.*

Kane: Right. I think that's probably one way that I'm different than some other swing artists—I'm doing what we call "twisted" swing songs. For instance, on my last record, *Diva la Grand*, there was a song called "I'm in Love with a Girl." I say this is the first bisexual swing song ever written— you won't see Big Bad Voodoo Daddy singing "I'm in love with a boy"! At the same time, I think some of the dancers aren't really concerned with the lyrical content of this music. They just want to dance, and that's fine with me. The audience ends up being really eclectic and colorful because of some my songs and their content. I get a lot of lesbians and bikers and a lot of just disenfranchised people at my shows—big women, people who feel like they don't belong along—along with fabulous swing dancers and fabulous blues fans.

Elwood: *And you try to make it all sexy.*

Kane: It's certainly not all sexy. In fact, one of the songs I do live is a song that I used to strip to a long time ago called "I've Got a Right to Cry" by Joe Liggins and the Honeydrippers. When I was a stripper I wasn't very popular, because I used to dance to all the old-timey songs like Joe Liggins and T-Bone—songs I loved to listen to and made me feel like dancing, not songs that necessarily were making the audience feel sexy or horny. I wasn't dancing to Donna Summer and Chaka Khan. I also didn't know you had to be erotic—I thought you just had to be naked. So now I'm not picking songs that are titillating for any particular reason. I just write songs that say what I have to say, and the songs I choose as covers are usually songs that I love the singer on or love the horn arrangement.

Elwood: *Are people starting to discover some of the older artists?*

Kane: Oh, definitely: Louie Jordan, "Five Guys Named Moe" and songs like that; Louie Prima with "Jump, Jive an' Wail"; and all of the big-band people like Buddy Johnson. A few years ago when David Lee Roth had a hit on "Just a Gigolo," I got into an argument with this kid who was trying to tell me that David Lee Roth wrote the song. Now kids are discovering who the original artists were. They're still making a distinction between swing and blues, and that's why I bring up people like T-Bone Walker—there's not that much of a distinction between swing and blues. If you take the same exact blues shuffle and put horns on top of it, they jump up and dance. But if you play the blues shuffle with a guitar starting it, they get confused because they're like, well this is blues—this isn't swing. As the dancers learn more about the beat and feel more comfortable in the groove, they will start dancing to anything and be able to swing to it. It's just a matter of listening to the bass and drums and what's happening.

I would like to see the swing DJs who are teaching dancing use songs by some old blues people who swung, like Johnny Guitar Watson or even Little Willie John or T-Bone Walker. It's just not the big-band Tommy Dorsey thing.

Elwood: *Is swing music and dancing a reaction to what's been happening the last 15 years?*

Kane: When I was growing up sexual experimentation was okay. Now because of AIDS and other diseases people aren't doing the sexual exploration they did in the '60s and '70s, so swing is a wonderful way to use your body creatively, to be close to a person and not necessarily have to be sexual. But anybody who is dancing or watching good swing dancers knows it has a wonderful sexuality about it. It's a healthy way to use your body and express your sexuality without any of the risk involved.

Elwood: *On your new record Sue Beehive Palmer plays the accordion, and she earned a place on the CD booklet.*

Kane: She's my musical partner and my band director, so she is in charge if I hire a new person or something. She's also my accountant. When we first met we found out that we had a lot in common musically. She was a huge Basie and Duke Ellington fan, and she loves a lot of early piano players like Camille Howard and Julia Lee. I love Julia Lee because she did all these dirty old songs like "Snatch and Grab It"—I love that risqué blues. Sue is a popular fixture at the shows because of her big hairdo. It's funny though; sometimes her picture comes out in the paper and they say, "Here's a picture of Candye Kane with a big red beehive." They get confused about who's who, but that's okay.

Elwood: *What songs on the new record stand out for you?*

Kane: I think "200 Lbs of Fun" is a great song—it's obvious I gravitate toward size anthems. I'm not saying that being big is necessarily better, but that being different is okay. If you are 200 pounds or 100 pounds or bald or short or too tall or too dark-skinned or whatever you think your weakness is, all of those things can be sexy in the right setting and at the right time. I try to encourage people to accept themselves.

JOHN MAYALL
Spreading the Word

> "The players that have come through my bands all started right at the very beginning— the roots of the blues."

As a bandleader John Mayall is the Miles Davis of British blues, nurturing such world-class musicians as Eric Clapton, John McVie, Peter Green, and Mick Taylor. In his own right, Mayall has maintained a long and successful career through his abilities as a songwriter, multi-instrumentalist, and crowd-pleasing performer, coupled with his deep knowledge of and love for the blues. Elwood talked to Mayall in 2001, shortly after the release of *Along for the Ride*, an album that featured budding talents such as Jonny Lang along with former Mayall bandmates like Taylor and McVie.

Elwood Blues: *You have been called the father of British blues. What makes the blues so important to you?*

John Mayall: Blues to me has always been a great means of expression because it's such an honest music, and it so correctly represents the things that are going on around us. Music added to the words provides the emotional impact that touches everybody.

Elwood: *How did you originally get turned on to this music?*

Mayall: I grew up in a household where I heard nothing but jazz and blues. My father had a very large record collection of Duke Ellington and Louie Armstrong and countless others. I rarely heard anything that was on

*Master collaborator John Mayall gets his inspiration
from the musicians he plays with.*

the radio in the popular-music vein—everything was blues and jazz when I was growing up. It became a part of me and has been with me ever since.

Elwood: *What instrument did you grab on to first?*

Mayall: Well, we didn't have a piano. I guess I started off with the ukulele, and when my fingers got strong enough I graduated to a guitar. When I was 13 I went to junior arts school, and of course they had a piano there, and I was able to start prodding away at my attempts to emulate people like Albert Ammons and Big Maceo and all those wonderful boogie-woogie pianists.

Elwood: *Who influenced you on the guitar back in those days?*

Mayall: People like Josh White, Leadbelly, Blind Lemon Jefferson, Big Bill Broonzy, Brownie McGhee.

Elwood: *Those are all the fingerpickers.*

Mayall: Yes, though I never did fingerpicking—I lean more towards chords.

Elwood: *Leadbelly is one of my favorites. What attracted you to his music?*

Mayall: His songs were so instantly accessible. In fact, when I first started listening to Leadbelly, his song "Goodnight Irene" became a No. 1 record in England. That was pretty much out of left field. He wrote such a wide range of songs, a vast selection, and I loved everything he did.

Elwood: *You were trained in graphic arts. When did it click that you could make a career of music?*

Mayall: I was 30 when Alexis Korner kicked off the blues movement in England, and that's what I'd been playing all my life, so I figured I would have a shot at it. He put me in touch with people in the London clubs to get me started and introduced me to a few initial musicians, and it rolled on from there. That was back in 1963. In the ten years prior to that, the music you heard in all the jazz clubs was traditional New Orleans jazz. But then Alexis and Cyril Davies brought amplifiers and guitars into the Ealing Club. People had been listening to blues records for a long time, and they just kicked the thing off. It was experimental, but it grew very, very quickly and inspired a lot of people to move in that direction.

Initially there was only Cyril Davies and Alexis Korner's Blues Incorporated, which at that time had Dick Heckstall-Smith on tenor sax, Graham Bond on organ, Jack Bruce on bass, Ginger Baker on drums, and Johnny Parker on piano. It was a great band. It didn't last very long in that particular lineup, but that was the group that kicked things off. They toured the country. Within six months there were so many groups. The Rolling Stones branched out from Alexis's band, and so many other things you've read about in the history books.

Elwood: *So many great players got their starts in John Mayall's Bluesbreakers. How did you originally put together that group?*

Mayall: When I moved from Manchester down to London I didn't know anybody, so it was hard to find the right people at first. Like I said, Alexis introduced me to a few people to get me started. But after a while it settled in with Peter Ward, who was my drummer at art college, and John McVie. He was just out of school and learning the bass, so he became the bass player. We had a succession of guitar players in the beginning. The first years I was working semipro anyway. I had my day job as a graphic designer, and evenings and weekends were devoted to the music.

Elwood: *You went on to bring great guitarists like Peter Green and Eric Clapton into your band. How do you choose players like that?*

Mayall: The players that I picked, regardless of the instrument, are people who know the music and have not come into it overnight and just picked up the latest thing. The players that have come through my bands all started right at the very beginning—the roots of the blues—and studied it way back to the earliest recordings. Blues is like passing the baton in a relay race. One player influences another, and it goes from fathers to sons and so forth and from city to city. And one learns from what has gone before. That's the important thing—all these guys did their homework and found out about the roots of the music.

Elwood: *Your former bandmate Eric Clapton has gone back to more rootsy blues in the past few years.*

Mayall: Well, he dedicated his album *From the Cradle* to some of the songs that were important to him when he was starting out. They're tributes to all those great blues players, most of whom are now gone.

Elwood: *One of the young stars of the blues, Jonny Lang, plays on your new album. Is it fair to compare him to a young Eric Clapton?*

Mayall: Well, not really, because everybody has their own style. I think the people who emerge from the pack are the ones who have a distinctive sound and something really special going for them. On this album I have two of the best, Jonny Lang and Shannon Curfman. She's only 15, but her singing and her guitar playing have maturity way beyond her years. I want to show people that there are absolutely no signs of the blues dying and not being passed on from generation to generation.

Elwood: *You've been doing Otis Rush tunes for a long time, and now you've recorded with him. What has he meant to you as a performer?*

Mayall: He has one of the most amazing voices in blues. I was listening to Otis Rush before there was even a photograph available to know what he looked like. His voice right from the very beginning on those Cobra 78s the '50s were my introduction to him. I've played "So Many Roads" for a long time. When we played Chicago last year, he came to the show, and he loved the way we treated the song, which is so different from the way he'd done it. It was great to have him sing it on the album.

Elwood: *Who are some of the other blues greats you've played with?*

Mayall: John Lee Hooker—when he first came to England in the '60s the Bluesbreakers backed him for his first club tour. We also backed T-Bone Walker and did some stuff with Sonny Boy Williamson and Little Walter and Eddie Boyd—quite a few blues players back then. Of course at that time I met just about everybody; I don't think there are too many blues players that I didn't meet and get to be great friends with. We're all part of the same family. It's just friendship and music, and we're all on the same side trying to spread what we believe in and do it well.

Elwood: *Can you describe what that is, what you believe in?*

Mayall: It's not something you think about. It's something you do. It really is that simple. If you're a painter you paint. You don't think about what you do. You see the colors and you see the brushes and the paint, and you just put it on the canvas. And for a writer or a filmmaker, they have their vision, but if they were to stop to think about what they were doing, maybe they'd freeze up. That's what we do as artists. We don't think about it too much. We express ourselves without analyzing it, and we just get on with it. The results are instant. You play a note, it's instant, and it sparks something which will lead to the next note.

Elwood: *Playing music and being on the road for so many years, how has that affected your life?*

Mayall: I haven't any idea, really. That's what I do for a living. It's also what I would do anyway if I wasn't earning a living from it, because it's pleasure, it's excitement. It's everything that's life itself to me, playing live and going around the world every year. We do at least 15 countries every year, and we play over 100 shows, so we reach a lot of people. For me, being on the road is very exciting. It's that communication directly with the people. A lot of bands who are playing by the book or whatever, it becomes more of a business than a pleasure. Of course, a lot of heartbreak goes on in that. A lot of casualties, too.

Elwood: *How important is your communication with an audience? What kinds of things do you and the audience share?*

Mayall: Well, you wouldn't play the way you do unless there was an audience there, because you feed off of them and they feed off of you. It's an intercommunication thing. The main thing is the music should not be contrived—it should be a reality, and you should treat it like a party. It's that kind of close communication. You can see their faces, and you can see their instant reaction to something you might do or play—it's right there. That's the main difference between recording an album in a studio and going out there and playing it. They are two different means of communication, but both are very valid and equally enjoyable.

Playing music is picking the right people that you enjoy playing with, and you feed off each other's ideas and excitement. One helps to propel the other, so when you get on the stage a certain magic takes place that becomes very physical as well as emotional. That's the thing that audiences pick up on, and the thing we share with the audience.

Elwood: *Do you think the audience for the blues is getting bigger?*

Mayall: The audiences have grown, definitely. There is a great consciousness about the blues right now, and there has been for the last five years at least. The prominence of people like Eric Clapton in the pop-rock arena and the Stones—I'm looking just at the really high-profile people— that helps to spread the word. Places like the House of Blues are spreading all over the place. It's great.

Elwood: *As opposed to somebody like the Stones, who have had almost the same lineup from the beginning, you've had a lot of people coming and going in your band.*

Mayall: Well, not that frequently. You mentioned the Stones: They are one of the only bands who have stayed together for that length of time. It's a slightly different thing. Theirs is a very set and organized production, whereas blues players and jazz players also have a structure, but it's a lot looser. They play what they feel, but it's still based around the discipline of certain tunes you select.

Elwood: *You've had an incredible career. What advice can you give to musicians who are just starting out?*

Mayall: It's so competitive and so tough out there because there are so few venues for people who want to play. So you really have to believe in yourself, no matter what people say. If they don't like you, you shouldn't try to guess what they want to hear. You have to believe in your own material and play it the way you want to play it, and hopefully something good will happen. I would also say that smoking, drinking alcohol, and all these things—and drugs particularly—are going to interfere with what you're doing. If you're clean and sober and dedicated to your music, that's the best way you can possibly go.

Keb' Mo'

Mo' Than the Blues

> *"I went to the university of 'get out there and see what you can do.'"*

Though his shows have an old-timey "one man, one guitar" feeling, Keb' Mo' brings a host of influences to his trad-based style. Born in Los Angeles, young Kevin Moore heard gospel music at home while exploring R&B and other styles on his own. After a string of sideman gigs in the '70s and '80s, Mo' made his solo-CD debut in '94 and has recorded and toured steadily since. He played Robert Johnson in the film *Can't You Hear the Wind Howl?*, and he hosted the public-radio series *The Blues*. Elwood talked with Mo' in 1998.

Elwood Blues: *B.B. King and Joe Cocker recorded one of your tunes, "Dangerous Mood," on* Deuces Wild. *Now that other guys are covering your stuff, do you feel like you have made it?*

Keb' Mo': It's not too bad when B.B. King does one of your songs with Joe Cocker thrown in there, too. But you never feel like you've made it. Once you get to where you saw yourself trying to get to years ago, you are looking at somewhere else to go. I am still trying to make it, working towards what I see now, trying to do a better show, do a better record.

Elwood: *How do you go about writing a song?*

Mo': First thing I need is something to write about. I spent a lot of years practicing writing songs, all different kinds of songs. That kind of educated

Keb' Mo' following his instincts at the New Orleans Jazz and Heritage Festival in 2001.

me into the songwriting process, so now I don't work so hard on the process. But I really work hard in finding something that I can speak about from the heart. Everything has to come out of that connection. If it doesn't come out of that, I don't really do it.

Elwood: *It sounds like you come up with the lyrics first.*

Mo': Well, sometimes. The idea is first. The lyric may not come, but the thing I want to say may come, then the music may came, then the lyrics start to come on that.

Elwood: *Do you ever think, Oh, they are not going to like this one?*

Mo': No. I don't consider that. *I* have to like it. I came up listening to a lot of music, the same music that maybe my audiences came up listening to. I have had the same experience in life. I've lived in the same world and I am a part of it. I am them, they are me. So whatever I write about, if I really feel it, I have more of a chance of connecting than if I go, Well, will they like it or not?

Elwood: *You come across with a lot of confidence when you perform. Is that because you are singing what is true to yourself?*

Mo': I don't know if it is so much confidence. I just like what I do. I have worked at it a long time, and I am still working at it. I really like doing it, and I am confident of the fact that I like it. But I don't know that I am so confident about myself going out there onstage. When you walk out there, the people give you the confidence.

Elwood: *You spend a lot of time on the road. What's that like?*

Mo': You get your guitar out the case, you open your suitcase. You put your guitar back in the case. You open your suitcase, you put your stuff back in. You pack it and you move on. In between that you do an hour-and-a-half thing that is just wonderful, that you really love to do. But everything else around it is pretty tedious, pretty crazy. Getting on the buses, getting on planes, going here and there. You are never in one place for that long, and you never really get grounded. If you don't love music, you will find out pretty quick if you get on the road because you won't make it. You will want to go home.

Elwood: *How did you get turned on to playing guitar?*

Mo': My uncle started teaching me, and then I had several other teachers—mostly guys in the neighborhood and friends and books that were laying around and classes here and there. I kept playing and playing. I didn't go to Berklee School of Music. I didn't go to UCLA. I didn't go to Juilliard. I went to the university of "get out there and see what you can do."

Elwood: *When you were young did you want to be a performer, or were you just playing because you were playing?*

Mo': I just played because I was playing, but I was actually performing. I was in bands from way back in the beginning—when I was 12 I was playing with this little steel band. But I didn't look at it like something I was going to do when I grew up. I didn't know how long it would last. I always had that thing of, well, one day I am going to have to straighten up and get a job and settle down, because everyone was telling me this wouldn't pay the bills and it was dangerous. So I was listening to all that BS, but you know, it worked out. I was very fortunate.

Elwood: *Were your parents supportive of your playing?*

Mo': Yes, they were as supportive as they knew how to be, especially my mother. She got me out of trouble when I got in trouble and made sure I was eating. She was the one who got me into music in the first place. She asked me did I want to get into music, and I told her no, and she said, "What? Well, you are going to get into it anyway." I got into it and I loved it.

Elwood: *Do you remember seeing a performance that blew you away and made you think, Hey, I want to do this?*

Mo': Maybe the Temptations at the Forum—I don't know. I was probably 30 before I saw somebody that really made me want to do it. I always liked the people in the background instead of the big star guy out front—I wanted to be the guy playing the guitar in the band. In my younger days I really liked David T. Walker. He had several albums out [in the late '60s–mid '70s], but mostly he was a session player—a premier kind of session player. If you ever listen to the Bobby Womack *Poet* album, David T. Walker is all over it. I tried to get into Jimi Hendrix, but I am just not a Jimi Hendrix kind of guy. It is hard to imagine him playing on a session—his style of playing would just be too big. But guitar players like Wah Wah Watson, even Ray Parker, Jr.—they had the art of ensemble playing down to a science.

Elwood: *Who did you see when you went out to hear music?*

Mo': I liked the guys that played in the clubs, the chitlin circuit cats—that is where my stuff comes from. I liked names that you don't know—Vernon Garrett and Charlie Tuna. Jimmy the Preacher, Doc Simco. I wouldn't go to big shows because I was always trying to get a gig on those nights—I was lucky I had a gig and wasn't going to pop 18 bucks or 20 bucks to go see someone play. I listened to their records instead.

I liked to take a record and follow the guitar or guitars all the way through, see what the guitar player was doing in the background. I paid attention to everything going on: the recording processes, the instruments they were playing, who was playing, why they were playing, how many guitar players were on the session, why they were on the session—what was going on behind, not up front. I never really got into one person.

Elwood: *Is there one player, though, who inspired you more than anyone else?*

Mo': The guy who inspired me the most would have to be Taj Mahal. He is a real blues man. He was doing it when it wasn't hip. Taj is more than a blues man, but when it comes down to the blues he has it down, he understands it. He is it. When I focus on the blues, I am focusing on Taj Mahal. But I pick my spot for people that I like. Like James Taylor—I like his songwriting, and I like Robert Johnson's songwriting. I like David T. Walker's guitar playing. I like Robben Ford's guitar playing, and Larry Carlton's.

Elwood: *Your slide playing is fantastic. What makes you decide whether you're going to play slide on a certain song?*

Mo': The song tells you, the moment tells you. And you know your instruments. You were at the store, you bought them, you know what all your gear sounds like. So when you hear the song, you just know what to do. It is like picking a microphone, like knowing which channel you are going into on the board. Maybe you don't know that, Elwood—you got engineers.

Elwood: *What's that guitar you use that sounds like a National Steel?*

Mo': I am playing a guitar made by a guy named Larry Pogreba in Lyons, Colorado. It's an aluminum-body guitar with an Oldsmobile hubcap on the front and a resonator. He brought it to me in Boulder, Colorado, and I started playing it and just loved it. A lot of times people bring me handmade guitars to see, but this one actually I bought.

Elwood: *Who did you listen to for vocal delivery?*

Mo': That's a hard one because I've always liked the real smooth crooners. I really like Bebe Winans. I love James Ingram. His voice fits everything—whatever it does it sounds great. I listen to singers like Donny Hathaway,

Stevie Wonder—real singers. I didn't really think of myself as a singer because when I thought of voices, I thought of those voices. So I listened to B.B. King, Son House—people who were more accessible, because I don't have a big range.

Elwood: *James Ingram has that jazzy feel, Stevie Wonder has the gospel flavor, and it all shows up in what you do. We say you are a blues guy, but you are really a musician, right?*

Mo': Well, I am working on it. I am all my influences, and the blues is a major influence in my music. But everything else is there too. I am not really killer at anything. I just take the little bits of everything that I do and put it all together, and it comes out to be Keb' Mo'.

Elwood: *What is it about Son House that grabs you?*

Mo': You have to listen to Son House for yourself. Put on "John the Revelator" or "Preaching the Blues." If it don't hit you, well, that is all right. But it is the real thing. Absolutely. He is one of the founders. When he was doing it, it was like being Usher or somebody—the latest thing in terms of the blues. He was plowing the fields for pop music to be what it is today. That is like the dirt. That is the fertilizer, the stuff that all the green stuff grows out of. That is my Son House.

Elwood: *What is it about the blues that grabs ahold of people?*

Mo': Because it is real. It doesn't just happen with the blues—it happens in any music around the world. But the blues is earthy, the soil. That is a gauge by which I can look at my music and go, is mine real for me? If it is real for me, then I can go, okay. That is the biggest influence the blues has had on me, more so than the songs, the riffs, the way Son House sings or Robert Johnson slides up the neck on his guitar—the biggest thing is that those guys are real and in the moment, and they are being truthful about who they are.

Elwood: *What advice can you give young players who maybe don't see the light at the end of the tunnel?*

Mo': All you have to do is follow the things that you want to do, the urges that push you. Follow your instincts about where you want to go and who you are, and you will never go wrong.

Elwood: *And stick with it.*

Mo': And stick with it. Stay with it, as long as you are feeling it. Your job is to not judge it, not to try to figure out if it is good or bad—I am quoting Martha Graham here—it is only your job to do it, and that is being yourself.

Elwood on the Air: Las Vegas

HOUR: 99/09
AIRDATE: 2/27–28/99
WRITER: MARY WINGS

[FX: music box theme for Mr. Rogers]
ELWOOD as Mr. Rogers—sings: It's a beautiful day in the neighborhood . . .
Could you be my neighbor?
I hope so.
Hi, boys and girls. I'm glad we're together.
Do you know what this is?
{FX: cards being shuffled]
A deck of cards. Can you say aces high? I knew you could.
And do you know what this is? Look carefully at the back. Can you see it?
     Good.
This is a marked card.
Can you say that?
Marked card?
It once got Mr. Blues into an awful lot of trouble.
Now do you know what this is? That's right. Kings over threes.
A full house. Can you say that?
That's right.
That is the hand that lost Mr. Blues his Bluesmobile to Glass Eyed Jack last
     night. But I know luck is with me right now. And I know it's with you, too.
Welcome to the neighborhood, boys and girls.
It is time to play a little card game.
Because this week our neighborhood is—LAS VEGAS!!!!!!
[Song: "Dead Ass Broke"—Big Bill Morganfield]

BIG BILL MORGANFIELD
Blues in His Blood

> *"I really felt the inspiration of my dad because those guys had walked the same road with him for so many years."*

When he was growing up in Florida, Chicago-born Bill Morganfield didn't show any inclination for pursuing the family business. Bill attended Tuskegee Institute and was selling insurance in Atlanta when he heard the news of his father's death, and not long afterward he decided to continue the legacy of his dad—born McKinley Morganfield but better know as Muddy Waters. Elwood talked with Big Bill in 1999 shortly after the release of his W.C. Handy Award–winning album, *Rising Son.*

Elwood Blues: *Do you ever feel pressure to be "Muddy Waters Jr."?*

Big Bill Morganfield: Not really, because all I can do is what I can do, so I do the best that I can and let people call it from there. You know, there's only one Muddy Waters, and there never will be another Muddy Waters. So I don't try to be him. I just try to be myself and do the best I can with my art.

Elwood: *You didn't set out to be a blues man, though.*

Morganfield: I had played basketball at Tuskegee and really was hoping that I would play professional ball, but it really didn't happen for me.

Elwood: *When did you get serious about playing the blues?*

Morganfield: It was about six months after my dad died. I've always tinkered with the guitar, and I decided I really wanted to learn a few of those old blues tunes and put together a tribute to him. I was around 26 or 27.

Son of Muddy Waters, Big Bill Morganfield didn't start playing guitar or the blues until he was 27.

Elwood: *Were you into the blues when you were younger?*

Morganfield: No, not really. R&B was the kind of music I was brought up on. I had heard blues as far as my daddy playing it—we listened to his records. But it was nothing that I was trying to get into. I grew up with Earth Wind & Fire and people like that.

Elwood: *Can you remember when you first heard his music?*

Morganfield: Probably at one of his shows when I was in my mother's belly. It's been a part of me probably for as long as I can remember.

Elwood: *Did you go to his shows?*

Morganfield: Not very many; we couldn't go to those clubs. My dad did a lot of one-nighters throughout the country—he would be on the road 310, 315 days out of a year. So it was hard to go to many of those shows.

Elwood: *Do you remember the first record you bought?*

Morganfield: There's one record I remember buying when it comes to blues. It was called *Muddy Waters Live at Mr. Kelly's.* I saw that thing and decided to grab it up. Oh, it was great, great. I had my little guitar, and I tried to play along with it.

Elwood: *Some of your father's old bandmates played on your album.*

Morganfield: Yeah. I had Willie "Big Eyes" Smith—he's one of the best shuffle drummers in the world; Pinetop Perkins, who's won over ten W.C. Handy awards—he's one of the best blues piano players; Paul Oscher, an underrated harmonica player who's really got that Little Walter style down; and, of course, Steady Rollin' Bob Margolin, who was my daddy's right-hand guitar player for about seven years. Bob has done a masterful job at going back and learning some of that old stuff, then taking that music and moving on with it.

Elwood: *What was it like working with those guys?*

Morganfield: Oh, it was awesome, man. It was like my feet wasn't touching the ground. I really felt the inspiration of my dad because those guys had walked the same road with him for so many years. For it to come full circle and have them help me get my thing started was just an awesome feeling. Those guys laid down incredible rhythms for me.

The album is my tribute to my dad, from son to father. But I tried not to cover any of the obvious tunes, like "Mojo Workin'" and "Hoochie Coochie Man." I think those songs have been covered just about by everybody—you might have even sung "King Bee," Elwood! So I tried to be creative and pick some of the songs that really meant something to my daddy. like "Screamin' and Cryin'," which is one of his favorite tunes.

Elwood: *You've been doing some live work with Bob Margolin.*

Morganfield: Bob had been backing me up on a lot of gigs. He's a caring kind of guy, and he's taken a big interest in my career. He's put his career aside for a little bit to help me and show me what I need to be doing—and what I don't need to be doing. I try to learn all I can from him, and some nights I try to give him a little run for his money. But, you know, Bob has still got the upper hand. Bob and I have a great relationship. We met way back when they were releasing a stamp of my daddy. We started playing guitars together and found that we really clicked when it came to music.

Elwood: *Bob Stroger was another guy on your album who goes back to your father's era.*

Morganfield: Even though he never got a chance to play with my daddy, he was one of the premier bass players in the Chicago area during that era. He played with some of the other greats.

Elwood: *Did your dad ever talk about some of the other people who played with him?*

Morganfield: Well, Jimmy Rogers and Little Walter—those guys used to ride around in the car, my dad say, and talk about the different parts and how they played together. My dad would do one thing and Jimmy Rogers would do another thing an octave higher, and stuff like that. Those guitars worked so close together. Little Walter, he was the innovator of innovators when it came to a harmonica. One day he was in a recording session with my dad, and he started playing some stuff that my daddy hadn't heard, kind of playing really close to his voice like Little Walter was known for—he could play right along with the vocalist. My daddy came back and asked him what kind of shit he was trying to do—you know, that he was messing up his record. So my daddy went back and listened to the record, and he was surprised how well that it did fit. Little Walter was like that. He was an innovator.

Elwood: *What other people were important to your father's career?*

Morganfield: I know that Big Bill Broonzy was instrumental when my daddy first came to Chicago—he took him around and introduced him to the other blues cats in town and really put him on the scene. I always keep that in mind. I added the "Big" part to my name; my daddy didn't do that.

Elwood: *Johnny Winter was another important figure in your dad's life.*

Morganfield: Johnny Winter produced several of my dad's Grammy-winning albums [including *Hard Again* and *I'm Ready*], and I really wanted to meet him. I finally had a chance to get backstage with him and check him out up close and personal. Johnny's a nice guy; we talk about my dad and how we miss him. His guitar playing is totally awesome.

Elwood: *Anyone else you'd like to talk with?*

Morganfield: Eric Clapton and my dad were great friends; that's one of the guys I really want to catch up with. My dad was like a father to him in a lot of different ways. I like that he's doing that old blues stuff and that he's really got it down. *Unplugged* was just beautiful with some of the blues tunes. He put in a tune that my dad wrote, "Rollin' and Tumblin'," and he even did [Robert Johnson's] "Walking Blues." He's got a love for the blues.

Elwood: *Does anyone ever tell you that you look like your dad?*

Morganfield: Well, I was over in Harlem and ran into Nappy Brown, who played many shows with my dad. He was saying, "Oh, you've got that moustache like your daddy." My dad was always known for the moustache—they said he had the best moustache in the business. So I guess it's the lips, you know; I'm forced to cut it a certain way because of the way my lips are shaped.

Elwood: *What other music do you listen to besides the blues?*

Morganfield: If I'm riding in the car I might listen to an R&B station, but I'm really just so deep into the blues that most of the music I listen to is blues. I'm still trying to learn and pick up new things.

Elwood: *What's your advice for someone trying to get into the blues?*

Morganfield: Well, go get some of the Chess recordings of my dad—I've always got to push those records. When you get tired of listening to those go grab some of the recordings of Robert Johnson. That will put you well on your way to understanding where it all came from—it's important to understand the roots of the music. If you are going to play the blues, go back and study the old stuff and then bring it on up to contemporary blues. My dad always said it's really easy to play that contemporary blues stuff, but if you take a man by himself with a guitar and put him in front of some people, that's a true judge of how deep he is into the blues. Just one man.

SUSAN TEDESCHI
Hub City Blues

> *"Sometimes you get so busy
> that you don't realize how
> you feel."*

Singer/guitarist/songwriter Susan Tedeschi brings gospel roots, a the-
ater-honed stage presence, and a love for the blues tradition to her own
brand of hard-hitting blues. Growing up in the Boston suburbs, she sang in
choirs and performed in musical theater at a young age, began working in
club bands in her teens, and then attended Berklee College of Music, where
she studied guitar and joined the resident Reverence Gospel Ensemble. In
1991 she formed her first blues band, and the group went from working in
the Boston blues scene to recording with locally based Tone-Cool Records
and hitting the festival circuit. Elwood talked with Tedeschi after the release
of her first record, 1998's *Just Won't Burn*.

Elwood Blues: *In your mind what's the link between blues and gospel?*
Susan Tedeschi: Singing blues is similar to singing gospel, except that in
blues you can sing about everyday stuff. That was the main draw for me. It's
funny; if you really have a passion for something, you seek it out until you
find it, and when you find it you know. That is what blues and gospel are for
me. Musical theater was great because it gave me an opportunity to emote
as a singer in front of large audiences all the time, when I didn't have band
or any other kind of an outlet. But my heart wasn't totally in it—I didn't feel
real comfortable. But when I sing gospel or soul or R&B or even country,

At home onstage: Susan Tedeschi plays at the Beale Street Music Festival in 2001.

especially blues, I feel like I can really look into myself, and I feel happy singing it.

Gospel is a healing type of music. It is a celebration of life, and everything about it is always good. Even if it is something devastating, there is still a wonderful outcome. So everybody is always way up high. Blues is way up high some of the time—as B.B. King would tell you, blues is not always about being sad. It is not just one thing, it is everything. When you are a human being, you experience lots of things, and that is what blues is. It is about being able to say this person left me or I totally hate living today or I love living today and I woke up and I can't find these shoes and I am late for work. Whatever it is, it is always about something that you deal with every day. And the great thing about blues is that other people in the world have to deal with those things too. It makes everybody realize that we are all the same—it becomes universal music.

Elwood: *It sounds like you enjoy taking that message to people.*

Tedeschi: The great thing about blues is you play a lot of festivals and outdoor gigs during the day, so you get all of these two- and three-year-olds that come up and start dancing. You realize a lot of these kids may have never heard of blues, and it is your responsibility to try to convey to them that this is fun music and a great style of music that nobody should be ashamed of.

It is funny to me that people are actually ashamed of the blues sometimes. I have had people say to me, "I don't play blues—that's simple music." The technical guitar guys say, "Anyone can play the blues," and other people say, "Oh, that is a little too close to home—I don't want to do that"—some people don't want to be personal with music. But singing gospel and blues, I have cried in the middle of a song and not been able to finish. Usually in a gospel song it is because I am just so incredibly happy and just so overwhelmed by the choir or something, and I get on a whole other level and start crying. But with the blues I am so emotional because either I am having a hard time or I just really relate to something I sang—even though I have sung it a thousand times, on that day all of a sudden it really hits home. When I get emotional I can't sing well, but I do know it's a good release for me. Sometimes you get so busy that you don't realize how you feel.

Elwood: *You say that when you are singing you actually feel the word that you are singing. Tell me more about that.*

Tedeschi: With blues, it should happen all the time, but sometimes I have so much on my mind that my band guys know I am not all there. But when I am singing gospel music I know what I am singing about, and I am always very aware of the lyrics. Mahalia Jackson, for instance—to just listen to her for an hour sing about going to Jordan or about her mother or about God, every word that she says gives you goosebumps. And you think, is it really the lyrics or is it the tone of her voice that is making you all of a sudden become very overwhelmed and emotional? I think the emotion comes because she is really believing what she is saying. You cannot sing gospel and fake it. When Mahalia Jackson sings, she is not just like a person—she is like a messenger. And you actually end up remembering the stories because of the way she sings it.

Elwood: *Who was your first big inspiration as a performer?*

Tedeschi: I had been doing musical theater since I was about six years old, but when I really started to think about being a singer, my influences were more from Aretha Franklin and Linda Ronstadt. I remember being 12 and I really liking Linda, but I never knew who Bonnie Raitt was. I was in a country music ensemble when I was about 18 and singing a song called

Susan Tedeschi

"Love Has No Pride." Bonnie recorded it, but I always knew Linda's recording, so that's the cover I was thinking of, though I tried to make it different. And after the show a lot of people were saying, "Wow, you sound like Bonnie Raitt." I was like, who's that? Then I heard her, and Bonnie became an influence later. Stylistically we had a lot of the same influences growing up—my father had some old records by Lightnin' Hopkins and Fred McDowell and Mississippi John Hurt. A lot of that kind of blues influence was also a big influence for Bonnie.

Elwood: *It sounds like you got turned on to blues at an early age.*

Tedeschi: Yes, but it really wasn't until I was in my early 20s that I started to get a hardcore blues influence. I had some friends that were running a blues jam in Boston, and for years they were telling me to come down and sing, because I always sang gospel and I was always inspired by old soul and R&B music. I didn't realize there was so much history to be learned about the blues, how it developed just in the last 100 years. When I finally discovered this whole world, it changed my whole way of singing and my whole life, and it's the reason I do what I do now.

Elwood: *How did you get into playing guitar?*

Tedeschi: I played clarinet for seven years and then I played piano. But I always had a guitar in the house, and I always wanted to play the guitar because that's what all the rock bands did—I think that was the main attraction. Anybody who ever made it played guitar. At the same time, I think I was really drawn to the guitar just because I liked the feel of it. I thought it was a neat instrument. But I didn't understand the technical side of actually getting your hands on it until later on. Also I thought that it would be neat to be known as a female guitar player just because there weren't a whole lot of them then.

Elwood: *Do you remember your first guitar?*

Tedeschi: My dad gave me a Martin that he had bought for $500 years ago. It's a 1970 Double-O 18. One Christmas he put it under the tree, and I said, "Dad, what's your guitar doing under the tree?" He says, "I'm giving it to you." I was so happy. I still have that; it's my favorite guitar. I do a lot of writing on it.

Elwood: *What's your approach to songwriting?*

Tedeschi: I like to write about what I am feeling at the time—and I feel a lot of different ways all the time. A feeling will come over me, and I'll sit down and concentrate on trying to put that feeling into words, with a nice melody that can baste that mood. Blues is at the root in all of my writing. I had a couple of songs that were a little disturbing, a little hardcore, that didn't go on my last record—they are more of what I think of as my '90s blues, like rap and hip-hop nowadays are a certain kind of cultural blues. It's basically kids talking about what is going on in the street. That is what all blues used to be, like when Robert Johnson was writing or when Lowell Fulson writes.

Elwood: *Did you take guitar lessons?*

Tedeschi: Most of the time I learn by watching other people and doing everything by ear. But I did take some lessons from Paul Rishell, and I learned how to play slide and Robert Johnson and a lot of country blues stuff. That was great because he would also teach me the history of a lot of those guys, about Son House, Robert Johnson, Charley Patton—that is exciting stuff. It's fascinating to be able to play the bass line and the rhythm and the lead all at once. And those guys' singing sounds so possessed, so spiritual. We can't even imagine what it was like to live back then. The times were so different, and yet the music is still very strong and very appropriate for the day.

Elwood: *When did you first start playing in clubs?*

Tedeschi: I started playing out when I was 13. I was in a band in Scituate, Massachusetts, which is right on the Atlantic Ocean. We used to play all sorts of covers; whatever the guys learned I would have to learn. Aerosmith was real big and the Stones and Zeppelin and all the classic rock bands. That was a great experience, just to be able to learn how to sing different styles of music. But I never really felt like I was showing myself off in a creative way. It took a long time to get into bands that were more original and out playing in clubs for different reasons.

Elwood: *You've done a lot of performing since then. Have you ever had the opportunity to be onstage with any of your musical heroes?*

Tedeschi: One time I was opening up for Irma Thomas at Johnny D's in Boston. I had played my set, which was about an hour long, and she came in and said, "I'm sorry, I only really heard the last song or two. But you have a beautiful voice. I'd love it if you would get up and sing with me sometime." I was like, "Oh, I'd be honored"—here's one of the most beautiful voices and beautiful women, really. I was totally in awe of her. So her band is up there playing their first set, and we're hanging out over by the ladies' room, and there's a whole bunch of people between us and the stage. She's talking to me and she says, "Do you know Bonnie Raitt?" I was like, well, I don't know Bonnie Raitt, but sure, I know who Bonnie Raitt is. She says, "Well, I just got off the road singing with her, and we did this one song. Do you know "Give Them Something to Talk About"? Oh, sure, of course I know that song. Irma had a wireless mic behind her back, so she pull it out and starts singing, and she says, "Come on, sing it." So the two of us are flipping back and forth singing the verses, and she grabs my hand and walks me up on the stage and the two of us finish a song. Then she says, "Let's do another song—let's make something up. I know you sing gospel." So we started making up a gospel tune. Her band is playing, and she's whispering into my ear an idea she's going to sing about—"sing something about this"—and words are just coming out. The two of us were having a blast, smiling ear to ear. It was great. That's what I live for.

JOHNNY WINTER
Roots & Branches

> **"I bought literally every blues record I could find."**

Fusing his own high-energy style with the tradition of blues masters such as Albert King and Albert Collins, Texan Johnny Winter shook the music world when he emerged in the '60s. Winter went on to forge an electrifying brand of blues-rock—often in collaboration with his brother Edgar—while maintaining a connection with blues roots through his work with greats such as Muddy Waters, who referred to Winter as "my son." Though he has long battled health problems related to his albinism, Johnny was still touring and recording when he talked to Elwood in 2002.

Elwood Blues: *You grew up in Beaumont, Texas, and traveled to Chicago in the early '60s. What was that like?*

Johnny Winter: It was great. Mike Bloomfield had this club for one night a week where he would bring in people who weren't very familiar; he had all kinds of people playing there. I started going to that club on my day off, and I'd sit there and play with Mike. He said I was the greatest guitar player in the world. I couldn't believe that.

Elwood: *You said you went there on your day off. Did you have a day job?*

Winter: No, a night job.

Elwood: *Were you mainly backing up people or did you have your own band?*

Winter: It turned into my band because I was the headliner—I was the lead singer and lead guitar player. I had a friend up there, Dennis Drugan, who had lived in Beaumont; in fact, his father had given me guitar lessons.

Johnny Winter captured the essence of Howlin' Wolf and Muddy Waters and turned it loose on the rock world.

That's how I got to start working in Chicago, because of Dennis. He was my first bass player.

Elwood: *When did you get into guitar, when you were a youngster?*

Winter: I started playing the ukulele at first.

Elwood: *Really? The ukulele?*

Winter: Yeah, I learned my first few chords on the ukulele. I played that for about a year before I got into the guitar. I started playing guitar when I was 11 or 12.

Elwood: *Were you mostly self-taught?*

Winter: Yeah, mostly. I learned a lot of chords from Dennis Drugan's father, Seymour Drugan, who was a jazz guitar player from Chicago. Then there was a country-and-western guy who was really good, Luther Nallie [later with the Sons of the Pioneers]. He was great at using the thumbpick; I learned a lot from Luther.

Elwood: *Besides your brother, did anybody else in your family play instruments?*

Winter: My father played banjo and sax, and he sang in barbershop quartets.

Elwood: *How did you discover blues? It seems like most kids wanted to play rock 'n' roll at that time.*

Winter: Yeah—I started listening to blues on the radio. There were several stations that had blues record shops with mail-order blues records. They'd do it all the time—"all time blues special, $7.98 for ten records," and deals like that. There were several stations down South—one in Nashville, one in Shreveport, one in Del Rio [Texas]. You got to hear all of the new blues records that were coming out. I bought literally every blues record I could find.

Elwood: *Do you still have them all?*

Winter: Yes.

Elwood: *Were there any in particular records that struck you as being really dynamite?*

Winter: Yeah, "19 Years Old" by Muddy Waters and "Somebody Walkin' in My House" by Howlin' Wolf.

Elwood: *You played on four of Muddy's records, including* I'm Ready *and* Hard Again. *What was it like to work with Muddy?*

Winter: He was a great guy. It was easy working with him, because I knew all of his records. He knew what he was doing when he went in and wanted to get it done real quick. I liked to do stuff in one or two cuts, and Muddy never did take more than three at the most—usually it was one or two cuts for everything. He just knew exactly what he wanted to do, and he did it. Meeting the guy was great. He was like a father to me.

Elwood: *Around the time you were working on your first album, the British invasion was happening. Meanwhile you were one of these guys in the States who was immersed in the blues scene. What was your take on the British guys recycling the stuff that you were already doing?*

Winter: It sure helped get jobs for the blues band over here; they really did get the blues going in the States. I didn't think they played it so great, but it still helps.

Elwood: *When Bob Dylan played electric, a lot of the folk purists turned their backs on him. Did you have a similar experience when you strayed from traditional blues and went more into rock 'n' roll?*

Winter: No, I was really lucky enough not to have too many people get irritated with me for doing that. In fact, *Johnny Winter And (Live)* was my first record that really sold big—it was my only gold record. So that was kind of a good thing for me to do. There was such a big blues revival in the United States in '68, '69, and '70, and we'd gotten so big that it was bound to explode. And it did. People just got tired of hearing blues. We didn't want to hear it anymore because it was so big for such a good while. People wanted to hear something else, so I decided to do more rock 'n' roll.

Elwood: *You and Tommy Shannon played Woodstock together. What was that experience like?*

Winter: Well, the main thing that I remember about it is it being all muddy and rainy. We stayed up all night. We played a festival the night before, so we went into a news trailer and found a bag of garbage to sleep on. We were doing shows like Woodstock regularly that year, so it wasn't that big a deal. We were playing big festivals all over. I didn't know it was going to be as big as it was.

Elwood: *Did you get to jam with Hendrix?*

Winter: I did, but at the Scene in New York in '69, not there at Woodstock. We recorded a little bit together. It was a lot of fun playing with Jimi. [Hendrix and Winter's New York tracks have been released as *New York Session*.]

Elwood: *When you guys all started putting out albums, who were some of your favorite players?*

Winter: Well, Muddy and the Wolf are still two of my favorites. Bobby Blue Bland, Lazy Lester, Lightnin' Hopkins . . . I could go on forever.

Elwood: *What about Howlin' Wolf grabbed your attention?*

Winter: His voice was just amazing.

Elwood: *Is there a particular song you get juiced about playing, either one of yours or a cover?*

Winter: There's so many records that do it for me that it's hard to pick one. "Little Boy Blue" by Bobby Blue Bland is one of my favorites. I love that one.

Elwood: *You played on Sonny Terry's last album,* Whoopin'. *He was another one of those seminal blues guys—what was it like working with him?*

Winter: That was a real thrill. He was like Muddy in a lot of ways; he knew what he was going to do and he wanted to do it quick. He was ready to go—he'd just start a song and tell you what key it was in, and start playing.

Elwood: *It seems like those guys had a natural professional attitude about recording and playing. Most bands today would do 20 or 30 takes and do a lot of overdubbing.*

Winter: Those guys weren't that way at all. They just wanted to get through with it. And they had to be good enough to get it right the first time.

Elwood: *Do you follow the current blues scene?*

Winter: I don't really listen to as many new blues people as I should. I still listen to the old stuff more—I miss out on a lot of the new blues guys.

Elwood: *It's pretty cool that after so many years the blues is still around and taking on new sounds. What helps it survive?*

Winter: That there are new people who want to do it. They have one or two guys who really start making it, and that starts a blues revival. The new guys keep it going. I don't think the blues will ever die.

ELWOOD'S PICKS
A Totally Opinionated Discography

Don't just sit there—listen to the blues! Here are some suggestions for getting into the artists in *Elwood's Blues.*

Aerosmith
Honkin' on Bobo
Live Bootleg (both on Columbia)

Luther Allison
Soul Fixin' Man
Blue Streak (both on Alligator)

Marcia Ball
Presumed Innocent
So Many Rivers (both on Alligator)

Bobby "Blue" Bland
Best of Bobby Bland Volumes 1 & 2 (MCA)
Midnight Run (Malaco)

Blues Traveler
Blues Traveler
Bridge
Four (all on A&M)

Charles Brown
A Life in the Blues (Rounder)
Driftin' Blues: The Best of Charles Brown (Collectables)

Ruth Brown
Miss Rhythm (Atlantic)
Fine and Mellow (Fantasy)

Eric Burdon
The Best of the Animals (ABKCO)
The Complete Animals (EMI)

R.L. Burnside
A Ass Pocket of Whiskey (Matador)
Wish I Was in Heaven Sitting Down (Fat Possum)

Ray Charles
The Birth of Soul (Atlantic)
Blues + Jazz (Rhino)

Popa Chubby
Booty & the Beast (Sony)
The Good, the Bad & the Chubby (Blind Pig)

Johnny Clyde Copeland
Texas Twister (Rounder)
w/Albert Collins and Robert Cray:
Showdown (Alligator)

Shemekia Copeland
Wicked
Turn the Heat Up! (both on Alligator)

James Cotton
100% Cotton (Universe)
Deep in the Blues (Polygram)

Luther Dickinson & the North Mississippi Allstars
Shake Hands with Shorty (Tone-Cool)
Polaris (ATO)

Bo Diddley
The Best of Bo Diddley: The Millennium Collection (MCA)
A Man Amongst Men (Atlantic)

Buddy Guy
Damn Right, I've Got the Blues
Blues Singer (both on Silvertone)

Michael Hill
Have Mercy
Bloodlines (both on Alligator)

Rick Holmstrom
Hydraulic Groove (Tone-Cool)
Lookout! (Black Top)

John Lee Hooker
The Healer (Razor & Tie)
The Best of Friends (Virgin)

Candye Kane
Swango (Sire)
Diva la Grande (Antone's)

B.B. King
King of the Blues (MCA)
Singin' the Blues/The Blues (Virgin)

Little Milton
Welcome to the Club: The Essential Chess Recordings (MCA)
Welcome to Little Milton (Malaco)

Taj Mahal
In Progress and in Motion (Columbia)
Shoutin' in Key (Hannibal)

John Mayall
London Blues (1964–1969) (Polygram)
Spinning Coin (Jive)

Brownie McGhee
The Complete Brownie McGhee (Columbia)
Sonny & Brownie (A&M)

Keb' Mo'
Keep It Simple (Sony)
Keb' Mo' (Okeh)

Big Bill Morganfield
Rising Son
Blues in the Blood (both on Blind Pig)

Charlie Musselwhite
In My Time (Alligator)
Sanctuary (Real World)

Robert Plant
Led Zeppelin
Led Zeppelin II (both on Atlantic)

Carlos Santana
Santana's Greatest Hits (Columbia)
Shaman (Arista)

Koko Taylor
Force of Nature
Royal Blue (both on Alligator)

Susan Tedeschi
Just Won't Burn
Wait for Me (both on Tone-Cool)

Rufus Thomas
Can't Get Away from This Dog
The Complete Stax/Volt Singles (both on Stax)

Bob Weir
w/the Grateful Dead:
Grateful Dead Europe '72 (Rhino)
Solo album: *Ace* (Arista)

Junior Wells
Hoodoo Man Blues (Delmark)
Buddy Guy & Junior Wells Play the Blues (Rhino)

Johnny Winter
I'm a Bluesman (Virgin)
Progressive Blues Experiment (Razor & Tie)

Bill Wyman
The Rolling Stones: England's Newest Hit Makers (ABKCO)
Various artists:
Bill Wyman's Blues Odyssey (Document)

ZZ Top
Greatest Hits (Warner Bros.)
Antenna (RCA)
Deguello (Warner Bros.)

Acknowledgments

We'd like to thank the folks at Backbeat Books who helped translate radio into print: Kate Henderson, Richard Johnston, Nina Lesowitz, Amy Miller, and Nancy Tabor.

We'd also like to tip the fedora to the many people who have worked so hard to keep *The House of Blues Radio Hour* going. They include:

Ellen Anderson, Matt Bauer, Monica Blakely, Jeannette Boudreau, Megan Bourne, Paul Bronstein, Kurt Brown, Brian Cady, Brian Carideo, Brian Chui, Martin Cohen, Charlie Columbo, Dave Cooke, Peter Crimmins, Ryan Crisman, James Dallessandro, Sarah Dekin, Andy Denemark, Scott Dirks, Melissa Dodd, Cilista Eberle, Jerry Embree, Carey Eyer, Johnny Fay, Marty Fitzpatrick, Jeannie Gant, Lisa Garelick, David Gibson, Daniel Handler, Karoline Hatch, Courtney Heller, Dave Herda, Jim Higgins, Wally High, Stu Jacobs, Juan Jermany, David Jorgensen, Jon Kalish, Joe Kaczorowski, Merle Kessler, Nick Kiernan, Bob Kipperman, Tony Kirk, Barry Korengold, Sarah Lockhart, Aaron Machado, Griffin Manilla, Lou Mann, Alex Martinez, Stephen Mayfield, Greg McKenney, Saundra McPherson, Chris Mergemekis, Jon Meyer, Jonathan Mitchell, Kevin Morrow, Theresa Murphy, Tom Murphy, Frank Murphy, Michael Murphy, Barry O'Neill, Mary Perez, Arthur Phillips, Rob Pierce, Alaina Provine, Lee Roman, Lauren Ryan, Catalina San Agustin, Bob Santelli, Cate Schley, Christine Sharkey, Shane Sharkey, Dick Silipigni, Alan Silverman , Jim Swenson, Issac Tigrett, Greg Trojan, Andy Valvur, Nick Verbitsky, Julia Weinberg, Paul Wells, Mary Wings, Brad Woodward, James Wynbrandt, Ben Yalom, Ian Zazueta, and all the many radio broadcasters across North America who have allowed us access to their airwaves.

Photo Credits

Page 4: © Robert Knight/Retna Ltd.; page 10: Clayton Call; page 17: Ken Settle; page 23: Ken Settle; page 31: © Retna/photo by David Atlas; page 38: © David Redfern/Redferns/Retna Ltd.; page 44: © Jon Sievert/Michael Ochs Archives.com; page 49: © David Atlas/Retna Ltd.; page 55: © Chapman Baehler/Retna Ltd. USA; page 60: Ken Settle; page 67: © Robert Knight/Retna Ltd.; page 73: Ken Settle; page 80: © Howard Denner/Retna UK; page 87: © Beryl Bryden/Redferns/Retna Ltd.; page 94: Ken Settle; page 100: © Howard Denner/Retna UK; page 109: Ken Settle; page 113: © Simon Ritter/Redferns/Retna Ltd.; page 119: Clayton Call; page 126: © Retna Ltd.; page 127: © David Atlas/Retna Ltd.; page 133: © Ian Dickson/Redferns/Retna Ltd.; page 137: © Retna Ltd.; page 144: © Retna Ltd.; page 150: © J. Scott Wynn/Retna Ltd.; page 157: Clayton Call; page 164: © Paul Bergen/Redferns/Retna Ltd.; page 172: Clayton Call; page 178: © Scott D. Smith/Retna Ltd.; page 185: Michael Kurgansky; page 189: © Retna Ltd.; page 194: Art Tipaldi; page 199: © Howard Denner/Retna UK; page 204: Art Tipaldi; page 210: Art Tipaldi; page 215: © Retna Ltd.; page 221: © Retna Ltd.; page 227: Art Tipaldi; page 232: © Robert Spencer/Retna Ltd.; page 238: Clayton Call

Blues Foundation

A portion of the proceeds from *Elwood's Blues* goes to the Blues Foundation. Headquartered in Memphis, the Blues Foundation has 125 affiliated blues organizations and a membership that spans the globe. The Foundation's signature programs—the W.C. Handy Blues Awards, Blues Hall of Fame, International Blues Challenge, and Keeping the Blues Alive Awards—as well as its informational and educational services place it at the hub of the blues world. You can support the nonprofit Blues Foundation by visiting www.blues.org or calling 901-527-2583.

Index

on segregation/racism, 55–56
Dixon, Willie
  Bob Weir on, 152, 155
  Buddy Guy on, 61, 64
  Charlie Musselwhite on, 103
  Koko Taylor on, 110
  Popa Chubby on, 185, 186
"The Dog," 114–115
Dowd, Tom, 187
Down South Summit Meeting, 91
"Drifting Blues," 16, 19, 21
Drugan, Dennis, 237–238
Drugan, Seymour, 238
Duke label, 9
Duke/Peacock label, 172–173
Dyer, Johnny, 205

E
electric blues, 150
Elektra label, 102
Elwood. *See* Blues, Elwood
Ertegun, Ahmet
  Ray Charles on, 40
  Ruth Brown on, 25, 26, 28
Estrin, Rick, 102

F
Fat Possum Records, 30, 33
Four Aces, 119
Franklin, Reverend C.L., 12
Fredricks, Henry St. Clair. *See* Taj Mahal
funk music, 115–116

G
Gibbons, Billy, 164–168
"Good Morning Little School Girl," 152
Gordon, Roscoe, 11
gospel music, 231–233
Grateful Dead, 149–153
Gray Ghost, 173
Guitar Slim, 62
Guy, Buddy, 59–65
  on B.B. King, 63, 76
  early years, 59–63
  on Guitar Slim, 62

on Lightnin' Slim, 62
  Luther Allison on, 6
  on Muddy Waters, 62–63
  on Rolling Stones, 64
  on Son House, 62
  on Willie Dixon, 61, 64

H
Hamilton, Tom, 125–130
  on Chuck Berry, 127
  on Fleetwood Mac, 128–129
Hendrix, Jimi
  Chan Kinchla on, 180
  Eric Burdon on, 134
  John Popper on, 180
  Johnny Winter on, 240
  Keb' Mo' on, 222–223
  Michael Hill on, 198–200
"Hey, Hey, the Blues is Alright," 96–97
Hibbler, Al, 27
Hill, Dusty, 163–166
Hill, Michael, 198–202
  on B.B. King, 200
  on Bob Marley, 201
  influences on, 198–199, 200, 201
  on Jimi Hendrix, 198–200
  on Luther Allison, 200–201
Holmes, Jack, 24
Holmstrom, Rick, 203–207
  on Chuck Berry, 203
  on Jimmy Rogers, 205–206
  on Johnny Dyer, 205
  R.L. Burnside and, 207
  on T-Bone Walker, 204
  on William Clarke, 205
  youth of, 203–204
Hooker, John Lee, 66–70
  on B.B. King, 70
  Bill Wyman on, 159, 160
  on Chuck Berry, 69
  early career, 66, 68
  Luther Allison on, 5
  Madison Square Garden tribute, 70
  R.L. Burnside on, 32
  Rufus Thomas on, 116

Billy Gibbons on, 164, 165
Dusty Hill on, 164–166
Frank Beard on, 165
Luther Allison on, 4–5
Popa Chubby on, 185–186
King, Riley B. *See* King, B.B.
King, Saunders, 147
King Records, 20
Korner, Alexis, 216

L
Leadbelly
Brownie McGhee on, 90
John Mayall on, 215
Steve Tyler on, 128
Led Zeppelin
influences on, 136, 138, 140–141
Shemekia Copeland on, 190
Ledbetter, Huddie. *See* Leadbelly
Lewis, Furry, 194
Lightnin' Hopkins. *See* Hopkins, Lightnin'
Lightnin' Slim, 62
Lipscomb, Mance, 151
Little Milton, 93–98
on Albert King, 96
on Ike Turner, 95, 96
influences on, 95
on Sam Phillips, 95–96
on Sonny Boy Williamson 2 (Rice
Miller), 93
on T-Bone Walker, 95
Little Richard
Eric Burdon on, 134
Ruth Brown on, 26–27
Little Walter
Big Bill Morganfield on, 228–229
Charlie Musselwhite on, 101
James Cotton on, 51
Junior Wells on, 121
Lockwood, Robert Junior, 32
Lomax, Alan and John, 90
Lucky Millinder Orchestra, 27

M
Maceo, Big. *See* Big Maceo

Maghett, Magic Sam, 4
Magic Slim, 52–53
Mahal, Taj. *See* Taj Mahal
Manfield, James, 44
Margolin, Bob, 228
Marley, Bob, 201
Mayall, John, 214–219
on Leadbelly, 215
on Otis Rush, 217
on touring, 217–218
McClennan, Tommy, 160
McDowell, Fred, 30–31
McGhee, Brownie, 86–92
early career, 88–89
on Harry Belafonte, 90
on Jackie Robinson, 89
on Leadbelly, 90
on Lightnin' Hopkins, 90
on Sonny Terry, 86–88, 89, 91–92
McGhee, Walter. *See* McGhee, Brownie
Mercury Records, 96
Merriweather, Big Maceo. *See* Big Maceo
"Merry Christmas Baby," 16, 20–21
Miller, Rice. *See* Williamson, Sonny Boy 2
(Rice Miller)
Millinder, Lucky, 27
Miniatures, 12–13
Mississippi blues, 35, 82, 85, 94–95
Mitchell, George, 31–32
Mo', Keb', 220–224
Bill Wyman on, 161
on Jimi Hendrix, 222–223
on Son House, 224
on Taj Mahal, 223
Modern Records, 11, 66, 68
Moore, Gary, 6
Moore, Johnny, 19, 21
Moore, Kevin. *See* Mo', Keb'
Moore, Winston, 76–77
Morganfield, Big Bill, 226–230
on Big Bill Broonzy, 229
Bill Wyman on, 161
on Bob Margolin, 228
on Eric Clapton, 229
on Jimmy Rogers, 228–229

Listen to Elwood Blues on the House of Blues Radio Hour

Heard on over 180 stations nationwide

Check your local listings for details

Produced by Ben Manilla Productions and distributed by United Stations Radio Networks

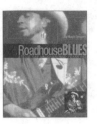